15

TO RENEW A.

Items should be returned on or before the
as displayed in the Library, will be charge

7

EUGENIE AND NAPOLEON III

David Duff

COLLINS
St. James's Place, London
1978

William Collins Sons and Co Ltd
London . Glasgow . Sydney . Auckland
Toronto . Johannesburg

First published 1978
© David Duff 1978
Set in Monotype Bembo
ISBN 000 211237 X
Printed and bound in Great Britain by
Butler & Tanner Ltd, Frome and London

Contents

Contents

Illustrations

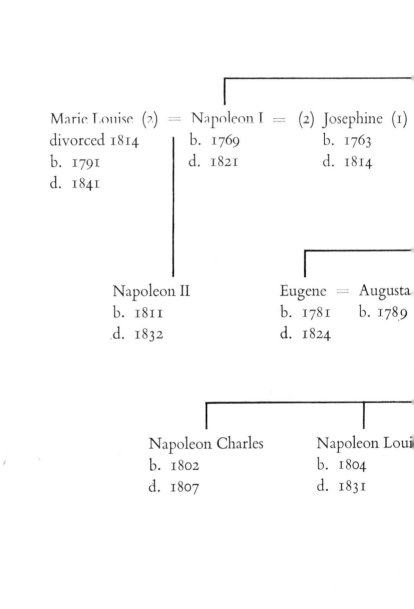

Marie Louise (2) = Napoleon I = (2) Josephine (1)
divorced 1814   b. 1769   b. 1763
b. 1791   d. 1821   d. 1814
d. 1841

Napoleon II   Eugene = Augusta
b. 1811   b. 1781   b. 1789
d. 1832   d. 1824

Napoleon Charles   Napoleon Loui
b. 1802   b. 1804
d. 1807   d. 1831

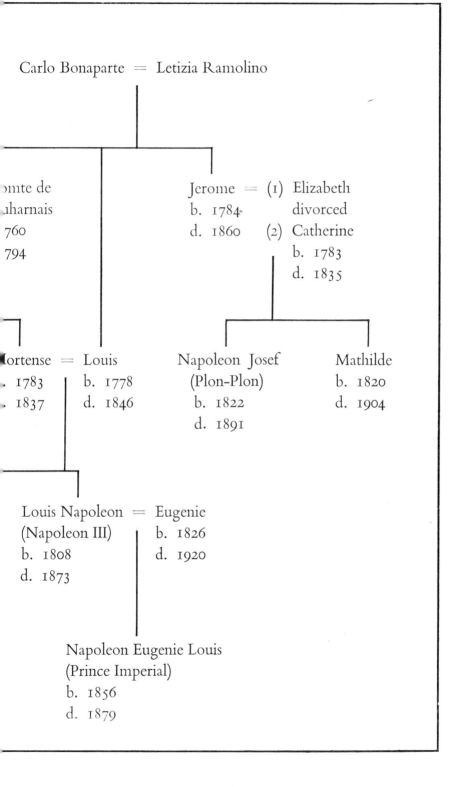

Carlo Bonaparte = Letizia Ramolino

᠊mte de
.harnais
760
794

Jerome = (1) Elizabeth
b. 1784   divorced
d. 1860   (2) Catherine
            b. 1783
            d. 1835

᠊ortense = Louis
. 1783   b. 1778
. 1837   d. 1846

Napoleon Josef
(Plon–Plon)
b. 1822
d. 1891

Mathilde
b. 1820
d. 1904

Louis Napoleon = Eugenie
(Napoleon III)   b. 1826
b. 1808   d. 1920
d. 1873

Napoleon Eugenie Louis
(Prince Imperial)
b. 1856
d. 1879

Author's Note

This is the personal story of the lives of Emperor Napoleon III and the Empress Eugenie, and, to a lesser extent, of their only son, the Prince Imperial. It is in no way a political and military analysis of France's Second Empire. It is an experiment in the resurrection of two outstanding characters, with its roots in the eighteenth century and its ending in 1920.

As the concentration is on the Emperor and the Empress and their background, many of the leading figures on the Second Empire scene have only been dealt with lightly. Napoleon's individuality and unfathomable mind made him largely independent of others. His handicap lay in his health, and perhaps also in his humanity, for he lacked the ruthlessness of the first Napoleon. The driving force behind him was his wife, beautiful, imperial, brave. That she was restricted to one child upset the balance of their married life.

I am indebted to many people in France—in particular the staff at Compiègne—for help in reconstruction of the scene. My thanks are due to Miss Jennifer Hassell for her encouragement and help since the inception and for her expert advice; to Mr Cecil Barclay for assistance with research and editing; to my wife, who has borne the main burden; to Dom Placid Higham, of St Michael's Benedictine Abbey, Farnborough, and Mrs Fenella Baines for reading and checking the manuscript; to Mrs J. M. Rochester and Miss Sarah Clay for typing it with infinite patience; and finally Mr Adrian House, of William Collins, for his advice and support.

David Duff

CHAPTER I

A Prologue

Paris – July 1870. The Emperor and Empress of the French were at St Cloud. They had separate bedrooms, for Napoleon III suffered from a stone in his bladder and slept only fitfully and for a few hours. He was due, the international situation permitting, to be operated on in London. He was sixty-two. Empress Eugenie was forty-four.

Napoleon held his Councils of State soon after dawn and granted interviews from his bed. Baron Alphonse de Rothschild, of the famous banking family, was well aware of this. He left his house in the Rue St Florentin as soon as the clock was striking four and drove to St Cloud. He sought the answer to a question of vital importance to his banking network throughout Europe. Was France about to go to war with Germany?

Baron Alphonse reached the Château St Cloud before the Council had been held. He was shown at once to the Emperor's bedroom. Napoleon, lying back on his pillows, assured his visitor that he fully understood his anxiety over the international situation. Then, taking Alphonse's hand between his, he said most earnestly: *'Ce n'est pas la guerre, mon cher Baron, foi de gentilhomme, ce n'est pas la guerre.'*

Relieved, delighted Baron Alphonse poured out his thanks and congratulations and bowed himself out. As he hurried along the corridor a door opened and a vision appeared. It was Eugenie in her dressing-gown. She moved smoothly towards him as if there were wheels rather than legs beneath her robe. It was a glide which has never been equalled. She paused and held out her hand to be kissed. Her beauty and fragrance swept over him, not unlike the loveliness of the palace gardens on that early summer morning. They exchanged trivialities and compliments for a while. Then Alphonse, bowing low, descended the stairs to his carriage and Eugenie entered her husband's room.

Thrilled by his encounters with the Emperor and Empress, Alphonse hurried to his bank in the Rue Lafitte. Away, on the telegraph, to the capitals of Europe, went the glad news that there was to be peace in Europe.

Two hours later a courier arrived from St Cloud, his horse reeking with sweat, for it had galloped all the way. Baron Alphonse tore open the missive. On the Imperial paper, hurriedly scribbled in pencil, were these few words: '*Tout est changé. C'est la guerre*' (signed) *N.*

And war it was. Life for Eugenie and Napoleon was never the same again; their fate was sealed.

Part I

LOUIS NAPOLEON

1807–1849

CHAPTER 2

Hortense's Boy

Carlo Buonaparte and Letizia Ramolino, the parents of Napoleon Bonaparte, had ten children. When they married in 1764, he was eighteen and she but fourteen.

Their first two children died in infancy. A son, Joseph, arrived in 1768. It was the time of the French conquest of Corsica and Carlo backed the island patriot, Paoli. He fought in the resistance movement and his wife and son were with him. Letizia was carrying another child, a child born of war. He was named Napoleon and she called him 'Napolione'. There followed three boys and three girls, Lucien, Louis and Jerome, and Marianne Elisa, Pauline and Caroline. The last of them was born in 1784 and the following year Carlo died. In 1796 the spelling of the family name was changed to Bonaparte.

In character, Napoleon stood head and shoulders above the rest. He alone inherited the will-power of his mother, *Madame Mère* as she was known in her widowhood. As a boy he was ambitious, possessive and resentful of being poor. His realm was his garden plot and he defended it against the ravages of other boys with military precision, his weapon a hoe[1].

In due season he was to heap upon his brothers and sisters the vain glories of this world, and the kingships of Spain, Holland, Westphalia and Naples were fruited on the family tree. Unsupported, it was unlikely that any of the brothers would have made an impact on the European scene. The sisters were better equipped. The most beautiful and gay of them was Pauline, whose second husband was Prince

3

Camillo Borghesi. Antonio Canova's statue of her as Venus reclining on a couch has assured her place in history.

Of the brothers of Napoleon, we are immediately concerned with Louis, who was nine years younger.

Louis was the favourite brother of Napoleon I, who had something of a paternal attitude towards him, supervising his education and military training. During the first Italian campaign Louis acted as A.D.C. to his brother and became his messmate, secretary and confidential adviser. The bond between them was very strong. Then, as a result of exposure in the field, Louis developed rheumatic gout and gradually the physical handicap changed his whole nature, character and attitude to life. The good companion and the gay adventurer became depressed, morose, suspicious and a hypochondriac. The elder brother simply did not understand the fate which had overtaken the younger, always believing that the mood would pass and that they would understand one another again. But the mood did not pass and with the years Napoleon's feelings became those of annoyance, impatience and disgust.

In 1802 Napoleon decided that it would be best, for the sake of his brother and the Napoleonic succession, that Louis should marry, and a wife was produced for him. She was Hortense de Beauharnais, Napoleon's step-daughter – daughter of his wife, the Empress Josephine, by her first husband, who had been guillotined during the Revolution. Hortense, though not beautiful, was most attractive, with blonde hair, violet eyes and great vivacity. She was also obstinate and awkward when crossed. Louis was in love with her, but she, realising his defects, not a bit with him. On their honeymoon there was a row, Louis having made rude remarks about his mother-in-law. He left Paris for several months and Hortense, pregnant, lived with her mother and Napoleon either at the Tuileries or Josephine's château of Malmaison.

During the summer, Josephine, whose thoughts were in the main centred around herself, went off, as was her custom, to Plombières to take the waters. Napoleon and Hortense were alone at the Tuileries. Tongues began to wag and none faster than those of Napoleon's sisters, ever jealous of Hortense. It was considered best that she leave the Tuileries, so a house was purchased in Rue de la Victoire, and it was there in October that her first son was born. A strongly worded message had been sent to the father by Napoleon, and Louis arrived just in time. The child was named Napoleon Charles.

Louis was restless. He changed their town house for a larger one and then bought a lovely country estate at Saint-Leu, twelve miles from Paris. But even here life with his wife and child irked him and once again he disappeared. Once again the tongues wagged, and in October 1804 Hortense gave birth to her second son. The Pope, who was in Paris for the coronation of Napoleon as Emperor, christened the child Napoleon Louis.

In 1806 Napoleon, following his plan for surrounding France with states in close alliance, made Louis King of Holland. Hortense went with him but soon it was she who did the disappearing. Louis took unto himself one of the ladies at court, at which his wife, somewhat unfairly, was furious.[2] When in May 1807 her eldest son died of croup, the bitterness and the grief shattered the marriage beyond repair. Heart-broken, Hortense retired to the peace of Cauterêts in the Pyrenees. There Louis visited her, but only for a short time. From this point dates and movements become of vital importance.

Louis left Hortense at Cauterêts on 6th July and went to Toulouse. There she joined him on 12th August and together they proceeded to Paris to attend the wedding of Jerome, the youngest of the Emperor's brothers, to Princess Catharine of Württemberg, at St Cloud on the 23rd, a big family gathering. As for Emperor Napoleon's movements, in the middle of July he left Tilsit for Warsaw, and then went on to Dresden. On the 24th he made his triumphal entry into Frankfurt, the capital of the states of the Prince Primate of the Confederation of the Rhine. On the 27th he was back at St Cloud. On 16th August he opened the sittings of the Legislative Corps and on the 23rd he was present at the wedding of Prince Jerome.[3]

These movements and dates have importance in view of the fact that Hortense gave birth to her third son on 20th April 1808. He was a month premature, a point confirmed by the doctors in attendance upon Hortense, among them being the Emperor's personal physician. So weak was the baby that, to save his life, it was necessary to bathe him in wine and wrap him in cotton wool.[4] That he was one month premature pinpoints the date of conception as within a few days of 20th August 1807. He was named Louis Napoleon.

Owing to the bad relationship between Louis and Hortense, rumours began as to the paternity of the child. But fortunately, or of design, it was not generally known that he was premature. Opinion was strong that the Emperor was the father,[5] but certain biographers have poured scorn and ridicule upon this theory propounded by 'calumniators'. They hammer home their point by stressing that, nine months before the birth, Napoleon and Hortense were a thousand miles apart. So they were – but the important figure is eight, not nine. Eight months before the birth, Napoleon and Hortense were together at St Cloud.

To spoil the trail, a red herring was dragged across it. The father, it was said, was really a handsome Dutch admiral, and certainly Hortense's friendship with this man made the theory feasible. Evidence was produced that someone of that name had called upon her when she was at Cauterêts. But in reality Admiral Carel-Hendrik had been at his post at The Hague during July and it was his brother who, in his position as Minister to Spain, had made an official and routine call upon Hortense.[6] In any case the call was too early to have incidence. But the story was fostered and grew in strength with the years and even during the Second Empire the guide showing visitors round the Royal Picture gallery at The Hague would point to a portrait of the admiral and say: 'And this, ladies and gentlemen, is the father of Emperor Napoleon III.'[7]

But it must also be remembered that Louis was with his wife for the Jerome wedding. That could be taken as grounds for establishing the child's legality, except for the behaviour of Louis. His jealousy had now become a mania and he openly accused his wife of infidelity. And in 1809 he arrived in Paris to seek permission from the Emperor to divorce her.

By this time Napoleon was becoming very impatient with his brother. He had placed him upon the Dutch throne as a representative of himself, expecting Louis to obey orders, but the King in name had espoused the Orange cause and become a patriot of his adopted country, turning down an offer to become King of Spain. Napoleon's views on his brother's attitude, both towards his wife and his country, were made clear in the following letter*:

> *Vous gouvernez trop cette nation en capucin. La bonté d'un roi doit toujours être majestueuse et ne doit pas être celle d'un moine . . . .*
> *Vos querelles avec la Reine percent aussi dans le public. Ayez dans votre*

*For translation see p. 299

6

intérieur ce caractère paternel et efféminé que vous montrez dans le gouverne-
ment, et ayez dans les affaires ce rigorisme que vous montrez dans votre
ménage. Vous traitez une jeune femme comme on mènerait un régiment . . . .
Vous avez la meilleure femme et la plus vertueuse, et vous la rendez
malheureuse. Laissez-la danser tant qu'elle veut, c'est de son âge. J'ai une
femme qui a quarante ans; du champ de bataille je lui écris d'aller au bal;
et vous voulez qu'une femme de vingt ans, qui voit passer sa vie, qui en a
toutes les illusions, vive dans un cloître, soit comme une nourrice, toujours
à laver son enfant? ... Malheureusement vous avez une femme trop ver-
tueuse; si vous aviez une coquette, elle vous mènerait par le bout du nez.[8]

In addition to the question of his divorce, the King of Holland had a further matter to discuss with the Emperor. He wished to obtain better terms for his country, threatened by invasion by the French forces because the Dutch would insist upon carrying on secret trade with England, thus diminishing the effects of blockade and economic warfare. But poor Louis failed on both counts. The next year he lost his throne, Holland was annexed to the French Empire and occupying troops took control of the coast and custom houses. While his wife and children remained in Paris, he fled to Bohemia, later moving to Italy and an obscurity from which he did not re-emerge. His plea for permission to divorce was refused, although he was allowed to separate from Hortense. This was fortunate, for in 1811 she had a fourth son by Comte de Flahaut. Hortense's third and fourth sons were to be of vital importance to France. The former, Louis Napoleon, became Emperor Napoleon III and the latter, the Duc de Morny, his friend and adviser.

To go back to 1809, the year in which Louis had sought his brother's permission to divorce Hortense, Napoleon was examining his own marital arrangements. Josephine was, as he put it bluntly, 'getting on,' and as yet had no children. The blame for that could not be put on him, he said, pointing to two of his bastards. Josephine felt the cold wind blowing down the long corridors of the Tuileries.

And so, five years after she had been crowned Empress, she faced the Bonapartes seated round a table in the Tuileries. She was dressed in white and wore no jewellery. Summoning all of her courage and all of her strength, she renounced her husband and stumbled out from their presence. That night she went to his bedside with her hair loose around her shoulders and her eyes wet with tears. In the morning, in the rain, she drove to Malmaison, there to hide and dream away her last few years. It was all very sad and rather shabby.[9]

Napoleon now looked around him for a young lady of about twenty to bear him a son. Not only must she have the physical attributes necessary for healthy child-bearing but she must be of a family sufficiently senior to promote the Napoleonic dynasty. Encouraged by the Austrian Chancellor, Prince Metternich, he married Archduchess Marie Louise, daughter of Francis I, Emperor of Austria, in 1810. She was nineteen. As they honeymooned at Compiègne, Metternich observed that Napoleon was so much in love with her that he could not conceal his feelings. The wine diet worked and within a year a son was born, destined to bear the empty titles of King of Rome and Napoleon II.

Hortense had always loved and admired her mother Josephine, overlooking her faults and weaknesses, and she was both shocked and hurt at the divorce, but she never for a moment lost her loyalty and reverence for the Emperor, bringing up her sons to regard him as the most magnificent hero that the world had ever produced.[10] It was that attitude that explained many things. She now spent some of her time at the Tuileries, some at her Paris house, but most at Malmaison, giving comfort and company to Josephine. Malmaison was looked upon by the two boys as their real home. Here 'Granny' spoiled them and interested them in her collection of curios and rare plants. Here they could walk in the woods and play in the wide gardens. Here they could make friends with the military guards and imitate them at their drill.

It was some time before the younger of the two surviving boys, Louis Napoleon, known as Louis and nicknamed 'Oui-Oui' by his grand-mother, overcame the handicap of his premature birth and was able to live the life of a normal child. His christening was postponed until he was two years and five months old. It was staged with pomp and splendour at Fontainebleau and the Emperor and the new Empress were his sponsors. Of the two boys Louis was the favourite of Napoleon and he showered him with presents. He needed no confirmation that the child was a Bonaparte – it was clear from the skull formation, the long body and short legs. When they breakfasted at the Tuileries, the Emperor would pick up Louis by the head and, laughing loudly, hold him high in the air. Hortense objected strongly, on medical grounds, and said so, but now she had to be careful in her dealings with Napoleon, for the ears of Marie Louise were ever listening.

Louis Napoleon was within a few days of his sixth birthday when the Empire collapsed. As Napoleon headed for Elba and Marie Louise, with her son, made her furtive way back to Austria, Hortense packed her children into a carriage and drove through the night, to the background music of gunfire, to Malmaison. The shock was too much for Josephine and, a few days after the Bourbon King, Louis XVIII, took over France, she died.

Hortense was allowed to stay on at Malmaison on condition that she behaved herself. As an insurance policy she moved under the protection of Tsar Alexander I of Russia, a tall and impressive figure in resplendent uniform to whom Louis Napoleon took an immediate liking. It was at Alexander's prompting that the new King bestowed upon Hortense the title of Duchesse de Saint-Leu and agreed that her State allowance of 400,000 francs should be continued.[11]

Early in March 1815 Hortense was told by an Englishman that Napoleon had left Elba and was heading north from Juan across the mountains. That night, with her two boys and their governess, she slipped out of the garden gate of her Paris house and led the way through the darkness to the home of an old nurse, a staunch friend of the family. There the four hid in the attic, the nurse keeping them in touch with the news and at length telling them that the Bourbon King had fled to Ghent.

Hortense was among the great ones of the Empire when Napoleon strode into the Tuileries late on the 20th March, the birthday of his son. What a change a year had brought – Josephine was dead, Marie Louise was in Austria and had renounced him, and his son he was never to see again. So, although there was initial chilliness in his greeting to Hortense, a few hard words concerning the favourable treatment that she had accepted from King Louis and Tsar Alexander, the drama of the reunion was too much for him and after a few minutes he took her in his arms and embraced her. Thereafter, for a short time, Hortense filled the gaps left by Josephine and Marie Louise. It was easier than either of the two women would have realised. Every night she dined with the Emperor. They drove together to Malmaison and there he went alone into the room in which his first wife had died. Then for an hour they walked together in the gardens, talking of Josephine. He had loved her very much – perhaps, earlier, he had not known how much.

Now that he had lost his son, Hortense's boys meant even more to him. After breakfast he would hold them up to the palace windows so that the troops gathered below could see them. And they were there, above the throne, on that great day when the Emperor took his oath to the new constitution and handed out eagles to his troops. That was a picture which remained for ever before the eyes of seven-year-old Louis Napoleon. On 11th June there was a dinner party at the Elysée, Hortense acting hostess. Napoleon was in good spirits, calm and collected, for once again he was in the role that he knew and loved, the commander of armies. His nephews were allowed in for dessert.[12] Next morning he left for Belgium and Waterloo.

Eight days later Napoleon was back in Paris. Once Hortense had received the black news that Wellington and Blücher had crushed the French forces, she again put her children into hiding, this time in the house of her dressmaker in the Boulevard Montmartre. But she was at the Elysée to meet her fallen hero, to comfort him and help him with plans for the future in the maelstrom of events which altered hourly. At dinner on the 24th he said to her: '*Je veux retirer à la Malmaison. C'est à vous. Voulez-vous m'y donner l'hospitalité?*'[13] So they spent three green summer days there together, alone but for the ghost of Josephine moving hauntingly among the flowers. The boys were brought from their hiding place to say their goodbyes. Hortense sewed her diamond necklace, which had so often sparkled at the Tuileries balls, into a black silk belt. It was an insurance policy and Napoleon fastened it around his waist – it was to be with him until his end.

At five o'clock on the afternoon of the 29th Napoleon Bonaparte, a strange and almost unrecognisable figure in civilian clothes, stood by a carriage saying farewell to a group of his friends. He was calm, but, when he came to Hortense, he clasped her tight to himself[14] in a long embrace, as if, by releasing her, he ended his world and his age. He jumped into the carriage and said no more. He sat looking back at the picture of Hortense standing before the back-drop of Malmaison until a corner came. West he went towards Rochefort and H.M.S. *Bellerophon*.

Now Hortense was a marked woman and there was no chance of a repeat of the comparative peace which she had been allowed in 1814. During the Hundred Days she had stood firm by the eagle, she had shown clearly her love and her loyalty for the Emperor, and there was to be no forgetting. The Napoleons scattered, spanning the western world from Trieste to the Delaware River. As the Bourbon King returned to Paris and the accusations against the Bonapartist supporters poured into his ears, Hortense made her preparations to leave. On 19th July her marching orders arrived, signed by a Prussian general. She was given twenty-four hours to quit Paris.

In her hour of pressing need an unexpected knight came to her rescue. He was Prince Karl Schwarzenberg, Austrian Field Marshal, one of the senior Allied generals to conduct the 1813 – 14 campaign which led to the fall of Paris. He had a personal link with Napoleon – it was he who had been sent from Vienna to negotiate the Emperor's marriage with Archduchess Marie Louise. Schwarzenberg detailed his adjutant to conduct Hortense and her children to that home of exiled emperors, Switzerland, and a dramatic and arduous journey it was.

Booking into the Hotel Sécheron at Geneva, Hortense looked forward to being allowed to rest for a while, but that was not to be. The Swiss had been quick to clamber on to the victors' band-waggon and in the dining-room of the hotel the local military were holding a banquet to celebrate the downfall of Napoleon. Shortly a message arrived from the authorities asking the ex-Queen of Holland to move on. There was only one place that she could go to – back to the second of her two homes in France.

Empress Josephine had lived in two lovely homes – Malmaison and the Château de Prègny at Aix-les-Bains. Under her mother's will Hortense received Prègny and the jewellery, while Malmaison went to Hortense's brother, Prince Eugène de Beauharnais, Duke of Leuchtenberg. Hortense judged that, in her own house in distant Savoie, she she would be free of the attentions of spies and the police of Paris, but she was much mistaken. 'Boney' had become a fetish throughout Europe, and particularly in England where certain statesmen would have liked to have seen him shot after Waterloo. What he had done from Elba, he might well do again and, if he did, it was believed that many in France would again rally to the magic call of the little man. Yet here, people said, was the woman who had been at his right hand during the Hundred Days, living free in France, in a strategic position to help him, and bringing up a boy ready to do the same thing all over again. So Hortense was spied upon and became the subject of urgent discussions at Allied conferences.

In fact Hortense was near to a break-down, physical and mental.

The strain of watching an Empire's fall, its resurrection and final collapse, had aged her beyond her thirty-two years. Sleepless nights and the hard flight from Paris had sapped her strength. And recently there had come another blow. Her husband, ex-King of Holland, had taken judicial action and the courts had awarded him custody of his elder son, Napoleon Louis. It was an act prompted by spite, for it was clear that the boys would be happier and fare better if brought up together. The elder boy was strong, gay and high spirited, while the younger, still suffering from the effects of premature birth, was physically weak and of a serious turn of mind. Napoleon Louis was the tonic which his mother needed, but in October he was taken from her and sent to his father in Florence.

Hortense took refuge in the pastimes which she loved, singing, composing, sketching, in all of which she was talented.[a] But those who watched her wondered what it was that she wrote, and put a second meaning to the sketches which she made in the autumn sunshine around the Lac du Bourget.

Once more marching orders arrived. This time she was to go to the unexciting town of Constance in Baden. In November she arrived there, and once again there was the experience of a dreary hotel and the request from the authorities to move on. But she had had enough, her deep obstinacy showed, and in defiance she went out and bought a small house near the spot where the lake flows into the Rhine. She was on firmer ground now for her brother Eugène had married Augusta of Bavaria, daughter of Duke Maximilian of Bavaria, and lived in Munich, while Stéphanie de Beauharnais, Napoleon's adopted daughter, was the wife of Grand Duke Charles of Baden. Both Eugène and Stéphanie owned summer houses by the lake.

The people of the Canton of Thurgau, in which the ex-Queen and her son Louis now resided, soon became attached to them and they were invited to make Constance their permanent home. In 1817 Hortense bought the Château of Arenenberg, standing on a wooded height six miles west of the town, overlooking the Unter See. One historian described it as 'a little old-fashioned château, commanding superb views of the lake and river and landscape, sheltered around by fine timber and approached on all sides through vineyards. The entrance

(a) She was the composer of several songs, including '*Partant pour la Syrie*', which was to become the anthem of the Second Empire.

was reached by an old drawbridge. It was just the spot to appeal to the romantic imagination of a woman like Hortense.'[15]

Now life had a new meaning for her and she set about the building of a reminiscence of Malmaison, of bringing the presence of Napoleon back from distant St Helena. She used the tented style of the Consulate for the reception rooms and, when her furniture arrived from France, she could look at it and float back to the past. Through the years she collected souvenirs, portraits, uniforms and letters and Arenenberg became a museum devoted to Emperor Napoleon I.

As for the present, Hortense and Louis lived in a world peopled only by themselves. She called him '*le doux ténébreux*'[16] – the gentle dreamer – and she herself cared for his education. She was a cultured and talented Bohemian and put slight store by morals. She cared little for boundaries and, when visitors came to Arenenberg, Louis Napoleon listened to French, German, Italian and Spanish, imbibed them, and became fluent in them all. It was fortunate that Hortense was the woman that she was, for she was able to see and understand the boy's handicaps and problems. Because of his premature birth and the after-effects of her post-natal depression, stemming from the allegations of her husband, Louis Napoleon was both physically and mentally backward. The signs ran true – a complete lack of concentration – and a great distaste for serious study.[17] When, thirty years later, the same signs appeared in the young Prince of Wales, Queen Victoria and Prince Albert were unable to recognise them and untold harm was done to their heir.

When the time came for her son to have a tutor, Hortense chose Abbé Bernard. This genial priest was more of a companion than a tutor. The two would ramble through the woods, learning of birds and flowers, and there were no fixed times for meals and bedtime. When Hortense saw that her son had grown in strength, was taking a healthy interest in the pastimes which are the natural outlet of boyhood, then – and only then – did she introduce an educational curriculum in parallel with that arranged for Albert Edward by Prince Albert and Baron Stockmar.

A new tutor arrived from Paris, one Phillippe Le Bas. Now the order changed – meals were served as the clock struck, lessons were regulated and the hours long. But the pupil was ready for the strain and learned fast. The example of Napoleon was ever held before him and led him on. When the sad news came from St Helena that the exiled Emperor was dead, thirteen year old Louis wrote to his mother: 'When I do wrong I think of this great man, and I seem to feel his shade within me telling me to keep myself worthy of the name of Napoleon.'[18]

In 1821 it was decided that Louis Napoleon needed the company of other boys and he joined the St Anna Gymnasium at Augsburg in Bavaria. With him went his French tutor and his mother, who rented a house there. It was at Augsburg that he picked up the German accent which he was never to lose, a point which Prince Albert was to note with satisfaction. School brought out the competitive spirit in him and, with the determination of one who had been forbidden games owing to poor health, he now set out to outstrip his companions. He excelled at swimming and shooting and became a superb horseman. Holidays were spent in travelling, staying at German palaces, climbing Swiss mountains, accompanying his mother to health resorts. Sometimes he visited his brother and his father, ex-King Louis, at Florence.

At seventeen he left Augsburg and was ready to begin his chosen trade of war. He reported at the Military Academy at Thun in Switzerland. His instructors were two former officers of Napoleon, Colonels Fournier and Dufour, and he took courses in artillery and military engineering.

The winters by Lake Constance, in the cold Château of Arenberg, did not suit Hortense and now, each autumn, she would make the long pilgrimage to Rome in search of the sun. On the way she would call upon her elder son at Florence, providing that her husband was absent. Louis Napoleon escorted his mother and it was by the banks of the Rubicon that he began to dream his dreams. By displaying the tricolour and arranging meetings with the male members of the Bonaparte family, he attracted the attention of the police. He also attracted the attention of Lord Malmesbury who, with some dismay, watched him gallop his horse through the streets of Rome. Malmesbury wrote of him:

Although short he was very active and muscular. He excelled in all physical exercises. He was a remarkable swimmer, an admirable horseman, and a noted gymnast. His face was grave and dark, but redeemed by a singularly bright smile. Such was the personal appearance of Louis Napoleon at the age of twenty-one years.[19]

Two years later, in 1830, came the 'July Revolution', when Louis XVIII's successor, Charles X fell, and the time of the Bourbons was over. Louis Napoleon was at Thun and wrote to his mother: 'France is free. Our exile is over ...'[20] Forbidden to enter France by the act of 1816, he moved to Geneva to be near the frontier should the call be made for his cousin, Napoleon II, to come from Austria.

But instead it was now the turn of the Orleans family and Louis Philippe was in the wings. On 7th August this friend of Queen Victoria's father, who had lived in both America and England, was created King of the French.

Across the frontier in Italy the July Revolution had its echo in the Papal States; the liberal uprising in France swept southwards. Italy, divided and oppressed, was a seed-bed for conspirators and secret societies. Some of them made their way to Hortense's home at Arenenberg.

In November, as was their wont, Louis Napoleon and his mother arrived in Rome. A few days later Pope Pius VIII died and in the subsequent upset the behaviour of Louis Napoleon was more than suspect. Papal police escorted him to the frontier of the Papal States. He headed north to join his brother in Florence, leaving his mother behind.

In February the revolutionaries staged a rising in the Romagna, aiming at the expulsion of the Pope from Rome. Hortense sent an urgent message to her sons, warning them of the dangers of becoming involved. But Menotti, one of the insurgent leaders, had already filled the two young men with talk of glory for the Bonapartes and freedom for the oppressed. Hortense, suspecting that something of the kind might happen, left Rome in a hurry to exert some maternal discipline. She arrived too late. In her hotel bedroom she found waiting a note from Louis Napoleon. It read: 'We have accepted engagements, and we cannot depart from them. The name we bear obliges us to help a suffering people that calls upon us.'[21] On the 20th they had left for the fighting, having been given officer ranking.

Next morning Hortense visited the husband whom she had not seen for twenty years. She found him fussy, flurried and rather pathetic. His contribution to the critical state of affairs was to suggest that Hortense should venture in among the warring forces and forcibly extract her sons from the field, while he undertook the less arduous task of calling upon the Austrian ambassador and enlisting his help. Hortense realised that, if she was to be seen driving about among the revolutionary forces, her political reputation would be gone for ever. She waited in the vain hope that her sons would come back. They did not.

Her sons had been in action at Civita Castellana, between Viterbo and Rome. On a plan prepared by Louis Napoleon, a result of his Swiss military training, the action had proved successful and the town had been taken. But this had led to jealousy among the leaders and the fear at insurgent headquarters that France would be prejudiced against their cause if Bonapartes were involved. There was danger that they would be declared outlaws. News also came in of Austrian troopships approaching the Adriatic coast and of the outbreak of fever in the east.

Early in March the news was such that she decided that she had no alternative but to leave for the fighting. On 10th March Hortense left Florence. In her possession was a British passport, which she had charmed out of the British Minister there, giving her passage through France to England. She headed south and contacted the insurgent forces, only to learn that her sons had left, making north for Bologna. She hurried in pursuit and at Perugia learned that they were further to the east and that the Austrian forces were in the field. She climbed into the mountains, hearing on the road that Napoleon Louis was down with fever at Forli.

At Pesaro Louis Napoleon met her. He told her that his elder brother was dead. He had died on the 27th after only three days illness. He was newly married and had been fully occupied with his business interests until caught up in this wild adventure. Fainting, Hortense was carried into the house where her younger son had been hiding.

She had no time to grieve. Not only was Louis Napoleon now an outlaw and a much wanted man, but he was in the first stages of the same fever – a virulent form of measles aggravated by cold and exposure – which had killed his brother. The Austrian troops were in command. She had to act very quickly. She knew that one of her nephews had a palace at Ancona and she made for it, fast, nursing her son and keeping him out of sight. On arrival, he was immediately put to bed.

The town was occupied by the Austrians and, as ill luck would have it, General Geppert, who was in command, chose for his billet the same palace belonging to Hortense's nephew. His choice of bedroom was next to the one in which Louis Napoleon lay sweating with fever.

Hortense had already taken the precaution of spreading the story that her son had taken ship for Greece, and this had been accepted. Her dual task now was to ensure that he did not give away his presence by coughing, and to gain the confidence of General Geppert. The second proved easier than the first, for few could surpass her in the handling of men.

For eight days Louis Napoleon fought the fever and, with the care lavished upon him by his mother, a care so sadly denied to his brother, he came through. Meantime Hortense had played her part of an ex-Queen superbly, suitably impressing Geppert with her reminiscences of the Empress Marie Louise and Field Marshal Schwarzenberg. She extracted from him a pass through the Austrian lines.

Early on Easter morning, before the Austrians were astir, Hortense entered her carriage. On the box was a young footman, servile and suitably dressed. It was young Louis Napoleon, whose first convalescent outing was to be a journey from the Adriatic to the Mediterranean. But for the sadness of death pervading the days, the long drive would have resembled a light operetta. Here was a very grand lady, with a British passport but speaking little English, flashing a pass at the Austrian guards, flattering and flirting with the Italian police, heading for London as if it were the most every day affair, while behind her on the box sat an outlaw and one of the most wanted men in Italy still pale and unsteady on his feet. Often they were near to discovery, sometimes near to arrest.

They travelled by Perugia, Siena, Pisa, Lucca, Genoa and Nice. Then, in defiance of the act which forbade them entry and on the strength of the British passport, they crossed into France. They rested for a while by the beautiful bay at Cannes.

It was April and France was green and fresh. They set out for Paris. Slowly now, for this was a nostalgic journey for Hortense, through places which she had known in the long ago. She was the guide and he, freed of the label of outlaw and the role of lackey, the sightseer. At Fontainebleau she showed him the font where he had been baptized, the rooms where she had danced in the fêtes of victory in 1807, the little table where the Emperor had signed the abdication in 1814.[22] Soon the fortifications of Paris came in to sight.

Hortense directed the coachman to the Rue de la Paix. Fittingly, she chose to stay at the Hotel de Hollande, and from her first floor apartment she could see the Place Vendôme Shortly a member of the Government arrived, suspicious, asking leading questions. She had already informed the King of her arrival and now she was bidden to meet him.

Louis Philippe was still, under his middle-class guise, flying the flag of equality. He had taken the royal lilies from the panels of his carriages and had not yet moved from the Palais Royal, which was open to all, to the Tuileries. To a ruler who had not yet found his feet, it was both embarrassing and compromising to meet the former Queen of Holland and the last woman in the life of Napoleon. But he had known her parents and understood well the problems of exile.

Hortense found the trappings of royalty drab and commonplace compared with the Empire days. At the Palais Royal she was shown into a small bedroom. After a while Louis Philippe entered. To make sure that he was not ensnared by this *femme fatale*, he brought with him his wife and sister. When Hortense revealed that she was on her way to London, on a British passport, and was only taking a short rest in Paris, there were smiles all round. But she received the clear impression that the sooner she went on her way the better the King would be pleased. When she got back to her hotel, she discovered that Louis Napoleon had suffered a recurrence of the fever and she decided that he could not be moved.

Daily the King sent round notes enquiring as to the progress of the invalid, each one more pressing than the last in the obvious wish that they should go. Hortense knew the reason behind the urgency – 5th May was the tenth anniversary of Napoleon's death and his old soldiers would be demonstrating in the streets. Finally an ultimatum came from the Government – leave at once, ill or no. But the departure of Louis Napoleon had been delayed long enough for him to be able to hear the crowds shouting '*Vive Napoléon*' as they placed their crowns of flowers around the column in the Place Vendôme. It was fine music to his ears.

CHAPTER 3

Dreams and Schemes

On 10th May 1831 Louis Napoleon underwent a useful, but uncomfortable, lesson in military planning. He learned of the dangers and impractability of attempting to invade England across the Channel in the area Calais-Dover. A westerly gale was blowing and dark nets of drenching rain blew in from full ahead. The coach was lashed firm to the deck of the steamship *Royal George*. Hortense lay prone along the seat and beside her moaned her faithful lady-in-waiting, Mlle Masuyer. This lady, who had uncomplainingly faced the perils of the Italian mountains and the dangers of insurgent warfare, now informed her Maker that, as far as she was concerned, He could take her now.

But, the channel crossing accomplished, and after a rest at Canterbury, the spring sunshine in the Kentish orchards and the interest to be found in a new country diverted attention from internal weaknesses. There was some cynicism expressed concerning English roads and traffic. Louis Napoleon took on the task of communicating with the natives and, with true Bonaparte confidence, dismissed as fools those who could not comprehend his halting words and strange accent.

Britain was in the throes of a general election and people were too much concerned with the policy and actions of the new King, William IV, and the progress of the Reform Bill to be interested in the arrival of a party of 'Boney's' relations in a shabby old coach. And shabby it was, for it had covered more than 2,000 miles since leaving Arenenberg in the autumn and had seldom been off the road. London was crowded and there was difficulty in finding an hotel which would take them in. Hortense, unaccustomed to such treatment, put the blame on the coach and decided that she must have a new one. At last accommodation was found on two floors at Fenton's Hotel in St James's at a daily rate of £4, but Mlle Masuyer, who handled financial matters, considered this to be excessive.[1] A few days later a house was rented in George Street, which had the advantage of being handy to the green of Regent's Park.

Hortense's acquaintances in London were thin upon the ground. A scattering of relations came to call: her niece, Amelie, married to Dom Pedro, first Emperor of Brazil; Lady Dudley Stuart,[a] daughter of Napoleon's eldest brother, Lucien; Achille Murat, son of Caroline Bonaparte and the ill-fated King of Naples, on a visit from America;[b] and Comte Walewski, a natural son of Napoleon by Marie Walewska. But this cocktail of mixed blood lacked influence and social contact and Hortense was ever a one to work from the top. She quickly sent a note round to King William and picked up links from the past with two of the most important houses, Holland and Woburn.

Lord Holland, a leader of the Whigs, had been a stern critic of the hard treatment meted out to Napoleon during his last years in exile and thus had much to discuss with Hortense. His wife, known as 'Old Madagascar', had built for herself a reputation as a hostess rivalling that of the great ladies who held 'salons' in Paris in the eighteenth century. Hortense was invited to Holland House and was well and truly launched.

Her other connection was with the Duchess of Bedford. They had met in Paris in the lull of 1802. The then Lady Georgiana Gordon had been taken to France by her match-making mother and had fallen in love with Hortense's brother, Eugène, but Napoleon had soon put a stop to that. So Georgiana married the sixth Duke of Bedford. She was rich, influential and dynamic – it was she who said to George, Prince of Wales, 'Come pree ma mou, ma canty callant.'[2] An invitation arrived to spend a few days at Woburn Abbey in June and off they set in their shining new carriage. The splendours of the Bedfords' stately home in England deeply impressed the Bonapartes, just as, ten years later, it was to impress Queen Victoria and her young German husband. The army of servants waiting to receive them at the door, the powdered footmen, the aviary, the modern dairy, the wide park, the great fête staged in their honour, left an unforgettable impression on the mind of Louis Napoleon.

But it was his mother, not he, who was considered the social catch of the season. He was still too young for his peculiar brand of ugliness to

(a) Lord Dudley Stuart, born 1803, son of the Marquess of Bute, married, in Italy, Christiane Alexandria Egypta, daughter of Lucien Bonaparte, Prince of Canino.
(b) He had emigrated to America in 1821 and settled near Tallahassee, Florida, where he was postmaster from 1826–38. He married a great-niece of George Washington.

appeal to women and, with his long body and short legs, he showed off better on a horse than on a chaise longue. So while his mother was invited to take tea at all the best houses, he occupied himself with broadening his mind. He inspected the defences of the Tower of London. Brunel[a] conducted him round the work in progress to bore a tunnel under the Thames between Wapping and Rotherhithe. He was present at the opening of Parliament. He became involved in an angry crowd demonstrating for reform, and was forced to take shelter. But his activities were not restricted to sightseeing and the educational. He again began to dabble in conspiracy. London was the nerve centre of those wishing to overthrow the Orleanist regime in France and they considered that Louis Napoleon was an asset to their cause.

In the event there were already sufficient suspicions around his head without him adding to them. After their Italian adventure, the French Government considered that Hortense and her son were capable of any degree of mischief. It was Achille Murat who first informed his aunt that there was considerable unrest in diplomatic circles concerning her presence in London and that Talleyrand, the new French ambassador, was particularly worried. There was a certain piquancy in this as it was rumoured that Talleyrand was the father of Comte de Flahaut, by whom Hortense had had a son[b] in 1811. Among the stories going the rounds was one that Louis Napoleon had his eye on the throne of Belgium, and this he denied in print. But in any case he would have had no chance, for the wily Coburgs had reserved this prize for themselves, Leopold being elected King of the Belgians in June.

Before leaving for his new country Leopold called upon Hortense, informing her that, if she were to return to Switzerland via Belgium, he hoped that she would not take his kingdom with her.³ The suspicions surrounding the visitors to London caused endless troubles over the issuing of a passport for their return to Arenenberg. First they were to go through Paris, then they were not to go through Paris, and it was August before their papers arrived.

In the meanwhile the combined strain of coping with the vagaries of Talleyrand and the conspiracies of her son upset Hortense's nervous system and this told on her physical well-being. She decided that she must leave London and take the waters in the peace of Tunbridge Wells.

(a) Sir Marc Isambard Brunel (1769-1849). The work was completed in 1843.
(b) Duc de Morny.

Here she deemed she would regain her strength and that her son would be clear of secretive callers and midnight meetings. Fortunately Louis Napoleon's interest was diverted in a more welcome direction. He became enamoured of a certain beautiful Miss Godfrey and his moonlight hours were occupied with a less hazardous occupation. On 7th August the return journey to Switzerland began.

Hortense decided that it would be wise to avoid Paris, as King Louis Philippe was showing no signs of hospitality and, even more important, because Louis Napoleon had informed her that, if he were to see crowds demonstrating in the streets, he would join them in their fight for freedom. So she decided that she would implant in him even more deeply the legend of Napoleon. She took him to Boulogne where, in 1805, she had seen the invasion fleet tied up ready for the assault on England. She showed him the little house where the Emperor had stayed. Then she drove on to Rueil where her mother was buried. In 1824 she and her brother had purchased one of the chapels in the church there and placed in it a white marble statue of the Empress at prayer, inscribed 'A Josephine, Eugène et Hortense, 1825'.[a] She had planned to visit Malmaison but it had been purchased by a Swedish banker and it was necessary to have a ticket to gain entrance. Hortense did not feel inclined to beg a ticket to see the spot where the Emperor had given her the last embrace before passing from her life, and from France.

Back at Arenenberg there came an interval of peace. Louis Napoleon built his own pavilion and crowded it with military memorabilia. He wrote pamphlets on the tactics of war and the aims of the Bonapartes.[b] He interested himself in parochial affairs and became quite the little squire. 'He became so great a favourite in the department where he resided, by uniform kindness to the inhabitants, and by the exertions, both personal and pecuniary, which he used to promote the education of the poor, that the Canton of Thurgau conferred on him the right of citizenship.'[4] He thus had roots for the first time since the age of seven.

The quiet life was shattered on 22nd July 1832 when the news came from Vienna that the Duke of Reichstadt, alias Napoleon II, alias the

(a) The church was afterward rebuilt by Napoleon III. There he erected a tomb to his mother, the figure of Queen Hortense kneeling and crowned by an angel.

(b) *Considérations politiques et militaires sur la Suisse; Rêveries politiques, suivies d'un projet de constitution.*

King of Rome was dead. He was only twenty-two and had spent all of his remembering years in the gilded captivity of his grandfather's[a] Austrian palace. Strange it was that three boys senior to Louis Napoleon in the Bonaparte dynasty had died in their youth. And now, it seemed to Louis Napoleon, that the mantle of the Great One was firm around his shoulders. Destiny had decreed that he should lead France and dwell in the Tuileries and, as the body of Napoleon II was laid to rest in the Church of the Capucins in Vienna, he looked to the future with excitement. Mlle Masuyer wrote of him at this time: 'Dressed in black, and wearing in his cravat a little eagle in diamonds, with a thunderbolt of rubies in its claws, he appeared to me as the man of destiny, although, with his serious features that light up with a singularly attractive smile, he is above all the man of mystery.'[5]

With the death of his nephew, Joseph Bonaparte, the head of the family, considered that, in America, he was too far removed from affairs and accordingly left his home at Bordentown, New Jersey, and came to London. There he called a conference of Napoleon's brothers. Lucien and Jerome answered the summons but ex-King Louis was crippled with rheumatism and could not leave Florence. Louis Napoleon was invited to take his place. Hortense agreed to his going as she considered that he would get into less trouble among all the varied interests of English life than he would at Arenenberg, where his devilish conspiratorial friends were for ever planning mischief for idle hands to do.

He arrived in London in the middle of November and was soon writing letters to his mother complaining of the lack of panache and planning of his uncles, whose only aim seemed to be to compromise on everything. He was, however, compensated by society, who now included him in the fashionable round. At one party he met Talleyrand, who ignored him. In revenge Louis Napoleon waited until the ambassador was talking to a lovely lady, then cut in and stole her away from him. He met a number of conspirators and made at least one secret journey across the Channel, and his uncle Joseph was mightily relieved when he returned to Arenenberg in May 1833.

Convinced that military training was an essential both to his character and to his future role, he again took up service with the Swiss forces, was promoted 'Captain Bonaparte' and wrote a Manual of

(a) Emperor Francis of Austria.

Artillery. But in the evenings, in his pavilion, he concerned himself with planning for the Second Empire, which he saw as '*un pouvoir national, c'est-à-dire un pouvoir dont tous les éléments se retrempent dans le peuple, seul source de tout ce qui est grand et généreux*'.[6]

Strangely enough Louis Philippe and his ministers played into the dreamer's hands. The leaders of France were middle-aged, middle-class and boring. But the Citizen King was wise enough to know that his people needed romance and so he gave it to them, in the form of the Napoleonic legend. Some twenty years had passed since Waterloo and the blood and the suffering, the massacre and the agonies, were but vague in the mist. Only the great moments shone in the sunshine of the present. So the people cheered as the statue of the Emperor swung back to its place in the Place Vendôme, as the names of victories were carved in stone at the Arc de Triomphe.

Once again the tricolour was the national flag of France. Poets immortalised Austerlitz and Elba. Actors portraying Napoleon played to full houses. There was talk of the body being brought back from St Helena – but then, some said, there would be two Kings in Paris, one at the Tuileries and one at Les Invalides. It was peculiarly the Napoleonic legend that was fostered, divorced from Bonapartism. The ageing brothers and their children played no part in it. They were forgotten, which was very fortunate for Louis Napoleon. He, too, had written off the family. It was the legend that he wanted, fresh and strong.

There then drove into Louis Napoleon's life Jean Gilbert Victor Fialin, a man of his own age. Fialin was a somewhat Byronic figure. The son of a tax collector, he had been dismissed from the army for insubordination. He had turned to journalism, writing for *Le Temps* in Paris. By this time he had assumed the title of Vicomte de Persigny, claiming descent from an old Brittany family. He was addicted to political causes and pretty women.

On a business trip to Baden he saw one evening a young lady who took his fancy. Learning of the whereabouts of her home, he drove out next morning to find her. His carriage passed a young man striding out along the road, whereat the coachman rose from his seat and shouted '*Vive Napoléon*'. On being informed of the walker's identity, Persigny forgot all about his feminine fancy. A dream came before his eyes. He saw a new Napoleon crossing the frontier of France, saw him gathering support as he marched towards Paris, saw delirious crowds greeting the Second Emperor in the capital. He obtained a letter of introduction and presented himself at Arenenberg. Shortly afterwards he took on the role of Louis Napoleon's Chief Planning Officer.

The two schemers built on the lines of the return from Elba but they made some miscalculations. Certainly La Fayette had written to Louis Napoleon: 'The Government cannot continue. Your name is the only one which is popular . . . . *Osez donc et je vous aiderai de tous mes moyens, quand le moment sera venu.*'[7] But that was only the view of a section in Paris and did not take into account the army. Emperor Napoleon had been a legend to his men, who had only been away from active service for a year when he came back from Elba. In 1836 the army had, in truth, grievances and was discontented, but Prince Louis Napoleon was an unknown and untried quantity both to officers and men and only the older among them were battle trained. The difference in the way of thinking and reacting between battle trained units and cantonment troops was not grasped by the planners. The regiments stationed along the Rhine frontier considered their duties to consist of parades, guards and customs duties. Their main considerations were with leave and ladies. They relied upon weekend visits to the casinos and cafés of Baden-Baden to relieve the monotony and rigours of their life. Only a long conversion course and some blood-letting would turn them to the kind of men whom Napoleon had led into battle at Waterloo. Louis Napoleon had many lessons still to learn.

Persigny made a reconnaissance of the frontier towns and decided that Strasbourg should be the starting point for the adventure. The 4th Artillery was stationed there and this same 4th had hurriedly joined Napoleon at the beginning of the Hundred Days. It was reasoned that, what this unit had done before, it might well do again. The next point to be settled was the composition of the headquarters staff. Besides the two principals, this consisted initially of Comte Francesco Arese, a former member of the *Carbonari*, who had been involved in the Italian affair and who had accompanied Louis Napoleon to London on his second visit; Colonel Parquin, husband of Hortense's reader and an enthusiastic Bonapartist; and Charles Thélin, Louis Napoleon's faithful manservant. In the summer of 1836 Persigny decided that it was time to move nearer to the scene of action and he rented a house on the German side of the Rhine handy for Strasbourg.

It was there that they were joined by a most useful recruit. She was strikingly beautiful, she was farouche, she was a contralto of repute and she was a widow.

Eleanora Marie Brault was born in Paris in September 1808. Her father was a captain of the Imperial Guards and she was educated at a convent in the Rue de Sèvres. Her loves being music and the theatre, she studied at the Conservatoire and for a time Rossini was her mentor. She developed a contralto voice and sang in Italy and around Europe. In 1831 she was in London and there married Sir Gordon Archer, an officer attached to the Anglo-Spanish legation. In March 1836 he died of typhus at Vittoria. His widow chose to be known as Mme Gordon. A very merry widow, she returned to her stage career and became the mistress of Persigny. She accepted an engagement to sing at Strasbourg and Baden-Baden and had quarters in both towns, which was most convenient for the planners.

Eleanora Gordon was described both as a 'woman-man' and a 'man-eater'. She was a woman who needs must be a fanatic about something and she divided her energies between Bonapartism and sex, with the emphasis on the former. She could fence and she could shoot – it was rumoured that, on a trip with her husband, she had shot a tiger in Bengal. Gossip was that she was also the lover of Louis Napoleon, but he denied it and she denied it, and it was her denial that carried more weight. She said that he was too much like a woman for her. But she admitted that she adored him politically.[8] The great advantage of Eleanora was that, if it became necessary to tempt a man, she was capable of tempting beyond man's endurance.

Louis Napoleon now began the task of making contacts. He frequented the casino at Baden-Baden and there got into conversation with a number of young officers on leave from Strasbourg. He was looking for those who had grievances. He was lucky enough to find a Lieutenant Laity[9] who was not only discontented with his lot but was also a fervid admirer of the Emperor Napoleon. Through him a group of some twelve recruits was gathered. The next step was to enlist the help of a senior officer. Louis Napoleon went to the top and tried his hand with General Voirol, commanding the 5th Division. He asked for but a word in reply. He received a few brief and very pointed words. They were to the effect that General Voirol would give the Prince a quarter of an hour to get back across the Rhine.[10]

The next to be approached was Colonel Vaudrey, commanding the 4th Artillery. Claude Nicolas Vaudrey was fifty-two. He had fought with the Grand Army in all the campaigns between 1806 and 1814, had been a prisoner of war and distinguished himself at Waterloo. In 1830 he had been recalled to service and promoted colonel three years later. But, like many another long serving officer, Vaudrey considered that he was deserving of better things. His application for a senior staff post had been turned down. He was a fine figure of a man, married with two children. But, discontented though he was, when approached it was discovered that he was not prepared to risk his career for any wildcat scheme. So other steps had to be taken and before the susceptible Colonel's eyes was dangled the carrot of beautiful Eleanora. She entranced him, twisted him round her finger. He begged her to be his mistress. She said: 'I will only be his, who is for the Prince Napoleon.' Vaudrey replied: 'Be mine. I am his.'[11] And so it was.

Early in October Louis Napoleon, in disguise, slipped into Strasbourg one day at dusk. In a room in Eleanora's house he addressed two dozen of his supporters. He spoke of the sanctity of his cause and uttered the old rallying calls of the Empire days. He returned convinced, from the reception which he had received, that he had sufficient support to make the attempt without further delay. He drove to Arenenberg to see Hortense and to receive her blessing. She slipped on to his finger a plain gold ring. It was engraved with the names of *Napoleon Bonaparte* and *Josephine Tascher*. It had been their wedding ring.[12]

On 26th October Louis Napoleon moved. He disappeared. He drove around the by-roads ensuring that he was not trailed. He spent the night of the 27th at Lahr. The next day he drove to Freiburg, crossed into France at Neuf-Brisach and headed north to Colmar. He entered Strasbourg late in the evening and spent the night at Eleanora's house, 7 Rue de la Fontaine. He brought with him a trunk containing proclamations and French uniforms. The 29th was spent in contacting his supporters. Late in the evening he met Vaudrey on the Quai Neuf.

There was little sleep in Eleanora's house that night. Shortly before six on the morning of the 30th the conspirators slipped out into the half light. It was snowing. Louis Napoleon was in the uniform of a colonel, Parquin in that of a general. They carried a tricolour surmounted by the eagle of the Empire.

Vaudrey had paraded his men early. He called them to attention and saluted Louis Napoleon as the party materialised out of the darkness. The would-be Emperor then made a dramatic and rousing speech. This was greeted by some half-hearted cries of '*Vive l'Empereur*', for the early hour and the inclement weather were not conducive to enthusiasm. The band struck up, the order was given and off marched the 4th Artillery towards the barracks of the 46th of the Line.[13]

At this point Persigny hurried off to arrest the *Prèfet*, and Parquin, the Military Governor. General Voirol, roused by the clamour, was in his combinations and in no mood for interference. He ran from room to room, banging doors in Parquin's face and struggling with his trousers. His wife and mother-in-law joined in the skirmish and through their efforts Voirol reached the street, dishevelled but recognisable as a general. He looked straight into the barrels of two pistols and, behind them, the excited face of Eleanora Gordon. She had spent the night with Vaudrey and now joined in the fun with a gun in either hand. Fortunately for Voirol, she mistook him for a supporter. Otherwise, as she later said, she would have blown his head off. She was the only real danger on the streets that morning.[14]

Unfortunately there was a hitch in the advance of the 4th Artillery. It had been planned that entrance to the barracks should be gained by scaling the ramparts, an entrance which, it was deemed, would impress the infantry. But instead the column was led up a narrow lane and only a few of its members could be distinguished in the poor light by the sergeant of the guard. He was not impressed. But the column pushed by and was confronted by a subaltern. He was ordered to parade the regiment. He refused. Napoleon or not, the infantry was not taking orders from the artillery. By this time a considerable number of men had collected in the barrack square. Louis Napoleon began his harangue, but was interrupted by the cry of 'Imposter'. The commanding officer appeared on the scene and ordered the party of the would-be Emperor to be driven against a wall. Louis Napoleon forbade his supporters to draw their swords or pistols. He was arrested and lodged in the town gaol. Persigny hid in Eleanora's house. When soldiers arrived to take him in charge, she fought so fiercely that he was able to escape through the back.

General Voirol sent an immediate report to Paris. It went by 'aerial telegraph', semaphore being used to transmit from one high point to

Queen Hortense, mother of Napoleon III

Prince Louis Napoleon

Portrait of Mlle Eugenie Montijo, afterwards Empress of the
French. A drawing by the Prince de Joinville, 1852

Above: Château Malmaison
Below: Château de Fontainebleau

another. But there was fog on the route and only half the message got through. Being translated it read:

> This morning, at about six o'clock, Louis Napoleon, son of the Duchesse de Saint-Leu, aided by the Colonel of Artillery, Vaudrey, appeared in the streets of Strasbourg with a party of . . . .[15]

This disturbed Louis Philippe and his Ministers immensely. Unless the fog cleared, there was no possible way of finding out what the rest of the message was. There was no way of estimating the size of 'the party'. It was within the bounds of possibility that a new Emperor was already well on his way to Paris, an insurgent column behind him. Next morning fog still shrouded the countryside and it was not until the evening that a messenger rode in from Strasbourg. Never has a king been more relieved. So much so, indeed, that he conferred an immediate title on General Voirol.

Some way behind the messenger, another traveller made for Paris. It was Hortense and she was in a hurry. She contacted Louis Philippe, begged for forgiveness for her son, pleaded that it was only youth's craving for adventure, and made promises. The King was anxious both to avoid trouble and not to tarnish the Napoleonic legend. So he forgave, provided that Louis Napoleon went to America. He also forgave the other conspirators and they were found not guilty at their trial. But this was the last time.

Louis Philippe was making no mistakes. Louis Napoleon was brought under guard to Paris and, after only a few hours there, was taken on to the fortress of Port Louis near Lorient. He was not allowed to see his mother. Another sadness was contained in a letter from his uncle Jerome. This informed him that, as a result of his outrageous behaviour, there was now no question of his marrying his cousin Mathilde. There had been an understanding between them and he was devoted to her.

On 21st November he boarded the frigate *Andromède*. At the gang plank there were two moments of cheer. He was handed a purse containing 16,000 francs in gold, as a present from King Louis Philippe. And an officer of the Gendarmerie whispered to him: 'France knows now that the Emperor has an heir.' Out in the Bay the captain opened his sealed orders. His journey to the United States was to take four months and his passenger was to be treated as a prisoner. So throughout the winter the *Andromède* pottered about the Atlantic, from the Canary Islands to Rio, and it was not until 30th March 1837 that she made landfall at Norfolk, Virginia. Louis Napoleon was given a farewell dinner by the officers. He was now on his own. The long sea voyage had dulled his aspirations and he was contemplating a life as an American farmer. He described the next step in his journey in a letter to Hortense, written from New York:

> The second of April the captain and officers conducted me to the steamboat that conveyed me up Chesapeake Bay to Baltimore. We left at four o'clock in the afternoon. There were two hundred passengers on board. The cabin, a narrow room, about 160 feet in length, extends the entire length of the boat. Supper was served at seven. Half an hour later, the tables were taken away and beds were made for everybody. The women have cabins apart. About four in the morning, being very hot, I got up and went on deck to get some fresh air. We arrived at Baltimore at six o'clock in the morning, and started immediately upon another boat. At the end of the bay we found a railway that conveyed us to the Delaware River, where we again took boat to Philadelphia. From Philadelphia to New York we travelled in the same way, partly by railway and partly by boat. I passed before Point Breeze, the residence of my uncle (King Joseph, at Bordentown, New Jersey). It is a pretty little house on the banks of the Delaware, but the surrounding country is flat. The only fine features are the width of the stream, and the steamboats which are magnificent.

Once in New York, the loneliness and the isolation came to an end. Waiting to greet him were two fellow conspirators, Count Arese and his faithful servant, Charles Thélin. There were also three cousins – Pierre, the son of Lucien Bonaparte, and Achille and Lucien Murat. He put up at the Washington Hall Hotel on the east side of Broadway, one of the finest buildings in the city,[a] and by virtue of his name and his adventures received attention from the newspapers. He dined with General Webb, editor of the 'Courier and Enquirer', and was introduced to Washington Irving. He was taken up by the Clintons and the Livingstons and so occupied was he by the social round that his plan to

(a) Later the site of a store owned by A. T. Stewart and afterwards the offices of *The Sun* and *New York Herald*.

make a detailed tour of the continent was postponed. He had only made a trip to Niagara Falls and inspected his uncle's house, known locally as 'Bonaparte Mansion', on the Delaware, when his life was interrupted by a letter from his mother. As he prepared to open the envelope he saw written over the flap the words '*Venez! Venez!*', and he recognised the hand of her physician, Dr Conneau. Then he read:

My dear Son,

I am about to undergo an operation that is absolutely necessary. In case it should not succeed, I send you my blessing. We shall meet again, shall we not? in a better world, where you will come to join me only as late as possible. And you will remember that in leaving this world I regret only you – only your gentle affection, that has given some charm to my life. It will be a consolation to you, my dear child, to know it was your care for her which made your mother as happy as it was possible for her to be. You will think of all my love for you, and take courage. Believe that we always keep a kindly and searching eye on all we leave here below, and that certainly we meet again. Have faith in this consoling idea; it is too necessary not to be true. I give my blessing also to good Arese as to a son. I press you to my heart, my dear one. I am quite calm and resigned, and hope we may meet again in this world. Let the will of God be done.

Your tender Mother, HORTENSE.[16]

He surmised cancer and realised that Hortense had been ill for some time and kept the truth from him. He booked passage on the first boat to sail out of New York, the *George Washington*, and was in London, at Fenton's Hotel, by 10th July. Now he wanted help, and quickly, to obtain a passport for the remainder of the journey. But he was a marked man. On hearing of his arrival, his uncle Joseph sent him a rude letter and immediately retreated to his home of Brettenham Hall, set in a park of 150 acres near Lavenham in Suffolk. Lady Dudley Stuart was more helpful. She used her influence with the Austrian Ambassador who approached the French embassy in an attempt to gain freedom of passage through France, but he met with a blank refusal. Then a welcome visitor in the person of Persigny called at Fenton's and offered his wealth of conspiratorial experience.

Meantime the French Ambassador had received instructions from

Paris: 'Neglect no means of obtaining exact information of the doings of this young man and his plans of travel. If he should leave England, you will kindly let me know at once, by courier and by telegraph, which direction he takes.'[17] The Ambassador visited the Home Office and Lord John Russell promised assistance.

Louis Napoleon received another letter from his mother and decided that he could wait no longer. He borrowed an American passport, and this was signed by the Swiss Minister without query. On 29th July he drove openly, with all his luggage, from Fenton's to Richmond, where he put up at an inn. Persigny was now in charge of planning and next day Louis Napoleon was rushed back towards London in a fast chaise. At the outskirts the passenger slipped out and the chaise went on. Louis Napoleon caught an omnibus and made his way to the Thames. There he boarded the Dutch steamer, *Batavier*. Persigny warned Mlle Masuyer of his departure, telling her to contact Mr Thomson at Mannheim. On the 31st the London Police informed the French Embassy that they had lost touch with the Prince Louis Napoleon. By this time the fugitive had reached Rotterdam and transferred to a Rhine steamer. He disembarked at Mannheim, collected his mail and continued by road to Arenenberg. He arrived late on the evening of the 4th August. His mother was sleeping and was too ill to be woken.[18]

When she saw him in the early morning, the delight brought strength flowing back to her. He sat beside her, reading to her, reminiscing, making her smile, through the warm, still months of August and September. She lasted until the leaves began to fall. She died before dawn on 5th October, her eyes fixed upon, her arms outstretched towards, the son to whom she had given all of her love.

CHAPTER 4

Invasion and the Prison Cell

The heart of Louis Napoleon was broken. In seclusion at Arenenberg[(a)] he sorted out his mother's possessions and carried out the many bequests in her will. In the room which she had decorated and furnished for him he read over and over again her last instructions:

> *Never be tired of claiming that the Emperor was infallible, and that he had a valid national motive for all of his acts.*
>
> *Do not fail to assert at all times that he rendered France powerful and prosperous, and that each one of his conquests brought to Europe institutions which will never be regretted.*
>
> *People end by believing that which is repeated often enough: one always obtains that which is demanded continuously and in every form.*[1]

But in January 1838 he could bear the loneliness, and the ghost of her, no more and he moved to the nearby Château of Gottlieben, a property which Hortense had left to him. It was to Gottlieben that his friends, who felt that his grief and hermit-like existence had lasted long enough, gathered to cheer him up. And among these friends were men who had taken part in the Strasbourg adventure.

The French authorities, who had followed a policy of non-interference during the mourning period for the ex-Queen of Holland, heard of these gatherings and became very much alert. A contributory reason was the publication of a pamphlet by Lieutenant Laity which attempted to show that the Strasbourg attempt was much more dangerous than had generally been supposed. This indiscretion earned Laity a prison sentence of five years. The French Government now obviously viewed Louis Napoleon as a serious menace. At the end of January the Duc de Montebello, son of Marshal Lannes, presented himself at Lucerne and demanded his expulsion from Switzerland.

This brazen demand annoyed the Swiss immensely. They had no

(a) A few years later Louis Napoleon sold Arenenberg. He repurchased it when he became Emperor and presented it to Eugenie.

intention of being dictated to about the movements of their honorary citizens, and they objected to interference with their custom of offering refuge to well-heeled exiles. They accordingly embarked on a plan of go-slow. When the French Minister asked what progress had been made in complying with the demand, he was told that the matter had been passed to another department, that a committee had been formed to consider it, that an international lawyer was being called in to give his opinion. It was a case of memo piling up on memo, minute on minute, of files passing slowly from hand to hand – 'Over to you', 'Passed to you for action'. But no action was taken. At length the mass of memoranda reached the Canton of Thurgau. Unaccustomed to dealing with matters of international import, the locals replied by inviting Louis Napoleon to become president of their shooting club.

The French, infuriated, could stand no more. In September an army corps of 25,000 men was mobilised at Lyons and moved towards the Swiss frontier. The commanding officer thundered: 'Our turbulent neighbours will see for themselves, perhaps too late, that instead of making speeches and insults, it would be better to satisfy the just demands of France.'[2] In Switzerland Louis Napoleon became a national hero. Honours were piled upon him. The Swiss and French press railed at one another. At Lucerne volunteers offered their services to fight for the honour of the Republic.

The Swiss army mobilised, trenches were dug in the streets, war seemed imminent. Summer tourists found the situation disturbing. Amongst them the Nightingale family, who were in Geneva at the time, hastily prepared to leave for Paris. Florence sat indoors with her mother, listening to the clamour outside as the barricades were erected in the streets.[3] Her father searched the town for horses for their carriage. This was Miss Nightingale's first taste of war.

Louis Napoleon was now a hero and it was the first time that he had enjoyed such a role. The French King had played into his hands by telling the world that an emperor stood in the wings. This time Louis Napoleon made no mistake. At the moment of crisis he calmly announced that he was leaving Switzerland of his own free will. The French looked foolish. The Swiss were delighted that they had made their point and extracted themselves from a difficult situation. At the beginning of October Louis Napoleon held an auction sale of his

34

carriages and horses and on the 14th drove, through cheering crowds, across Germany towards the Rhine, Rotterdam and London.

As a result of his mother's will and the sale of land in Switzerland, Louis Napoleon was now a rich young man and he spent lavishly. He rented a fine house, 17, Carlton House Terrace, later moving on to 1, Carlton Gardens. In his suite were Persigny; General Montholon, who had stayed at St Helena with the Emperor Napoleon until his death; Colonel Parquin; and Dr Conneau, who had promised Hortense before she died that he would never leave her son's side. Below stairs were the faithful Charles Thélin and two retainers inherited from his mother. He engaged the best cook in London. Imperial eagles were painted on the doors of his carriages. His clothes were made in Savile Row and he wore a diamond studded eagle in his black caravat. He attracted much attention when he rode in the Park and he was sketched by John Doyle. The Hollands and the Duchess of Bedford were quick to renew their acquaintance. As Society was flocking to Leamington Spa for the winter, thither travelled Louis Napoleon, staying at the Regent Hotel. He hunted with the Warwickshire and received invitations to stay at the great houses of the Shires.

He met the Duchess of Somerset, the Duke and Duchess of Beaufort, Lord Eglinton, Bulwer Lytton, Captain Marryat, Michael Faraday, Rossetti, Marie Taglioni and Benjamin and Mary Anne Disraeli. After breakfast one day at Bulwer's place on the Thames, Louis Napoleon took the Disraelis for a row. He grounded the boat on a mud bank and the wash from passing craft threatened to overturn it. To the amusement of her husband, Mary Anne laced into the oarsman. 'You should not undertake things which you cannot accomplish. You are always too adventurous, sir.'[a][4]

The Duke of Wellington showed marked interest in the nephew of the Emperor whom he had defeated. He commented: 'Would you believe it, this young man Louis Napoleon will not have it said that he is not going to be Emperor of the French!'[5] Others noticed the same fixation about the future. In Scotland he stayed at Brodrick Castle with the son of the Duke of Hamilton, who had married his cousin Mary, daughter of the Grand Duchess Stéphanie of Baden. Among the guests was the Duke of Newcastle, who wrote: 'Prince Louis

(a) Twenty years later, at the Tuileries, Mary Anne recounted the story. The Empress Eugenie's eyes turned up to the ceiling and she commented: 'Just like him.'

Napoleon and I often went out to shoot together, but neither of us being very keen for the sport, we preferred to sit down in the heather and discuss serious subjects. He always opened the conversation by speaking of what he hoped to do when he wore the crown, and I am convinced that this thought never left him for a single moment.'[6]

His summit of achievement in the activities of British society was when he took part in the famous Eglinton Tournament of 1839. Sightseers in their thousands flocked to the Ayrshire site to watch the tilting, admire the armour and the striking dresses of the ladies, but sadly one of the best rehearsed and most ambitious spectacles of the nineteenth century was all but washed out by drenching rain. 'A grand cavalcade, in which Prince Louis Napoleon rode as one of the knights, left Eglinton Castle on the 28th of August at two in the afternoon, with heralds, banners, pursuivants, the knight-marshal, the jester, the King of the Tournament, the Queen of Beauty, and a glowing assemblage of knights and ladies, seneschals, chamberlains, esquires, pages, and men-at-arms, and made their way in procession to the lists, which were overlooked by galleries in which nearly two thousand spectators were accommodated; but all the while the rain came down in bucketsful . . . .'[7]

Despite Louis Napoleon's determination to be seen with the right people at the right time, he was nevertheless regarded with distrust by real society, and particularly by mothers of pretty daughters. To them he was both an adventurer and an upstart. As a debutante, Lady Dorothy Nevill was somewhat taken by him – he made her laugh. 'My sister and I saw a good deal of him – so much so, indeed, that we were often told to see less of him; for at that time society did not view this Prince with any too favourable an eye, nor consider him an ideal companion for young ladies.'[8]

Another reason for suspicion of Louis Napoleon was his constant attendance at Gore House, Kensington, reigned over by Lady Blessington and Count D'Orsay. True, most people-who-were-anyone were seen there on occasion, to laugh for a while and leave, to paddle and not to bathe. Louis Napoleon bathed. Leveson Gower damned the place. 'I was never in Gore House myself, but I was told by others who knew it that with some few exceptions the company was inferior and to compare it with that of Holland House, as has sometimes been done, is simply ridiculous.'[9] Greville was little kinder: 'Lady Blessington's existence is a curiosity, and her house and society have at least the merit of being singular, though the latter is not so agreeable as from its composition it ought to be. There is no end to the men of consequence and distinction in the world who go there occasionally ... she *has been* very intimate with Byron, and *is* with Walter Savage Landor. Her house is furnished with a luxury and splendour not to be surpassed; her dinners are frequent and good; and D'Orsay does the honours with a frankness and cordiality which are very successful, but all this does not make society, in the real meaning of the term. There is a vast deal of coming and going, and eating and drinking, but little or no conversation . . . .'[10]

Apart from the point that Lady Blessington wrote books for money, which definitely was not the done thing, it was the past record of herself and D'Orsay to which people took exception, in particular their treatment of D'Orsay's young Countess, known as 'the virgin wife'. Lady Harriett Gardiner, born in 1812, was the only legitimate daughter of the Earl of Blessington. Harriett's mother died when she was young and her father married Marguerite St Leger Farmer, witty, farouche, handsome, extravagant and a very bad stepmother. Leveson Gower continued with his damnation: 'Lord Blessington's daughter was brought up in Ireland by two pious old aunts in the principles of religion and morality. When she had reached the age of sixteen her step-mother, Lady Blessington, brought about a marriage between her stepdaughter (Harriett) and her own lover, Count D'Orsay, in order that he might get hold of her fortune. After the marriage she induced him entirely to neglect his young wife. She, moreover, endeavoured to undermine her faith and her morals by getting her to read books calculated to do so, and what was still worse, she promoted the advances of other men, who made up to this inexperienced and beautiful young woman. Her life at Gore House became at last so intolerable that she fled from it, never to return.[a][11]

One of the reasons why Louis Napoleon was so often at Gore House was because D'Orsay was an enthusiastic supporter of the Bonaparte cause, his father having received his title from the Emperor. But with the passing years he realised the snags of tying himself too closely to

(a) After the death of her husband in 1851, Countess D'Orsay married the Hon. Spencer Cowper, of Sandringham Hall, Norfolk, later the home of the Prince and Princess of Wales.

these two talented but unscrupulous adventurers. Friends of a Prince on the loose in London were not necessarily the right friends for a leader of a nation. When after the *coup d'état*, Lady Blessington visited Paris, she expected some return for her hospitality and an invitation to the Tuileries. But no invitation came. At length she met him at a reception and he had no alternative but to recognise her. He assumed his slow and distant smile. '*Ah, Miladi Blessington! Restez-vous longtemps à Paris?*' She looked at him straight and snapped back: '*Et vous, Sire?*'[12]

It was, however, not to one of the belles of fashionable London drawing-rooms that Louis Napoleon gave his heart, but to the daughter of a rich Kentish builder, Henry Rowles. Emily was very beautiful and, through her mother, Spanish blood flowed in her veins, an admixture which the French pretender seemed to find attractive. He gave Emily many presents and often stayed at her home, Camden Place, Chislehurst. Strangely enough when, as an exiled Emperor, he took refuge in England in 1871, it was to find that his wife was installed at Camden Place, Chislehurst.

Louis Napoleon's social activities were in part a means of keeping his name before the public and in part a blind. Behind the scenes he was concentrating on the cause to which he had devoted his life. From six o'clock in the morning until the time came for his afternoon ride and his evening engagements, he was hard at work reading the political and industrial news, researching and writing. In the summer of 1839 his book, *Des Idées Napoléoniennes*, was published. The language was rich, the creed elysian. Napoleon was revealed as a social reformer upon whom military campaigns had been forced. The future lay in '*une idée sociale, industrielle, commerciale, humanitaire, . . . à travers la gloire des armes une gloire civile plus grande et plus durable.*' A cheap edition was published in France and became a best seller.

More and more mysterious callers came to Carlton Gardens, among them Eleanora Gordon. The French Government made a request to the British Prime Minister that Louis Napoleon should be forbidden to reside in London. Lord Melbourne replied that such a veto would be impossible in England. The French Ambassador was therefore instructed to keep a close watch on his activities and report his movements to Paris. Spies were now never far away and steps to blacken his name with the British authorities were taken. Among them was a plan to involve him in a duel. A natural son of Emperor Napoleon, the wastrel Comte

Léon, was sent to London to pick a quarrel. This he did most efficiently, being rude beyond endurance. Accordingly Louis Napoleon called him out. They met early one morning on Wimbledon Common. Léon played for time, making an argument about the choice of weapons and, as had been foreseen, the police arrived before any damage could be done. The contestants and their supporters were arrested and driven to Bow Street police station, where they were charged with committing a breach of the peace. On production of securities they were bound over. But it was Louis Napoleon who stayed in London and Léon who crept back to Paris, penniless and disgraced.[13]

Louis now embarked upon the most stupid and reckless escapade of his career. He decided once again to invade France. Fired by the news that the Emperor Napoleon's body was to be brought from St Helena, borne in triumph and placed under the gilded dome of Les Invalides, he decided that his moment had come. He overestimated the power of the Napoleonic legend in France and underestimated the intelligence of the Embassy spies in London. In June 1840 he raised, on dubious security, a sum of £20,000 through his Florentine banker, Count Orsi, who also agreed to take charge of planning for the invasion. Muskets were ordered from Birmingham, uniforms from Paris and proclamations were printed in London. In July a steamer, the *Edinburgh Castle*, was hired for a month – 'for a pleasure cruise', the owners were told. A force of fifty-six men was recruited, more than half of them being refugees from the Continent and menservants. Only four persons knew the true purpose of the voyage – Dr Conneau, Orsi, Charles Thélin and Persigny. Not even old General Montholon and Colonel Parquin were fully in the secret.

On the morning of the 4th August loading began at London Bridge. Nine horses and two carriages were swung on board. Cases, all labelled to an address in Hamburg, were stowed in the hold. They contained muskets and pistols, uniforms and proclamations. Less disguised were the cases of wine, spirits and food, fitting companions for a pleasure cruise. The invasion force was picked up, in parties, at various points on the way down river. At two o'clock the *Edinburgh Castle* reached Gravesend. Here Parquin boarded with a party of ten. Louis Napoleon was also supposed to be there, but he was having trouble throwing the watchers from the French Embassy off the trail and it was nearly six when he eventually arrived. Parquin went ashore to buy some cigars and returned plus a dishevelled vulture, a caricature of the Imperial eagle, which was tethered to the mast.[a] The final embarkations took place at Ramsgate, reached on the morning of the 5th. Then the *Edinburgh Castle* steamed out over the horizon.

Once beyond the point of no return Louis Napoleon paraded his passengers, informed them of their destiny, issued them with uniforms, paid each man one hundred francs and counteracted the effects of shock and trepidation by opening the cases of liquor and food. Unaccustomed as they were to the trappings of a luxury cruise, they soon passed beyond the stage of argument, and fell asleep.

At three o'clock on the morning of the 6th, before dawn on a dead calm sea, the invading force, only half awake, stumbled about the deck adjusting their strange uniforms. To the south were the lights of Boulogne harbour. A mile away, to the east, the silhouette of Wimereux materialised in the dawn.

Two coastguards patrolled the shore. They picked out the outline of the *Edinburgh Castle* in the mist, and the dark shape of a rowing boat moving in. They were waiting at the Pointe aux Oies as it grounded thirty yards out and its occupants waded ashore. On being challenged by the coastguards they said that they belonged to the 40th Regiment, were en route from Dunkerque to Cherbourg and that their paddle wheel had broken down. But an irresponsible member let out the truth and the effect on the coastguards was shattering. They shook with fear. Instead of regarding the second coming of Louis Napoleon as the arrival of the Messiah, as he would have liked them to have done, they behaved as if they were in the presence of Attila the Hun. Misguidedly, Louis Napoleon let them go and they made off smartly towards the safety of Wimereux.

Three times the boat made the trip from the steamer to the shore. As the sun was rising, the leader marshalled his men and marched over the hill into Boulogne. His objective was the infantry barracks where a certain Lieutenant Aladenize[14] was in the plan and had promised his support. The column proceeded without hindrance until it reached the guard-house on the Place d'Alton. Impressed by the spearhead of officers, the sergeant turned out the guard but, on being requested to join the invaders, excused himself on the grounds of duty. On they

(a) It ended its days as the pet of a merchant in Arras.

went. They met a lone officer on his way to duty at this early hour. He was greeted cordially and invited to join the column. He did not, however, appear to appreciate the honour and slipped away to warn his commanding officer.

Better luck awaited them at the infantry barracks. The guard saluted and Lieutenant Aladenize had the men on parade and called them to attention. Louis Napoleon addressed them in true imperial fashion and was handing out promotions and francs when a very irate colonel arrived. There then began a shouting match, during which Persigny had to be restrained from killing a royalist supporter who shouted '*Vive le Roi*'. Meanwhile the order had gone out for all officers to parade immediately and, when they arrived, it was all over. The colonel assumed full command and a very angry Louis Napoleon marched his men off towards the upper town where there was an arsenal. It was now about six o'clock and people were about in the streets and leaning from the windows, roused by the drums of the infantry. They were offered proclamations and largesse but only stared, as if they were witnessing publicity for a travelling circus.

When the column failed to force the Porte de Calais, the older and less enthusiastic members decided that discretion was the better part of valour, broke away and ran for the harbour area in the hope of avoiding capture. With his remaining supporters Louis Napoleon made for the *Colonne de la Grand Armée*,[a] determined there to make a desperate stand. But the National Guards were now out on the streets and it was clear that the end was near. Louis Napoleon planted his flag at the column and then, protesting, was at last persuaded to make a dash for the Wimereux shore and the waiting boat. Away they ran, a crowd of officials, soldiers, police and onlookers hard on their heels.

The rowing boat from the *Edinburgh Castle* lay off the Pointe aux Oies. As the 'remnants of an army' reached the shore, those at the rear were overtaken and made prisoner. Only those at the head, still with heart and wind, took to the water. Among them were Louis Napoleon, Persigny and Conneau. As they reached the boat and clambered on board, the National Guards opened fire. One man was killed. Then the boat capsized and another man was drowned. A craft was launched from the shore and Louis Napoleon and the other survivors were

(a) Begun in 1804 and finished under Louis Philippe, in commemoration of Napoleon's projected invasion of England.

dragged from the water. They were landed at the stone steps of Pidou jetty. Louis Napoleon was allowed to change his dripping clothes at the Custom House and then, in a varied assortment of carts and carriages, the prisoners were taken to the Vieux Château of Boulogne. By nine o'clock the invasion was over. The *Edinburgh Castle* was escorted into harbour and the cataloguing of her strange cargo began. The news was flashed to Paris and Louis Philippe laughed with delight.

A few days later Louis Napoleon began his journey to Paris. The police in the carriage with him were armed and had orders to shoot to kill if he attempted to escape. A night was spent at the dismal Château of Ham on the river Somme. He was brought into the capital at midnight on the 12th and lodged in the Conciergerie. On 28th September he was arraigned with his principal accomplices before the Chamber of Peers, sitting as a High Court of Justice. In a brilliant and forceful speech, Louis Napoleon expounded his political beliefs and reasons for the Boulogne landing. To some extent he salvaged himself from the flood of ridicule which he had brought upon himself. But there was no question of his guilt. He was sentenced to life imprisonment in a French fortress. Those who had accompanied him received terms varying from two to twenty years, and were to be confined at Doullens. Louis Napoleon and the other principals, Montholon, Conneau and Thélin, were taken back under strong guard to the dark fortress of Ham.

Ham lies thirty-six miles south-east of Amiens on the Laon road. It had been dominated through the years by its tenth century castle, a fortress which had defied the passing of time but was to crumble to the guns in the retreat of 1917. Before Louis Napoleon was enclosed by its ramparts, other famous prisoners had languished there – Joan of Arc, Louis of Bourbon and, more recently, the ministers of Charles X.

It was dark, it was dank, and the low lying mists from the river Somme condensed into cold trickles on the thick stone walls. During Louis Napoleon's five and a half years of incarceration, the damp and the draughts and the lack of exercise ate into his body, reawakened his childhood weaknesses and he aged the equivalent of a decade of normal living. He was thirty-two when he went in under escort and thirty-eight when he slipped out alone. A slice of the best years of his life were lost, yet he would never have made the Emperor that he was to become without those two thousand days of solitude.

Oh, the grey weariness of the enclosure between those enormous walls, mixed with the dull mouldy smell of the cellars, on the vaults of which is graven the heraldry of the lords of Saint Pol. And on the horizon nothing but these ever-sleeping waters, with their unending melancholy, and yonder Ham, with its small streets and lanes with such strange old names – rue Saint Vaneng, rue du Grenier à Sel – where in the monastic silence which muffles them, the clattering sabot re-echoes.[15]

Cross two drawbridges, enter the central courtyard, and a two-storeyed building lies to the right. Pass through a door, locked and guarded, and into a white-washed passage. This was the prison of the adventurers of Boulogne. Off the corridor opened the two rooms of General Montholon, the guardroom, the chapel and the bathroom. Upstairs were the quarters of Louis Napoleon, Dr Conneau and Charles Thélin and the communal dining-room. Louis Napoleon had a bedroom, a study and a third room, which he later converted into a laboratory. In the study were a bureau, a deal table, a sofa, an armchair and four rush-seated chairs. At his request planks were put up on the walls to act as bookshelves. A most necessary screen kept off the worst of the draughts. The grimness of the place was relieved when books arrived for the shelves and portraits of the Emperor, Josephine and Hortense graced the walls.

Except for services in the chapel on Sundays, there was little to distinguish one day from another. Each day Louis Napoleon worked through from breakfast until lunch – reading, writing letters, composing articles for such newspapers as would print them, researching for his pamphlets and books. In the afternoons he took exercise, walking on the ramparts. Soon he was allowed to ride a horse round the courtyard and work on a little garden which he fashioned on the mound. But it was only from the ramparts that he could see the horizon. It was fifty strides along the rampart and fifty strides back. Then about turn and once again. There was little to see but the slow barges creeping along the St Quentin canal and the sentries on the further bank of the river, so posted to ensure that the prisoner could not communicate with the outside world. There were four hundred men at the fortress, sixty being on guard at a time. But they had other duties, for Ham was a school for bandsmen, and their discordant notes and clashes rendered life even more intolerable. The evening was the best time of the day, for then there were endless games of cards, the Governor making up a four with his three senior prisoners.

Louis Napoleon referred to Ham as his 'university' and the sobriquet was fitting, for it was while there that his education was widened and that he learned to see beyond his previous narrow conviction that only the resurrection of the Bonapartes was of any account. He studied British history and published a pamphlet entitled *Fragments Historiques, 1688 and 1830*, comparing the relevant revolutions in England and France. He drew, and invented, improvements to contemporary small arms. In an age when exciting discoveries were being made in the field of chemistry, he obtained the aid of a local practitioner and together they constructed a small laboratory, and dabbled in gases and electricity. For a while he became engrossed in the growing of sugar beet, and a paper he wrote on the subject aroused considerable interest in the sugar trade. He switched to the advantages of a tideless canal through Nicaragua, linking the Atlantic with the Pacific. This delighted the Nicaraguans but in the end the idea lost to Panama. He ended his 'university' course by studying the possibilities of eliminating poverty from the world, but he had, by now, developed a great longing for people.

Visitors were not encouraged but a few got through, including the redoubtable Eleanora Gordon and influential friends from London. They told of Louis Napoleon's wan complexion, how he talked ceaselessly from the moment of their arrival, asking questions and not waiting for the reply. They told also of the look of haunting sadness in his eyes as he bid them goodbye. There were visitations of another kind which it fell to the lot of the Governor to consider. These visitations were for the purpose of sex. Fortunately the France of Louis Philippe was more tolerant and understanding in this direction than the England of Victoria and Albert.

Louis Napoleon's first requests for female company were apparently misunderstood. A local lady, who had watched him striding along the ramparts and developed princely dreams, was introduced and retired with the words, 'I had a kiss, which still burns on my hands.' Pauline

Virginie Déjazet, the famous actress who played 'breeches' parts at the Gymnase, was far more enticing, but she only blew him kisses and that was not enough. So Louis Napoleon applied, through the Governor, to the Home Secretary for permission to indulge fully. 'The Minister replied that he could not grant such an immoral request, but that he would shut his eyes to the prisoner's morals.'[16] The Governor interpreted this as licence to admit females of the lower order.

A number of local women moved freely in and out of the fortress. They came to cook, to launder, to mend clothes. They came to sell vegetables, fish and wine. They were a distinct asset to an establishment of four hundred men and the guards knew them well. Alexandrine Eleanora Vergeot worked as an ironer, living in the house of one of the gatekeepers. She cared for such items of an officer's apparel as needed ironing. She was twenty, voluptuous, with chestnut hair and blue eyes. The garrison knew her as 'la belle Sabotière', but the reason is lost – may be she danced well in wooden shoes. She stayed at nights in the room of Louis Napoleon and the Governor shut his eyes. She was not only a mistress, but also a link with the outside, and Louis Napoleon taught her grammar and how to speak, as well as treating her to lectures on historical subjects. Two sons were born to them.[(a)] He never forgot his 'belle Sabotière' and during the Empire she lived in comfort in an apartment in the Champs Elysées.[17]

Early in 1846 Louis Napoleon heard that ex-King Louis of Holland was very ill and he applied for permission to visit him in Florence. On his application being refused, he decided that he could now, with free conscience, escape. General Montholon had but a year to serve. Dr Conneau and Thélin had both completed their sentences but out of loyalty had stayed on, to keep their leader company and to care for him. Both were free to leave the fortress.

A visitor, carrying two passports, arrived at Ham. One passport he left behind. Louis Napoleon then complained about the state of repair and decoration of his quarters and the Governor agreed that workmen from outside should come in and put matters to rights. Thélin smuggled in a set of clothes similar to those worn by the workmen. The conspirators waited until the job was almost complete, and the guards well accustomed to the comings and goings of the men, before they took

(a) Alexandre Louis Eugene (1843–1910). In the Foreign Service. Created Comte d'Orx. Alexandre Louis Ernest (1845–82). Created Comte de Labenne.

action. Dr Conneau described the happenings of the morning of
25th May:

> We rose at six o'clock. The Prince put on his workman's disguise,
> consisting of a coarse shirt, a blue blouse, and a pair of blue trousers,
> with an apron, and a pair of sabots over his boots. As his face was
> naturally pale, he coloured it with some dye, which gave him a
> ruddy complexion. He also painted his eyebrows and put on a black
> wig, which completely covered his ears. Shortly after seven, he
> shaved off his thick whiskers and moustaches . . . .[18]

The work force arrived and Thélin invited them downstairs for a
drink. Louis Napoleon put a pipe in his mouth, a plank across his
shoulder and strolled off towards the door, open but guarded. He
tilted the plank so that the sentry could not see his face. He was through
and out in the courtyard. He was unaccustomed to a pipe and half
way across it fell from his mouth. He bent down and unconcernedly
picked up the pieces. At the main gate the sergeant of the guard was
reading a letter and did not even look up. Louis Napoleon walked on
through the little town and on to the St Quentin road. He dropped
the plank into a ditch. He came to the pre-arranged rendez-vous,
a roadside graveyard. There, by a cross, he knelt down and
prayed.

Meantime Conneau had contrived a dummy in the empty bed and
informed the Governor that Louis Napoleon was ill, asking that the
daily inspection should be waived. It was. Thélin left the fortress on
the excuse of taking his master's little black dog, called Ham, for a
walk, for Louis Napoleon could not bear the thought of being parted
from his faithful companion of so many lonely days. Thélin had booked
a cab the day before. He picked it up and drove to the graveyard.
Louis Napoleon materialised from among the tombs and the cab made
all speed on the twenty kilometre journey to St Quentin. Here they
parted, the valet going into the town to hire a chaise, Louis Napoleon
and Ham walking along the Valenciennes road. Thélin soon overtook
them and the chaise sped over the forty odd kilometres to Valenciennes,
the driver being constantly bribed to go faster, for the danger of pursuit
was real. It was two o'clock in the afternoon when the two men, and
the dog, reached Valenciennes station, but now they had the worst

part of the journey to face. For two hours they sat on the platform, scanning faces, keeping out of sight. At last a train came in and soon they were over the frontier and in the safety of Belgium.

By the evening of the next day Louis Napoleon was in London. He arrived for dinner at Gore House with dye on his face and stubble on his chin and Lady Blessington all but swooned. Even more upset was a French attaché who, knowing nothing of the escape, left his dinner and raced back to his Embassy.

CHAPTER 5

Elysée at Last

The gay adventurer who had tilted at the beaches of Boulogne in 1840s summer days was no more. Youth had faded during the dismal years at Ham. People scarcely recognised the Prince Louis Napoleon as he strolled around the streets of St James's or in the Park, the little black dog at his heel. He limped now, for the mists of the Somme had left their mark in rheumatism. An eyeball was dilated, from over-study by bad light, and, as a cure, leeches were applied. For a while dreams of the mastery of France were pushed aside. He had but two objectives – to regain his health and to visit his acknowledged father, the ex-King Louis of Holland. Although they had seen but little of one another and, in former days, their views had clashed, during the years in Ham a regular correspondence had been kept up and an intimacy and understanding had developed between the old invalid in Italy and the prisoner in France.

Having obtained from the Prime Minister, Sir Robert Peel, permission to reside in England, and having assured the French Ambassador that there would be no more invasion attempts, Louis Napoleon asked various authorities for the necessary passport to make the journey to see his dying father. But no one was taking any more chances with Hortense's son. The Italian adventure, followed by the attempts at Strasbourg and Boulogne, were too fresh in the memory. The Austrians did not even bother to reply. So the ex-King of Holland died alone at Leghorn on 25th July. In his will Louis Napoleon received the palace at Florence, an estate at Civita Nuova and over three million francs in good securities. There also came to him a collection of decorations, family heirlooms and many interesting souvenirs of the Emperor.[1] This inheritance was both welcome and necessary, for Louis Napoleon had spent much of the fortune received from his mother in backing schemes for the Bonaparte revival, the Boulogne attempt and, it must be added, in gambling. He had also been most generous to those who had served Hortense and himself and when Dr Conneau arrived in

England, having served a short sentence for his part in the escape from Ham, the Prince bought him a London practice.

Realising that it would be futile to seek permission to attend his father's funeral, Louis Napoleon left his London hotel and set about his rehabilitation programme. He smartened himself up. At his tailors, Henry Poole and Co., of Savile Row, he purchased a superfine double-breasted frock coat with silk body linings for six guineas, a pair of check doeskin trousers for fifty shillings, a silk-lined black Venetian cloth overcoat for five and a half guineas, and a fancy-figured cashmere waistcoat for thirty-eight shillings. He then exchanged London's soot-laden air for purer climes. For several months he lived at Bath, taking the waters and walking with Ham on Claverton Down. He moved on to the bracing sea air of Brighton, riding regularly to regain his fitness. He received many invitations to stay at large houses and was the guest of the Damers in Dorset, the Duke and Duchess of Beaufort at Badminton, the Marquess of Anglesey in Staffordshire, the Eglintons in Ayrshire and Duke and Duchess of Hamilton at Brodrick.[2] By the end of the year he was back in his Napoleonic stride. And, of natural course, he looked towards the ladies. While, prior to 1840, he had been regarded as a flirt, apt to disturb a girl's emotions but little else, his experiences in the hard and narrow bed at Ham with 'la belle Sabotière' had converted him into a much more dangerous animal. Even then, the number of women with whom Louis Napoleon was said to have slept in the period 1846–8 bordered on the impossible, even for a visiting Frenchman with time on his hands. The truth was that he had only to be seen paying attention to a pretty young lady for the worst to be surmised. And some young ladies considered that it was rather a cachet and did not bother with denials. Anyway, in those 'hungry forties' before Prince Albert's cold fingers had throttled the serpent of sex weaving around the Court, it was the done thing to sleep around. Lord Palmerston shared the bed of a lady-in-waiting when called to Windsor. The Queen's cousin, Prince George of Cambridge, had set up the actress, Louisa Fairbrother, in a house in Queen Street and had three sons by her.

Louis Napoleon was, at heart, a snob. Demanding though he was for sex, he never knew a love for which he would put aside his personal aims and ambitions. He was grateful to his ladies, certainly, and he cared for them, but that was all. He hankered after seducing those whom he considered looked down upon him – as happened in the case of Lady Jersey and her daughter – but it was the triumph that he sought. An extrovert, he liked to picture himself as the gay adventurer and handsome seducer. There was a mystique about him, yes, and an attraction for some – including Queen Victoria – in the slow smile and the emanation of ruthlessness and mischief, but the handsome lover – never. The women who intrigued him sexually, and obtained a grip upon him, were of the courtesan class, experts in their field, giving of themselves for background reasons of power or money. It was essential for his ego that he knew himself as a great lover and that he gave himself as a favour to the chosen. In the event this was far from the truth. There exists a record of one of his nights of love, and there is no reason to believe that one night was much different from another:

> The Marquise Taisey-Chatenoy, who was the only one of his mistresses indiscreet enough to give a detailed description of his prowess in bed, described his appearance in an elaborate uniform at a ball, followed by the secret assignation in her bedroom and his arrival in the early hours of the morning, looking rather insignificant in mauve silk pyjamas. There follows a brief period of physical exertion, during which he breathes heavily and the wax on the end of his moustaches melts, causing them to droop, and finally a hasty withdrawal, leaving the Marquise unimpressed and unsatisfied.[3]

The woman who came the closest to capturing both the body and the soul of Louis Napoleon was Elizabeth Anne Howard. He met her at Gore House, where she had been dallying with D'Orsay. She was only twenty-four, but had already crammed into her few adult years more adventure and experience than come to many women in a lifetime. Why she had adopted the family name of the Dukes of Norfolk is unknown. Her real name was Haryett and she stemmed from Brighton and a background of inns and horses. She rode superbly and in her teens became the mistress of Jem Mason, who rode Lottery, the winner of the first Grand National in 1839. She moved on to James Young Fitzroy, a notorious gambler on cards and horses. He had a lucky win and gave her money. Stepping up the ladder, she became the lady of Francis Montjoye Martin, major in the 2nd Life Guards, by whom she had a son in 1842. But as the major was married, this led to trouble and he deserted her, leaving the child well cared for. She was sad but there were many to take his place. The Duke of Beaufort, the Earl of Chester-field and the Earl of Malmesbury were reported to be her 'friends'.[4] She was an expensive toy with which to play and received a number of settlements, including property at Civita Vecchia.

By the time that Louis Napoleon met her, Elizabeth Howard was a woman of independent means. She was described as blonde, beautiful, with classical features, magnificent shoulders and a graceful carriage. She was not firmly tied to anyone. She was strongly attracted by the would-be Emperor, with his big head and lanky hair, long body and short legs, and became his alone. This inconvenienced her former friends and they resented it. Particularly was this so in the case of author A. W. Kinglake, who took his revenge in the printed word.

The proprieties were observed. Louis Napoleon took a lease, at £300 a year, of 3, King Street, St James's.[a] She was installed at 9, Berkeley Street. It was an easy stroll. He had been master in his own house for so little of his life. He revelled in the experience, converting King Street into a museum of the First Empire. In the middle of February 1847 he wrote to his old tutor, M. Vieillard, in Paris:

> For two weeks now I have been settled in my new house, and I am delighted once more to have a home, for the first time in seven years. I have brought together all my books and family portraits; in short all the precious objects which escaped from the wreck.[5]

He was in no hurry for power now. He knew that the sands were running out for Louis Philippe, and he let them run. The French King was seventy-four and concerned only with dynastic matters. Having exchanged visits with Queen Victoria, and made the most of the point that his daughter, Princess Louise, was married to her Uncle Leopold, King of the Belgians, he had blotted his Windsor copybook in the affair of the 'Spanish marriages', an attempt to revive the Bourbon policy of French predominance in Spain. He had thus earned for himself in Britain the reputation of being two-faced. But, as regards his position at home, he considered himself secure in the folds of the middle-classes. Louis Napoleon knew otherwise. Persigny was sending him underground news from Paris and this pointed to growing Republican and Socialist strength and opposition. The pretender was not to be

(a) Then known as King Street Houses.

trapped again by risky adventure. This time, France would come to him.

His was a Jekyll and Hyde existence. Some days he gambled at Crockford's, attended the races and cavorted with Elizabeth Howard. On others he gave bachelor dinner parties to statesmen and politicians, authors and scientists. He continued with his scientific studies, as if in a separate world. He was at the meeting of the British Association at Oxford in the summer. For feminine companionship there he relied upon Florence Nightingale. What strange contrast here with Eleanora Gordon at Strasbourg, 'La belle Sabotière' at Ham and Elizabeth Howard at Newmarket.

The conversational excitement among the dreaming spires concerned the naming of the new planet simultaneously discovered by the Englishman, Adams, and the Frenchman, Leverrier. Each wished to be immortalised and there was some Franco-British rankling. Peace came when the planet was named Neptune. Peace was everywhere, for the sun was shining, the lawns were green and the roses sweet-smelling. Florence commented that she had 'never imagined so much loveliness and learning'. She strolled and chatted in a posse of Richard Monckton Milnes, Henry Hallam, Sir Robert Inglis and Louis Napoleon.[6] She liked the Frenchman well enough in the cloisters and the 'quad', but, when he reached the Tuileries, she dubbed him tyrant.

1848 was a year of revolution. It was crisis time for Kings and Emperors, Princes and Presidents, Queens and Grand dukes. Young *Punch*, now to be seen on all the best hall tables, published a drawing of all of them at sea in cockleshells. Some were already 'in the drink', and the question was – who would be the next? There was trouble in Austria, Poland, Prussia, Hungary, Sicily, Spain, Portugal, Switzerland, France, Piedmont, Venetia and Greece. To Prince Albert's horror, there was even anarchy in his beloved Coburg. In England the bark of the revolutionaries was more disturbing than their bite, but in Ireland the position was dire, the peasants being urged to pour molten lead over the rich. Queen Victoria was pregnant. As the bulletins came in from Europe and her world tottered about her, she commented that any child born under such conditions of strain could not fail to be odd. In the event Princess Louise proved to be somewhat out of the usual.

On the morning of 22nd February Paris was comparatively calm.

Then a rally demanding political reform was refused permission to march by the Government. This annoyed the would-be marchers, and buses were overturned and park seats burned. Gunsmiths were looted during the night. On the 23rd the King dismissed Prime Minister Guizot. In the evening a crowd gathered outside Guizot's house, in hostile mood. The infantry on guard were jostled. A sergeant opened fire, killing a man. The edgy troops followed suit with a volley, and over thirty dead and wounded lay on the *pavé*. The powder barrel went up and Louis Philippe took carriage for the coast just in time. Two days later he and his Queen arrived at Newhaven, without luggage. They travelled as Mr and Mrs Smith and, as disguise, he wore a flat hat and goggles. They put up at the inn by the quay.

On the morning of the 27th Louis Napoleon took his seat in the boat train for Paris. He was accompanied by his banker, Orsi, and Charles Thélin. He was wearing a thick muffler, not only to keep out the cold of the English Channel but also useful as a means of avoiding recognition. At Folkestone the steamer *Lord Warden* was discharging friends and relations of Louis Philippe. There was little traffic the other way. At Boulogne the trio lunched at the station, reviewing the scene of the 1840 disaster. Rail services were chaotic and it was not until the following morning that they reached Paris. Having found shelter with his former tutor, Vieillard, Louis Napoleon informed Lamartine, head of the quickly formed Provisional Government, of his presence. He was given twenty-four hours to get out of France. Not wishing for a repeat of the Ham experience, he left at once. He was a very tired man when at last he reached King Street and his marble bath. *Punch* was rather unkind. 'Humph! Here's France! Poor France! and LOUIS-NAPOLEON – hatched from goose-egg in eagle's nest – at this moment sitting to imaginary tailor for measure of imperial robe of moonshine!'

Still there was work to be done for the country which had given him shelter. A few days afterwards a mob gathered in Trafalgar Square, chanting '*Vive la République*'. The rioters moved off towards Buckingham Palace, breaking street lamps as they went. On arrival they wrecked Prince Albert's skittle alley.[7] A voluntary corps of special constables was formed and Louis Napoleon enrolled at Marlborough Street Police Station. On the vital day, 10th April, when a mammoth march of Chartists was planned from Kennington Common to the

Houses of Parliament, he was on duty in the West End. The march fizzled out, the leader having been told, most forcefully, that he would be shot if he made trouble. Louis Napoleon's contribution was to assist in the arrest of a very drunk old woman.[8]

Meantime the road was rough for Lamartine's Provisional Government, split down the middle, as it was, by moderates and extremists. Louis Napoleon, wisely advised, did not put his name forward for the general election for the Constituent Assembly held in April. Economic conditions worsened and in mid-May a mob attacked the Hôtel de Ville. As Louis Napoleon wrote to the President of the Chamber demanding his rights as a French citizen, his supporters, headed by Persigny, Montholon, Eleanora Gordon, Laity and Mocquard,[a] opened up an enthusiastic campaign on his behalf. They used every trick in the publicity circus. Posters appeared on walls and hoardings overnight. Paragraphs found their way into the Press. Pamphlets and handbills were circulated from shops and at street corners. Portraits and medallions were issued free. Songs were written and street singers paid to render them over and over again. Actors were bribed to make 'plugs' from the stage. No chance was missed to push the Napoleonic legend.

By-elections were to be held in June and at the last moment Louis Napoleon put forward his name. He was elected by four Departments, Seine, Yonne, Charent-Inférieure and Corsica. While crowds in the Place de la Concorde called his name, the police were ordered to arrest him the moment that he landed in France. Louis Napoleon resigned his seat, sending the message: 'If the people impose duties on me, I shall know how to fulfil them.'

To cope with unemployment the Government had instituted 'National Workshops', giving everyone 'the right to work', and, of course, be paid by the State. The difficulty was to find the right kind of work and such unproductive efforts as excavating the Champs de Mars were embarked upon. By June there were over 100,000 men attached to the 'Workshops' in Paris alone, while there were jobs for only one sixth of this number. Most of the men were armed. The cost was astronomic. On 21st June a tactless order was issued that all the workmen should be discharged within three days and that the able-bodied should enlist in the army. All hell was let loose.

(a) Later to be Louis Napoleon's secretary.

The men were starving, and they fought without hope, without leaders, without cheers, shooting sullenly in a dreadful silence behind great barricades of stone. For four days Paris was alight with the dull glow; guns were brought up against the barricades; a great storm broke over the smoking town; women were shot without pity, and on a ghastly Sunday a General in parley with the barricades was shamefully murdered; the Archbishop of Paris, with a supreme gesture of reconciliation, went out at sunset to make peace and was shot and died. It was a time of horror, and for four summer days Paris was tortured by the struggle.[9]

The man who quelled the rebellion was General Cavaignac, Minister of War. He was an experienced and disciplined soldier, devoted to the Second Republic, and, to his lights, he acted justly and with the necessary degree of ruthlessness. He emerged from the blood bath as the outstanding figure in France, a candidate for dictatorship. But civilians, no matter how strongly they may back a cause, have no liking for the use of military methods to quell internal disorders. As stories from the barricades spread through the country and mass deportation took place of those who had been involved, it became clear that General Cavaignac would stand little chance at the polling booth. At dinner at Gore House, Louis Napoleon commented, 'That man is clearing the way for me.'[10]

His priority now was to raise funds, to pay for the work of his supporters in Paris and to allow him to live in a fitting fashion when he returned to France. While Orsi trudged round the banking houses raising loans, Louis Napoleon mortgaged his estate at Civita Nuova, inherited from his father. The total of the loans and the mortgage topped half a million francs. But the path which led to the foundation of the Second Empire was paved with the gold of Elizabeth Howard. She sold her property at Civita Vecchia to Louis Napoleon on credit, and on the deed he was able to borrow sufficient money to ensure that he would have no financial worries on the way to the top.

There were to be supplementary elections in France in September and on 28th August Louis Napoleon wrote to his uncle, Jerome, King of Westphalia, the Emperor's only surviving brother:

Your wise councils on the subject of the elections about to take place have only anticipated the letter which I was about to write to you to the intent. I believe, as you do, that at this time it will be my duty to accept the mandate of my fellow-citizens, if they shall honour me with their suffrages. Under circumstances, which, happily, no longer subsist, I have not hesitated to prolong my exile, rather than suffer my name to be used as a pretext for pernicious agitations. Now that order is established, I hope that unjust prejudices will no longer prevent me from contributing, as a representative of the people, to the consolidation of the Republic, to its happiness and glory.[11]

On this occasion he was returned by five departments, and could no longer be denied his seat. Once again he joined the boat train, this time not to return. On 24th September he took rooms in the Hotel du Rhin in the Place Vendôme. Shortly afterwards Elizabeth Howard was spotted on the Dover train, her jewel case, firmly clasped, on her knee. She was installed at the Hotel Maurice in the Rue de Rivoli.[12]

Citizen Louis Napoleon Bonaparte made no great impact upon the members of the Constituent Assembly. He was inexperienced in governmental matters, his speeches lacked the necessary clarity and emphasis, and his German accent offended some. In fact a motion that had been tabled precluding any member of the Bonaparte family from becoming President, was withdrawn, as the proposer considered the possibility as nil. But Louis Napoleon was not seeking hand claps from politicians – it was votes that he wanted. In the time of Louis Phillippe there had only been 200,000 entitled to vote in the whole of France. With the extension of the franchise, the number had risen to eight million. These newcomers knew nothing of voting procedure and recognised few of the candidates. But they knew the name of Napoleon. It was an echo from their childhood days, it was written into their songs. All a Napoleon had to do was to offer them security, work and the means to live.

The Presidential elections were held on 10th December. 'Citizen Bonaparte' received 5,434,226 votes, against General Cavaignac's 1,448,107. On the 20th, in a crowded Chamber, he was proclaimed President of the French Republic, from that day forward until the second Sunday of May 1852. He retired to the Elysée Palace, which was to be his official residence. He had not been there since the evening in June 1815 when he had said goodbye to the Emperor before Waterloo. The authorities there were taken by surprise by the quick arrival of another Napoleon. No room had been prepared for him and he spent the night in a chair, by a table, writing, dozing, dreaming.

He had not been Prince President for a month before he had decided that a term of less than four years was insufficient for his aims. He began the task of slicing the opposition to his views into sections, manipulating one section against the other until there would be no major front against him. He said: 'The name of Napoleon is in itself a programme. It stands for order, authority, religion and the welfare of the people in internal affairs, and in foreign affairs for the national dignity.'[13] From the standpoint of his own security in the future, he made an error in placing too great an emphasis on nationalism and allowing over-much power to the Church.

One of his early problems was in dealing with the flood of relations and friends who looked upon his election as the opening of a door leading to office and perquisites. Bonapartes now materialised in surprising numbers, each with a hand outstretched. The most demanding of them was his uncle Jerome, the last surviving brother of the Emperor, who had been more of a handicap than a help on the hard way up. On one of his demands being refused, he called his nephew a bastard before the assembled company.[14]

But Louis Napoleon cared well for those who had played a worthy part in the struggle. Charles Thélin was promoted to Privy Purse. Colonel Vaudrey was reinstated as Brigadier-General, made Governor of the Tuileries and decorated with the Legion of Honour. Persigny became Minister of the Interior and went on to ambassadorial heights. Old General Montholon sat in the Legislative Assembly. Princess Mathilde acted hostess at the Elysée. Elizabeth Howard was set up at 14, Rue du Cirque, which was convenient as the President, on his evening stroll with Ham, had but to pass through a door in his garden wall to be by her side. Miss Howard was, at first, discretion itself, only being seen in public when sandwiched between M. Mocquard, the President's secretary, and his wife. But she soon tired of being chaperoned, appeared alone by the side of her lover and drew attention to herself by driving around in a carriage with a horse painted on the panels.

A faithful supporter to whom only sadness came was Eleanora Gordon. She was past forty now. For twelve years she had fought for the Napoleonic legend and the eyes of the police had ever been upon her. What was to be her reward? With the years her feelings towards

Louis Napoleon had changed. When full of the fire of life at the time of Strasbourg, she had spurned him as a lover. But now, tired, she was looking forward to the accolade of being his Number One. Instead of which he had arrived in Paris with the magnificent Elizabeth Howard. Eleanora was granted a pension of 4,800 francs, paltry thanks indeed. She went, in her fury, to the Elysée, and there was handed a purse containing 5,000 francs and shown firmly to the door. She became ill and died on 11th March 1849 – of a broken heart, people said. The President paid for her funeral. The bill was 720 francs.[15]

In April Louis Napoleon spotted, at an Elysée reception, a tall and beautiful Spanish girl with auburn hair – Eugenie de Montijo. He paused, and she was presented to him by the Rothschilds. She told him that she had spoken much of him with Madame Eleanora Gordon. A coldness came over him, as when the freezing shadow comes fast across the bright snow of winter as the sun goes down behind the mountain. He moved on and spoke to her no more. It was a strange way to meet his future wife.

Part II

THE BRIDE'S STORY

1849-1853

CHAPTER 6

Enter Eugenie

Marie Eugenie Ignace Augustine de Montijo,[a] the last Empress of the French, was born at Granada, Andalusia, on 5th May 1826. On her mother's side she was Scottish, stemming from the Kirkpatricks of Closeburn, Dumfries, a family strong for the Stuarts. One of her ancestors was sent to the scaffold in 1746 for backing Bonnie Prince Charlie.[1]

Her great-grandparents were William Kirkpatrick of Cowheath and Mary Wilson of Kelton, Kirkcudbrightshire. One of their sons became her grandfather.[2] He was ambitious and physically strong and, finding opportunities in Scotland restricted, he decided to try his luck in Spain.

He set up business in Malaga as a wholesale fruit and wine merchant trading with England and America. He prospered and bought a high yellow-washed house in the Calle San Juan. He fell in love with Françoise, daughter of Baron de Grivegnée, an immigrant Belgian in the wine trade, and married her. Their eldest girl, Maria Manuela, was born in 1794, six years before William was appointed United States Consul at Malaga.[b]

Manuela was dynamite. She was dark and flashing and beautiful, in a hard way. She could sing and act and dance and converse in five languages. She was a *maîtresse femme*, and she liked to see people enjoy themselves, as long as they did it in her fashion. Her sights were set

(a) Spanish baptismal names—Maria Eugenia Ignacia Augustina.
(b) He later retired to America where he died in 1837.

59

on power and high society and she had every intention of tasting life from the very best cup. She helped her father by acting hostess in the 'club' behind his wine shop. Here officers and foreign visitors came to taste and to buy, to gossip and to flirt. There could have been no better place to learn of the ways of men. In 1817 Manuela was twenty-three.

Owing to the marriage of his wife's sister to Count Mathieu de Lesseps, a member of a distinguished French family and, in 1805, to become the father of Ferdinand de Lesseps, the famous builder of canals, including the Suez Canal, the loyalties of William Kirkpatrick were given to Emperor Napoleon in preference to King George III. Manuela and her sisters were sent to school in Paris, returning, in 1814, as eligible young ladies.[3] Manuela, outstanding among the trio, had ambitious ideas.

In Paris in 1813 she had made the acquaintance of a certain 'Colonel Portocarrero', a Spaniard fighting for Napoleon, of whom he was an enthusiastic admirer. The Colonel had one eye, one sound arm and one sound leg, the result of various actions beginning with Trafalgar. Despite his physical handicaps, he took an active part in the defence of Paris in 1814 and rallied to the Emperor during the Hundred Days. On his return to Paris, Louis XVIII, quite naturally, took exception to the actions of the Spanish 'soldier of fortune' and declared him to be a prisoner of war. The Colonel was fortunate in being able to slip across his native frontier before being arrested.

In 1871 he visited Malaga and there renewed his acquaintance with the Kirkpatricks. 'Colonel Portocarrero', a name of military convenience, had disappeared into the past and he was now travelling under his true title – Don Cipriano Guzman de Palafox y Porto Carrero, Comte de Teba.[(a)] He was the second son of the Comte de Montijo and a Grandee of Spain.

Opinions on this mutilated Grandee of Spain are sharply divided. Latter-day writers have tended to see him as a romantic figure, the hero of the wars with a black patch over his missing eye, experienced, cynical, just the man to sweep a romantic girl off her feet. Those who wrote nearer to the time of the happening took a differing view. In the light of after events, it would appear that the latter were nearer to the truth. William Kirkpatrick saw clearly the advantages of an alliance.

(a) The title of the first Comte de Teba was created in 1492, by Ferdinand and Isabella, for his gallant conduct before Granada.

Although Don Cipriano was not unduly rich, his elder brother, Don Eugenio, Comte de Montijo, was. Don Eugenio was a confirmed bachelor of middle age so Cipriano was the heir to the Montijo empire. Thus it was that when Cipriano approached William Kirkpatrick and asked for the hand of his daughter, with the qualification that it would be necessary to prove to King Ferdinand that the Kirkpatrick ancestry was worthy of a Grandee, William was ready for him. He said to his proposed son-in-law: 'You trace up to King Alfonso the Eleventh. If I trace to King Robert Bruce, I suppose His Majesty will be satisfied?' He then laid before the King a patent from the Heralds' Office at Edinburgh, certifying his descent paternally from the ancient Barons of Closeburn. Whereupon the King, who did not like Don Cipriano, remarked cynically, 'Let the noble Montijo marry the daughter of Fingal!'[4] Accordingly, on 15th December 1817, Maria Manuela Kirkpatrick was married to Don Cipriano, Comte de Teba. He was eight years older than she.

The marriage was doomed to failure from the start. The two were opposites and neither would change their views or way of life. She loved entertaining – he could not abide people about the house. He was mean with money – she was open handed and generous. He believed in the benefits of privation and hardship – she revelled in luxury. He took politics in deadly earnest – she was prepared to shift her ground to suit her convenience. He lived much in the past – she walked in the present and dreamed of the future. They soon began to drift apart, saw less and less of one another until, in the last years of their marriage, they did not see one another at all.

They were handicapped by the turbulent conditions in Spain and by the fact that Cipriano, owing to his past activities and loyalties, was suspect and under police surveillance. King Ferdinand was cruel, cowardly and cunning and he persecuted those of a liberal way of thinking. The '*liberales*' such people were called and they included many soldiers who had served in France and become indoctrinated with foreign ideas. Cipriano was among them. In 1820 revolution broke out and Ferdinand became a prisoner of the insurgents. But the '*liberales*' were divided against themselves and the disturbed conditions in Spain caused the monarchies of the Holy Alliance to take action. In 1823 a powerful French army crossed the Frontier, quelled the insurgents and restored Ferdinand to power. Having given his oath to grant an amnesty to those who had opposed him, he immediately broke his word and, to the disgust of the French, began an orgy of cruelty and torture that earned the label of Inquisition. Cipriano was arrested and thrown into prison in the north of Spain. There he languished for a year and a half. Thereafter he was allowed to complete his sentence at Granada, living with Manuela at 12, Calle de Gracia. He was kept under close guard and his movements were restricted. Life was only tolerable because Manuela laughed at the restrictions, bribed the sentries and flirted with those whose task it was to watch over them.

She was now thirty and there were still no children. Bearing in mind the custom of the times and their religion, this was strange indeed. But on 29th January 1825 a daughter was born. She was christened Maria Francisca de Sales, and she was known as Paca or Paquita. If Cipriano was the father, then conception must have occurred while he was an inmate of the grim prison at Santiago de Compostella, where the *'libérales'* were undergoing the tortures of the Inquisition. On 5th May 1826 a second daughter, Eugenia, was born. The two girls grew up to be in complete contrast to one another, both in looks and character. What, then, were the movements of Manuela while she was parted, by prison sentence, from her husband? It has been suggested, and not without reason, that she was staying in Paris with her aunt, Catherine de Lesseps, with whom she had lived during her schooldays. In that case the view, commonly held in France during the Second Empire, that the father of the Empress Eugenie was George Villiers, afterwards fourth Earl of Clarendon and British Foreign Secretary, bears consideration. We know that Villiers was in Paris in the summer of 1825[5] and we also know, from his sister's letters, that he was being 'very wicked'.[6]

As Manuela coped with two babies and a husband who was a virtual prisoner, a dramatic happening claimed her attention. Her brother-in-law, Eugenio, married. His bride was a woman of easy morals and uncertain past and her motive was obvious – the capture of the Montijo empire. But the entry of this sexual temptress into the life of an ageing recluse proved too strong for Eugenio and he had a stroke which left him partially paralysed. This upset the lady's plan for giving birth to an heir, whose arrival would have placed both title and wealth firmly in her hands. So she thought up the idea of placing a supposititious child in her bed. Knowing that both Cipriano and Manuela were forbidden to enter Madrid, she thought herself safe. But she underestimated her sister-in-law, who knew full well that fatherhood was beyond Eugenio's physical capacity. Although Madrid was forbidden to her, Manuela gained permission to visit Valladolid where she knew King Ferdinand was staying. She obtained an invitation to attend a royal ball and, as the wife of a Grandee, was placed in the same quadrille as the King. The rest was easy for her. She charmed him. She extracted permission from him to visit the capital.[7]

Unannounced, Manuela arrived at Eugenio's house and thoroughly upset the arrangements, which were well advanced, for the arrival of the changeling. The unpregnant 'mother' ran screaming to her room and there attempted to stage a birth scene with the aid of an orphan baby. Manuela pursued her, pulled back the bedding and revealed the truth. There was nothing that could be said. Out of the generosity of her heart, and also to make sure that there would be no more such nonsense, she took the changeling away with her, adopted the boy and brought him up with her own children.[8]

As King Ferdinand aged, he lost his appetite for persecution and torture and even sampled the pleasures of domestic life. In 1830 Cipriano became, at last, a free man. He adored his daughters and his interest in them sustained him during his long period under restriction. But he clashed with their mother over their upbringing. She wished to lay the foundation for brilliant careers in society for Paca and Eugenie. She put stress on education and social graces. He was determined to bring up the girls to be tough and self-dependent, living on a plain diet and wearing simple clothes. He put little store by lessons. In 1832 the family visited Paris. Relations between husband and wife were strained – Manuela led a gay life and a frequent visitor to her apartment was George Villiers, working in Paris on a Customs Commission. They had first met there in 1825.

In the *diligence* on the return journey to Spain the family met a twenty-seven year old novelist and archaelogist, Prosper Mérimée. In him Manuela gained a friend and adviser who was to be beside her and her daughters until the Second Empire fell. Manuela and Mérimée became devoted to one another, in love without the complications of physical contact. They did much for one another – it was she who gave him the story for Carmen.[9] And he was in the nature of a godfather to the girls.

The years of peace were few. In 1833 King Ferdinand died, having, by legal contrivance, in defiance of the existing Salic Law, arranged that his daughter Isabella should succeed him, with her mother as regent. This infuriated his brother, Don Carlos, who had been generally accepted as the next King. The Carlist civil war began and lasted until 1839.

Cipriano moved his family to Madrid. It was there that the last link in his marriage snapped. George Villiers had been newly appointed British Minister.[10] Manuela became his mistress. Cipriano could tolerate a random affair in Paris, but not an open flaunting of unfaithfulness on his own ground. It was noticed that Villiers showed a particular interest in the younger daughter, Eugenie, an interest which advanced with the years until it became one of *in loco parentis*.

To further complicate matters, Don Eugenio died and Cipriano became Comte de Montijo. He inherited the Montijo palace in the centre of Madrid and the delightful country estate of Carabanchel not far from the capital. Soon afterwards the shooting began and cholera broke out. From the window of her new home little Eugenie watched monks being tortured and stabbed to death in the square below. Manuela decided that it was time to move and on 18th July 1834 she started, with her children, for the French frontier. Two days later Maréchal de Castellane, Governor of Perpignan, wrote in his diary:

> Many Spaniards are passing through Perpignan; most of them come from Madrid and are on their way to Toulouse; they are flying from cholera and the civil war. The Countess of Teba, a woman of thirty-five – extremely intelligent – is going to Toulouse. She has a very considerable fortune. Her husband has remained at Madrid for the session of the Cortes. Madame de Teba did not leave Madrid till the 18th; she saw dreadful things done there. The City Guard maimed and assassinated the monks and the Jesuits, even in their churches. The troops of the line were under arms, but looked on without interfering.[11]

On arrival in Paris Manuela's first thought was for the education of her daughters and she sent them to the convent of the Sacré Coeur in the Rue de Varennes. The 'Ladies of the Sacred Heart', as they were called, were a comparatively new order, having been formed in 1799. They liked their pupils to be rich, but they combined admiration for wealth with an intense piety and high intellectual efficiency. The girls referred to them as 'female Jesuits'.[12]

After two years at the convent Manuela considered that her daughters needed a change from the cloistered life and sent them to the *Gymnase Normal, Civil et Orthosomatique*, an establishment specialising in physical training on co-educational lines. Here was strong contrast with the Sacré Coeur and it suited Eugenie well. She was a high-spirited girl, reflecting the influence of Cipriano. She was apt to leap, without warning, over sofas or dive under the table. Her instructor reported that she was temperamental and excitable, but full of spirit, with a great taste for exercise – kind, generous, firm.[13]

The girls had other teachers in the evenings. Prosper Mérimée would call in to correct their French essays and teach them how to write letters. Then he would take them for a walk, an exercise which ended at the sweet shop. One evening he brought with him an author friend on a visit from Italy – Henri Beyle, who wrote under the name of 'Stendhal'. He was not well known then. Laughing, he would say that his day lay far ahead in time – in 1935. Stendhal was a fervent admirer of the Great Emperor and, for the girls, added to the Napoleonic legend begun by Cipriano. He had been a dragoon under Napoleon in the Italian campaign and at Moscow in 1812. The girls looked forward eagerly to his visits, sitting on his knees spellbound as he told them of Austerlitz and Waterloo. But there was one mentor whom they sorely missed – their father. Cipriano made only rare visits to Paris, and then stayed under another roof. He would take them to the circus and the theatre and shower them with presents. Yet Paca and Eugenie could not understand why they did not see more of him, and their frequent letters were full of longing.

Another influence was introduced to their lives. An English governess arrived, but the experiment was not altogether a success. She could not cure her charges of the habit of dropping their 'h's'. In addition she found them rebellious. More discipline was required and in 1837 Paca and Eugenie crossed the Channel and were deposited at a school at Clifton near Bristol.

Eugenie was not happy there. The typical English girls regarded a contemporary who had divided her time between Spain and France as an oddity, and teased her. They ragged her about her red hair and called her 'Carrots'. But she made friends with two Indian pupils, a trio homesick for other lands. She became fired with excitement by their tales of the Orient and in the dormitory a plan was hatched by which the three would stow-away on an east-bound ship from Bristol. They made good their escape from the school but were recaptured before they reached the docks.[14]

Eugenie wrote to her father, begging him to come and see them, saying that the place was dull, and that there were no amusements, not even nice people to watch passing along the street.[15] As a result of the girls' pleas, their stay at Clifton was curtailed and they returned to Paris in the care of a new governess, Miss Flowers. Miss Flowers belonged to that select band of export nannies and governesses who devoted their lives to reigning over foreign nurseries and schoolrooms and she was to remain in the service of the Montijos until the 1880s. To her Eugenie, even when Empress, was always 'Miss Eugenie.'

Early in 1839, as the Carlist war drew towards its end, Manuela heard from Madrid that Cipriano was seriously ill. She set off at once to care for him, arranging that her daughters should follow in the care of Miss Flowers. George Villiers, by this time Lord Clarendon, was still at his post in the Spanish capital, though under notice to return to London. The two had kept in touch, meeting as he passed through Paris on his way home on leave. It was fortunate for Manuela that he was there, for she had had little time to familiarise herself with the Montijo properties and possessions before the civil disturbances had driven her to France in 1834. She needed someone to help her. As it was, when Cipriano died in March, Clarendon was far from satisfied with the 'testamentary arrangements' as they affected the widow, but, taking into account her behaviour towards her husband, she had in truth little grounds for complaint. Sadly, the girls and Miss Flowers did not reach Madrid until after the funeral was over.

Soon a change came into the relationship between Eugenie and her mother. Manuela was rich – her personal income was over £4,000 a year – and propertied, and she had control of her daughters' money until they came of age. Free from the watching eye of Cipriano and his restrictions on finance, she spread her wings. She was in her forties and highly sexed, and this at a time when Spanish society was noted for its lax morals. She gathered around her a group of women of the same age and tastes and her Sunday night parties at the Plaza del Angel lasted well into Monday morning and became the talk of Madrid. Her goings-on at country houses were notorious. If she and her cronies were short of male company, they were not above kidnapping. Thus did an anonymous diarist describe the practice and the result:

> The Comtesse de Montijo possessed lovers galore, and had a most delightful habit of kidnapping any male biped whose society she wished to enjoy. It would appear to be the best way; it seems the most practical, and saves a most lamentable waste of time. A very dear and intimate old friend of ours, a man to whom I was personally greatly attached, the late José Hidalgo, was thus captured. One day, when a mere stripling, he was sauntering in the Prado; a carriage suddenly stopped; a man alighted and approached Hidalgo, and bowing and smiling asked the youth to accompany him. My friend had had more than a mere inkling of his impending doom, and was prepared for the worst (or should I say, the best); so when what De Soveral always called the sword of 'Damokuls' fell, he faced the music like a hero, and was spirited off to La Granja, where he stayed many weeks under the tyrannical governance of Mme de Montijo and a few other equally fascinating and pitiless lady pirates and a handful of young men, who like himself, after the fashion of Ganymede, had been stolen from their families. One of their pastimes, as recounted by Hidalgo, was for the men to get down on all fours on the floor, and for the ladies to straddle across their backs and tilt at each other as mounted knights might do at a tournament.[16]

Her affair with Clarendon may have contributed to Manuela's outbreak of middle-aged lechery. With Cipriano dead, she might well have hoped to become Lady Clarendon. The two had been close. Hard for her to appreciate that English mi'lords regarded marriage and personal alliances abroad in a very different light. He had, in fact, written from Spain to his sister, urging her to find him a suitable wife.[17] This she did, and on his return home he married the daughter of the first Earl of Verulam, a widow. This caused Manuela to transmit to her lover, via friends in England, a series of most sarcastic messages.

A danger stemming from her wild behaviour was the effect and impact this might have upon her daughters, both of impressionable age. Fortunately, Paca was immune. Dark, integrally Spanish, she took life as it came. Obedient, unquestioning, she accepted the situation. But

Eugenie was a very different proposition. Romantic, egotistical, a dreamer, devoted to the memory of her father, she lived in a world of fantasy, in a world of heroes and chivalry, of ideals and unbending beliefs. With her auburn hair and her classical features, she savoured more of an English stately home than of a palace in Madrid. She did not approve of the outlook and way of life of her Spanish contemporaries, and so she told Stendhal.

Eugenie drew further and further away from her mother, staging a silent rebellion. The result was that Paca became Manuela's favourite while Eugenie received the stick, as if, she said, she were a donkey. Matters came to a head when the girls became of marriageable age, for Manuela, Comtesse de Montijo, was an unrivalled matchmaker, and ambitious to boot.

While in Paris the girls had become friends with an unassuming young man who was eighth Duke of Berwick and fifteenth Duke of Alba and twelve times a Grandee of Spain.[a] He was short, slightly built, with a pale complexion and a voice that was hollow but attractive. Both Paca and Eugenie liked the quiet Duke and they were happy to share him, free of the disturbing influence of adolescence. It was when Eugenie met the Duke in Madrid, as she changed from girl to woman, that her feelings switched to those of love. He was in such contrast with other young people she met, who were concerned only with clothes and the social round and scandal. He talked to her of culture and travel and of the treasures in his beautiful home, the Palacio de Liria. She admitted her love, saying that she would go begging for him, even sleep with him. Here she was safe. The Duke was not prone to carnal desires.

Manuela was little concerned with the romantic notions of her daughters. She had decided that Paca should become Duchess of Alba, and that was that. She summoned him to a *tête-à-tête* conversation, put forward her views, and the passive young man acquiesced. Unfortunately Eugenie was eavesdropping outside the door and, on hearing the result, rushed to her bedroom and staged a scene in which suicide or

(a) The first Duke of Berwick was the eldest of the three children of James II and his mistress, Arabella Churchill, sister of the first Duke of Marlborough. James, Duke of Berwick, fought for his father's rights, and after the battle of the Boyne fled to France, where he joined the army. He died at the siege of Philipsburg in 1734. His grandson married a daughter of the Duke of Alba, who had no male heirs, and the two titles were merged.

withdrawal to a convent were threatened. Her plans were thwarted, but not before she had rushed off this letter to her future brother-in-law:

16th May 1843

My Very Dear Cousin,
You will think curious that I should write you a letter like this, but there is an end to all things in this world and my end draws near. I wish to explain to you, all that is in my heart, it is more than I can endure.

It is true my character is strong and I do not wish to excuse my behaviour, but on the other hand when one is good to me, I would do anything they want, but when I am treated like a donkey and beaten before people, it is more than I can bear: my blood boils and I cease to know what I am doing. Many people think there is no one happier than I. They are wrong. I am miserable because I make myself thus . . .

I fear ridicule more than death itself. My loves and hates are extreme. I do not know which is the stronger, my love or my hate. I am a mixture of passions, which are terrible and strong. I fight against them but ever lose the battle. My life will finish miserably in a turmoil of passions, of virtues and follies.

You will say that I am romantic and silly, but you are good and will forgive a poor girl who has lost all those who loved her and is now looked upon with indifference by everyone, even by her mother, sister and also by the man whom she loves the most, the person for whom she would have gladly have begged alms, and for whom she would have even consented to her own dishonour.[18]

There came a welcome diversion. Manuela decided that the trousseau must be bought in Paris and off she set, taking her two daughters with her.[19] The beauty of the seventeen year old Eugenie turned many a young man's head and one in particular wished to marry her without delay. He was the son of William C. Reeves, American Minister to Paris. As far as Manuela was concerned it would have been a good match, both from finance and status, and it would also have freed her from the tantrums of a recalcitrant daughter. But the Reeves family insisted that all children born of the union should be brought up to be Protestants. That Eugenie would not consider and her suitor surrendered to his parents' wishes and retired.[20]

Paca's marriage gave Eugenie one consolation – she now had a house where she could escape from the fault finding of her mother. She spent as much time at the Palacio de Liria as she did at home. There was no question of a continuing love for her brother-in-law. Her love had found a new target – it was for Paca, her sister or half-sister, as it may be. From this relationship may have stemmed the belief that Eugenie leaned towards sapphism. Certainly this new love was not returned by Paca. A few years after her marriage she received the following letter from Eugenie:

> Whilst reading your letter I wept. I do not know whether it was from sorrow or for joy. I certainly do not believe that your affection for me has lessened but believe we may love each other sincerely but it is not in the same way. I shall always regret the days when we were in Paris when you would not have fallen asleep if you were annoyed with me – since then how often you have bade me a cold 'good night'.[21]

Throughout her life, there was no love for a man which rivalled her feelings for Paca. It was only exceeded by her devotion to her son.

Although the young men of Madrid found her fascinating, they kept their distance, preferring the more orthodox approach to love prevalent among Spanish girls. Her temper was quick and violent. Her energy and physical achievement rivalled the masculine, and her voice was hard. She was often *difficile* and made clear her independence. She set high standards and was cruel in her censure if those standards were not met.

Let us see her, as a contemporary saw her, at a bullfight, the one experience that seemed to satisfy her craving for excitement and splendour. She had been selected to present the prize to the victorious toreador. She arrived, riding bare back, on a wild Andalusian horse, a cigarette between her lips. She was wearing national costume, the rich bodice clinging close to her. There was a dagger in her belt and, instead of the customary fan, she was carrying a whip. Her boots were of red satin, and high. Her auburn hair, coiled in broad plaits on the crown of her head, was decorated with pearls and flowers.[22]

Meantime the volcano of Spanish politics rumbled on, with frequent minor eruptions. Palace intrigues and military *pronunciamentos* were the order of the day and changing Generals held power. In April 1847

Manuela was appointed a lady-in-waiting to Queen Isabella and in October she rose to be *camerara mayor*, the highest position in the Household. Eugenie became a maid of honour.[23] But Manuela's escapades, intrigues and many affairs proved too much for Isabella and after a few weeks she appointed the Marques de Miraflores to be Governor of the Palace, taking precedence over the *camerara mayor*. Miraflores was an old friend of Cipriano's and consequently no friend of Manuela's. He made a dossier of her dubious activities and wrote to the Queen: 'For me to remain in my post is impossible as long as the Countess of Montijo remains in hers . . . . Since 1839, when I represented Your Majesty as Her Ambassador in Paris, I had encounters as heavy as they were unpleasant with this lady.'[24] On 16th December Manuela resigned – she had no choice. Eugenie, humbled with shame, considered entering a convent. Instead she fell in love.

The man was the Marques Pepe de Alcanizes. He was witty, ambitious and wealthy. He called often upon her and wrote many letters. But she discovered that Pepe was really in love with her sister, Paca, and that she was only being used as a means of access to the Duchess of Alba. Eugenie was shattered. She made up a foul concoction of ground up match heads and milk, and swallowed the poison. She then resolutely refused to take the antidote prescribed by the doctor. Manuela, well versed in the twistings of the feminine mind, sent Pepe to her bedside. There he asked if, before she died, he could have his letters back. In disgust, Eugenie agreed – and swallowed the antidote. She said: 'Like Achilles spear, you heal the wounds that you have made.'[25] Yet, ever desirous for that which she could not obtain, Eugenie hankered for Pepe. It was said that, before she agreed to marry Louis Napoleon, she sent him a note asking if he would have her, with or without love. Alcanizes refused.[a] [26]

Her fall from grace, an unfortunate affair with a young Italian who stole her jewels, and Eugenie's dramatics, prompted Manuela to leave Madrid, and for the next four years mother and daughter flitted around Europe, alighting at the gayest of places, the newly laid railways taking the hardship out of travel. They explored Spain. They walked by the sea at Biarritz and took the waters at Spa and Eaux-Bonnes.

(a) In 1868 Alcanizes, then Duke of Sexto, married the widow of the Duc de Morny. He was largely responsible for the restoration to the Spanish throne of Alfonso XII, whose father he was rumoured to be. He died in 1909.

They wintered in Brussels. Their Paris headquarters was an apartment in the Place Vendôme and, as has been related, they were introduced, by the Rothschilds, to Louis Napoleon shortly after the tragic death of Eleanora Gordon.

Much time was spent in England. They were entertained by Lord Clarendon. They stayed with Ferdinand Huddleston at Sawston Hall, where Eugenie aroused considerable attention as she rode around the Cambridge countryside.[27] At a reception given by Lady Palmerston in the spring of 1849 Eugenie was described as being 'a vision of youth and beauty'[28] and it was noted that she looked more aristocratic and British than the aristocratic British.

While Eugenie was making her social conquests throughout Europe, Louis Napoleon was planning and executing the most successful manoeuvre of his life.

Coup d'Etat

Thus did *Punch*, on 2nd February 1850, deal with the progress of Louis Napoleon, Prince-President of France, since his accession to office in 1848. The sketch was both concise and true. Nobody had expected the little man with a beaky nose and big moustache to be anything but a passing incident in the story of France. He had been placed where he was by the mass of the people because he was the nephew of the great Emperor and because they knew his name. Those who were experienced in politics and who pulled the strings of power still saw him as an upstart who had made a bloody fool of himself at Strasbourg and Boulogne. They were not impressed by his performance in the Assembly and considered that he cut a sorry figure. The Monarchists had accepted his presidency as a stage towards the return to kingship. His term was due to end in the spring of 1852 and, according to the Constitution, he could not be re-elected. They had not long to wait.

But they underestimated their man, for Louis Napoleon had grown up during his long years in the 'university' of Ham. Behind his expressionless face was a cold contempt for those who stood in his way. He played the parties of politics off against one another – Monarchists against Socialists, Socialists against Republicans. He put little value on the opinions of the men who played the power game in Paris and said their elegant pieces in the Assembly. He worked on numbers, the number of votes, the number who would say '*Oui*' to Louis Napoleon. He knew that the plebiscite was the ultimate answer. So he went out into the vast countryside of France, changing his speeches to suit the views of the people of each area. Whenever a new railway or bridge was opened, the Prince-President was there. His aim was the acquisition of absolute power. This could only be obtained from the people, and thus among the people he went.

To gain his end he cooperated with the elected members of the governing body. Curbs were placed upon the Press. The holding of meetings was forbidden. By the Falloux law of March 1880, the control of education fell into the hands of the Catholic Church, thus putting into reverse the intellectual emancipation born in the eighteenth century. When the Assembly attacked universal suffrage and reduced the number of voters from nine million to six million, by introducing a rule that a man must have been resident in one place for a minimum of three years, Louis Napoleon stood apart.

His strength grew with the passing months. He courted popularity with the army. He gathered around him a band of determined men wedded to the creed of Empire – Persigny, Rouher, Saint-Arnaud, Fleury, Maupas, Magnan and, last but not least, Morny. Louis Napoleon did not entirely approve of or like his half-brother, for he was a walking slur on the memory of Queen Hortense. But Morny was ruthless, ambitious, quick witted, a true grandson of Talleyrand. When in July 1851 the Assembly threw out a proposal for the revision of the Constitution, a revision which would have allowed Louis Napoleon to continue as President, it was Morny who insisted that the only answer was a *coup d'état*. Through August and the autumn the planning went on, in great detail and absolute secrecy. *Coup* day was finally fixed for Tuesday, 2nd December, the anniversary both of the battle of Austerlitz and the crowning of Emperor Napoleon.

On the evening of the 1st the President held his customary Monday reception. He was calm and appeared very much at his ease, standing before the fire conversing of railways, slum clearance and routine matters of a municipal nature. But he was acting, and he acted well, for he knew that there were men watching him, men who knew that a *coup* was in the offing and were looking for signs of excitement or unusual action. In the event there were two embryonic *coups*, for the Monarchists were planning on like lines. It was rumoured that two sons of ex-King Louis Philippe were already in France, ready to take over military commands, and that the Duchesse d'Orléans was standing by in London ready to leave for Paris with her young son.[1] Many Parisians were wondering which *coup* would mature first. But no clues were being given away at the Elysée that night.

At nine o'clock Louis Napoleon excused himself for a few minutes and went to speak to his secretary, Mocquard, in the study. Mocquard was busy checking the secret instructions for the hours which lay ahead. Louis Napoleon picked up the file and wrote across it 'RUBICON'. After a few minutes he rejoined his guests.

Morny had not yet arrived but came in soon after. He had attended the first night of Limmandier's new opera, '*Le Château de la Barbe-Bleue*', at the Opéra Comique.[2] *The Times* correspondent had spotted him sitting next to M. Thiers and General Cavaignac. It was a master stroke, for, people said, if Morny was at the Opera there could be no *coup*.

At ten o'clock the reception broke up, the last to leave being Saint-Arnaud, Minister for War, and Maupas, Prefect of Police. Having said their goodbyes and walked out through the main door, the two doubled back and returned a few minutes later by a side entrance. They joined Morny, Mocquard and Louis Napoleon. Louis said tersely, 'There is general talk tonight of an imminent *coup d'état*. But it is not ours. The National Assembly is going to send *me* to Vincennes in a *panier à salade*.[a],[3]

One by one the Palace lights went out. Paris slept.

Louis Napoleon, sharp, nervous now, instructed Morny and the others who had been joined by Persigny. The final touches were put to the plans. Each man was briefed. The conference ended at eleven o'clock. Saint-Arnaud, having given his final orders to Magnan,

(a) Black Maria.

Commander of the Army of Paris, went off to the Ministry of War where Colonel Emile Fleury was awaiting him. Morny produced his final, and tastiest, red herring. He strolled round to the Jockey Club for a rubber of whist. Maupas meanwhile drove to the *Imprimerie Nationale* carrying with him the handwritten copies of the Proclamations. For secrecy's sake the printing had been delayed till the last moment. By dawn the Proclamations, the ink upon them still wet, were posted all over Paris. Their message was that Louis Napoleon was omnipotent.

Maupas had another duty to fulfil as the *Deux Decembre* dawned. It was his task to arrange for the arrest of those who would oppose the *coup* and make trouble. A long list had been whittled down to seventy-eight names, those of politicians, recalcitrant military, journalists – Republicans and some British. For this operation a force of eight hundred police, divided into squads of ten – a squad for each arrest – had been decided upon. The leader of each squad was to be briefed individually, so that none knew the orders given to the others. At three o'clock Maupas began his briefing and he was hard at it for an hour and a half. He was insistent that the police were to be respectful and to avoid violence if possible. By five o'clock the squads were on the move, making towards their respective targets all over Paris. Their watches were synchronised. Zero hour was set for a few minutes after six. The striking of the hour was the alert. Then all were to move in on the same second.

The arrests were made with extreme efficiency. The slumberers were slow to wake to their senses in the deep sleep before the dawn, and made little trouble. A few reached for the pistols hidden beneath their pillows. A few, including Thiers, treated the police to political harangues, but most obeyed orders without question, climbing into their clothes as if in a trance. By seven o'clock they were all safely lodged in the Mazas prison.

In the early light six brigades moved silently through the streets, taking up their positions. In the barracks forty thousand troops stood by at the alert. Morny entered the Ministry of the Interior and announced to such as were there that he was their new chief. The Assembly, the Palais de Justice and the Hôtel de Ville were occupied. And simultaneously, all over France, police and military were taking over public buildings, telegraph offices and railway stations.[4] At seven o'clock

Persigny reported that stage one of Operation Rubicon had been safely accomplished.

When Louis Napoleon came downstairs after breakfast, the anterooms of the Elysée were packed with friends and supporters. He had planned to ride out in the streets at half past nine, but so enthusiastic was his reception that he was delayed for an hour. The cavalcade left from the Court of Honour. The President, in a general's uniform, was in the lead. He rode his magnificent English charger – many had commented that he had imported his lady and his horse from London. Behind him, to his right, was King Jerome, brother of the Great Emperor, a sight which brought glittering memories back to the old. On his left was General Saint-Arnaud. Behind came Flahaut, Magnan, Fleury and Ney, and a suite of forty general officers, gold braid flashing, plumed helmets tossing. As they rode out the Cuirassiers roared, '*Vive l'Empereur*'. Infantry lined the streets all the way to the Place de la Concorde. There the crowds were thick. Cries of '*Aux Tuileries*' could be heard. The gates of the Palace were open and Louis Napoleon cantered through. King Jerome raced up alongside and warned: 'Louis, you are going too fast. Better not enter the Château yet.' The President took the hint, wheeled the column and came from the Tuileries, crossed the Pont Royal, passed the Palais Bourbon and returned to the Elysée by way of the Pont de la Concorde. It was a magnificent piece of showmanship.

While this display of pomp and power was taking place, some two hundred Deputies gathered at a private house and then marched on the Assembly. They were greeted with 'savage shouts and brutal insults'[5] from the African Chasseurs in occupation. When the more daring tried to force an entry, they were repulsed by blows from musket butts. Considering discretion to be the better part of valour, the Deputies retreated to the comparative peace of the Mairie of the 10th *arrondissement* and there held their last meeting. They decreed that the President was deposed, that power was vested in the Assembly, and that those who had been imprisoned should be released immediately. Their deliberations were disturbed by the arrival of troops. The elected representatives of the people were seized by the collar and frog-marched through the streets to the military prison of Fort Valérien.

Apart from these displays, the *Deux Decembre* passed by very much as any other day. The *coup* had been too quick for the impetus of a city's life to be halted. The workers poured into the factories, cases were heard in the courts of justice, the banks carried on with their business, the shops and the theatres were open. But for the absence of eight opposition newspapers and the closing of certain cafés frequented by Republicans, there was little unusual. But there was bound to be reaction to such drastic steps. Louis Napoleon's political adversaries went underground and began their counterplanning.

On the 3rd there were a number of incidents. Barricades appeared in the streets and the young hot-heads who had been persuaded to man them tried the temper of the army. As troops advanced to clear the obstacles they were met with a barrage of *pavé* and insults, after which the defenders beat a very hasty retreat. Odd shots came from windows. Two men were killed and the sight of their bodies being wheeled away boded ill for the morrow.

On the morning of the 4th there were no troops in the streets. This unexpected development caused the Republicans to consider that the *coup d'état* was failing and that the regiments had been withdrawn to deal with disturbances in the provinces. Barricades were rushed up without hindrance and efforts were made to persuade the public to man them. But cries of 'Vive la République' met with little response from the crowds which had gathered to watch, while the working class of the east of Paris hardly stirred.[6] The active participants consisted of die-hard fanatics and young hot-heads and in all numbered little more than a thousand.

The absence of troops was not because of trouble elsewhere, but of design. General Magnan had decided to keep his troops off the streets in order that he could cope with the opposition with one stroke. The troops rested throughout the morning, were given a good dinner with ample wine and at two o'clock they were let loose, having been exhorted 'to make an end of it'. They were not instructed, as was the accepted practice, that they must not open fire on civilians except under specific order from an officer. So began the carnage which was to stain the reputation of Louis Napoleon throughout many years ahead.

Column after column appeared in the British Press describing the events of that Thursday afternoon. As movement was forbidden, and in any case highly dangerous, observers were limited to their individual field of vision. Here is the correspondent of the *Illustrated London News*:[7]

If the Boulevards, thronged by busy and animated crowds, their brilliant array of shops and *cafés* all open, be a sight to raise the wonder and delight of foreigners, anything more desolate and blank than their appearance when completely deserted by their peaceable inhabitants can hardly be imagined. Such was the picture presented to those who ventured within eyeshot of the scene on Thursday, in the afternoon, when every shop was closed, and the interior of the *cafés*, dimly lighted by a solitary *réverbère*, left scarcely the possibility for the few who hazarded to come within their precincts to recognise each other's faces. At the mouth of every street and every passage a picket of soldiers stayed the further progress of the people, who remained behind the barrier as spectators. But, while the open thoroughfare of the Boulevards was abandoned, the windows and balconies of every house, from top to bottom, were alive with anxious faces, eagerly watching the growing numbers and inexplicable evolutions of the military, who soon filled up the space as far as the eye could reach, from the point of the Boulevard des Italiens, at which I was situated. That something of consequence was about to be enacted, was evident to every looker-on. Circulation, which at first had been partially allowed, was at length imperatively forbidden, and the half-opened doors of the cafés, from which the unemployed *garçons*, and even the *cuisiniers*, had been furtively peering, were shut by command. Unconscious of what was going to happen, however, the inhabitants remained at the windows and in the balconies, their curiosity outweighing their fears. The rapid passage to and fro of heavy artillery, directed to unknown points; the sound of distant cannon, which told an undeniable story; the *croque-morts*, as those members of the *ambulances* are called whose business it is to carry away the dead and wounded; the army surgeons in their regimental guise; the incessant departure and return of the *guides*, all at the gallop – these and other appearances no less suggestive were insufficient to drive the people into their houses; the windows and the balconies continued to be busily occupied. At length, however, two or three successive motions of the hand from the general who was superintending the manoeuvres of the troops gave warning that danger was at hand, and the greater number of the curious retired from the windows, although those in the *balcon* of the Café du Cardinal failed to take the hint; and it was not till two tremendous volleys of musketry made the Boulevards ring again, that they became aware of the peril to which they stood exposed, and scrambled through the windows of the *premier étage* . . . .

The man from the *Morning Chronicle* found himself in the thick of it:

At half-past three in the afternoon the troops extending along the Boulevard des Italiens, the Boulevard Montmartre, and the Boulevard Bonne Nouvelle, were drawn up the whole way across the street, so as to touch the *trottoir* at each side. The foot-pavements were crowded with spectators, and in the balconies of the houses of each side were to be seen hundreds of ladies and gentlemen. There was not a barricade within a considerable distance, and certainly not within sight. Things were in this position when, all of a sudden, a running fire was opened on the people on the foot-pavements and at the windows. Fortunately it was not by platoons, but by a running fire, so that a considerable number had time to escape, but still the carnage was dreadful. To one house, at the corner of the Rue Bergèrel there were carried not less than 35 dead bodies, besides those carried elsewhere; and it may truly be stated that among this mass of victims there was not a single insurgent.

One Press artist stationed by a barricade saw six young men lined up against a wall and shot, and then bayoneted. He recaptured the utter horror of the moments in a dramatic sketch.

By the evening the firing had ceased and the streets were empty except for patrols, ambulances on their way to the hospitals and big vans conveying manacled prisoners to the railway stations. Estimates of the casualties varied widely, but in all some one hundred and fifty were killed and between 600 and 800 wounded. The large number of innocent spectators who suffered was tragic, but they had been warned to stay off the streets and away from windows. Many paid dearly for their curiosity.

It was all over and Louis Napoleon was supreme. On the fourth night after the *coup* his cousin, the Marchioness of Douglas, gave a ball in his honour at the Hotel Bristol. He was completely cool and collected. He chatted with many of the guests, spending considerable time with Lord Cowley, who had only arrived in Paris that morning to fill the post of British Ambassador. As the clock struck twelve the President's carriage was announced and Lord Douglas,[a] with a wax candle in either hand, led his guest down the stairs. To his amazement Douglas found at the door a plain, one horse brougham.[8] There was no military escort and not a policeman in sight. Louis Napoleon was indeed the master now. A few days later a plebiscite confirmed his ten year period as President by seven and a half million votes to 650,000. Lord Clarendon wrote to his brother-in-law:

> I have no sympathy with Louis Napoleon, who has committed wholesale high treason and trampled his own obligations and the rights of others under foot with an audacity that has no parallel in history; but I can't quite agree with you that he is such a *chétif* creature. The man who conceived this *coup d'état* and made all the arrangements for it with such secrecy and completeness – who pounced upon all his actual and probable enemies at once – who had the courage to show himself in the streets when he had no assurance that his blow was finally struck or popular – and who, during and after the carnage, appears not to have been troubled by the ordinary feelings of humanity – can be no common mortal . . . .[9]

(a) On the death of his father in 1852, Lord Douglas became 11th Duke of Hamilton.

CHAPTER 8

Falling in Love Again

Louis Napoleon's victory at the polls in 1850 led to changes in his personal life. First, he was now granted an income of a million francs a month, a rise which freed him from the financial troubles which had plagued him throughout his career. Second, he was faced with the task of providing an heir to the Empire which he intended to establish in the near future. So priority one became, *Cherchez la femme.*

Elizabeth Howard was by this time well established, at least in her own estimation. In addition to her house in the Rue du Cirque, she had a ground floor apartment at St Cloud. With her lived her son by Major Francis Martin and the two bastard sons of Louis Napoleon by *la Belle Sabotière.* She was devoted to all three. The President was thus able to enjoy the comforts of family life.

There was bound to be criticism of such a liaison by certain members of the public. On his long journeys through France Louis liked Elizabeth to be with him. Unfortunately, on a visit to Tours, the presidential party was lodged in the spacious home of General André, who was absent on a holiday in the Pyrenees. The General was both Puritan and Protestant and when he learned that his linen had been soiled by sin, he let off a rocket at the Prime Minister, Odilon Barrott. 'Have we returned to those times when a King's mistresses promenade their vices throughout the length and breadth of France?'[1]

Barrott arranged that the letter be seen at the Elysée and the President was furious. He reached for his pen and returned the General's fire:

> I detest that pedantic severity which always half hides a cold, unfeeling mind, indulgent towards itself but inexorable towards others. True religion is never intolerant, and does not go about trying to stir up storms in a glass of water, to make a scandal about nothing, and turn a simple accident or an excusable oversight into a crime .... If M. André really thinks, as he says he does, that his

house has been soiled by the presence of a woman who is not married, I pray you tell him from me that for my part I sincerely regret that a person of such pure devotion and high character should have happened by chance to visit a house where the ostentation of bombastic virtue without any christian spirit reigns under the mask of religion . . . .[2]

The Prime Minister decided that it would be in the best interests of the parties involved that this letter should go no further.

Although Louis Napoleon would tolerate no criticism of the women with whom he associated – seeing such as criticism of himself – in his life's race they ran a very poor second to the Bonaparte aims and legend. Sex and female company were essential to him, but he chose the time and the place. He was in parallel with those actresses who may dally while resting but will leap, ice cold, from the bed at the chance of capturing a leading part. He preferred to be pursued than to pursue. He took sex as a right. It was only women of the lower orders, or ladies who did what ladies usually do not do, who drew him, inexorably, to their couches. It was the body, and not the soul, of which he dreamed. Yet he always wished to remain on friendly terms in the *après* period and failed to understand the depths of a woman's feelings. He had already made that mistake with Eleanora Gordon – now he was to do the same with Elizabeth Howard.

He never had any intention of making Elizabeth his Empress, and early in 1852 he told her so. She did not believe him. She had but recently lent him 200,000 francs to finance the *coup d'état*. It was thanks to her that he was what he was. Louis Napoleon, however, continued fashioning his dream Empress in his own detached way. He must have someone whose standing and title was fitting for the role. His first thought was of Princess Mathilde, the daughter of King Jerome. He tried to resurrect this romance of his younger days, but Mathilde said no. Her unhappy marriage could easily have been annulled, but she already had a lover. Moreover she prized her independence, and wished to remain free of politics so that she could indulge in her love of the arts. Louis Napoleon was not perturbed. He did not in any case approve of marriages between cousins. He assured her that she would always sit at his right hand at the dinner table until such time as an Empress materialised. Too late, Mathilde discovered how much she prized that seat on the right hand. It was one reason why she hated the woman who deposed her.

Louis Napoleon's next candidate was a Princess of Sweden – Caroline Vasa. Here there was family 'pull', for Caroline was a granddaughter of Stéphanie de Beauharnais, Grand Duchess of Baden.[a] It was an ambitious plan, for the union would have forged links with Russia, Austria, Prussia and Sweden. It nearly came off. Louis Napoleon sent an emissary to Baden and Princess Caroline, although still in her teens, agreed to a bridegroom of forty-four. '*Au revoir. A Paris*', she said as she bid the envoy goodbye. The Prince-President then paid her a visit, liked her and returned to Paris convinced that the wedding was on. A few days later a letter, breaking off the engagement, arrived from the Grand duchess. She had been under pressure from Russia and Austria, and Caroline was quickly married off to the Prince of Saxony. It was a slap in the face for Louis Napoleon but he was philosophical. He commented: 'If the royal families of Europe do not want me among them, it is better for me. It certainly is hardly consistent for us Napoleons, who are of plebeian origin, to seek alliances with families whose distinctions come to them by Divine right.'[3]

He was a man who always learned the lessons of defeat. The farces of Strasbourg and Boulogne led to the triumph of the *coup d'état*. He did not lower his eyes when he lost, but raised them higher yet. Now he focussed them on the woman whom he saw as the future star of Europe and the world – the Queen of England. He had seen Victoria as girl-Queen and, after escaping from Ham, as wife and mother. He had stood beside her on one occasion – the opening of public baths in a poor part of London. Hardly a romantic setting, but he was ever drawn towards her as, later, she was to be towards him. Albert and territorial obligations forbade him coveting the large wooden bed at Windsor Castle, but Victoria had a niece of seventeen named Adelaide who neatly fitted the role of bride.

(a) Stéphanie de Beauharnais was the daughter of Claude de Beauharnais, brother-in-law of the Empress Josephine. On the death of her mother, Stéphanie was cared for by Josephine and subsequently adopted by Napoleon I. In 1806 she married the Grand Duke of Baden, whose sisters had married the Tsar of Russia, the King of Sweden and the King of Bavaria. They had three daughters. The eldest, Louise, married Prince Gustavus Vasa and Caroline was their daughter. The second, Josephine, married Prince Anthony of Hohenzollern and it was their son, Leopold, who was the indirect cause of the Franco-German war. The third, Mary, married the Marquess of Douglas and became Duchess of Hamilton.

Before tilting for that prize, Louis Napoleon decided that he must attain the status of Emperor, thus boosting his claim with the diadem of inheritance. He planned in secret. In the meanwhile he suited his own pleasure. Heartlessly, he turned a blaze of late summer sun upon the somewhat sad Elizabeth Howard. At a ball at St Cloud he retired with her to *rest* at half past ten. The couple later rejoined the guests.[4] The diarists made the most of that.

In September he set off south on the long tour that was to ensure, by a plebiscite, his goal of Emperorship. At Bourges the troops roared '*Vive l'Empereur*'. 'Down the river to the sea the shouting grew louder; all Avignon was roaring on the walls; Arles, Marseilles, Montpellier joined the dance and set their flags waving in a flutter of Bonapartism.'[5] His last speech was at Bordeaux and there he made his aims clear.

He came back to Paris on 16th October. He was met by a mounted column of generals, members of the Senate and cavalry. But he entered the capital alone, riding well ahead of the column, along a path hedged thick by crowds. He rode the magnificent chestnut charger which he had brought from London. His horsemanship was superb. His face was calm and inscrutable. Watching him, from the apartment one of her admirers, Huddleston of Cambridge, was Eugenie de Montijo.

It was on that day that Eugenie decided that he was the man for her and that she would share her life with him. It was both the figure and the courage which touched her heart. He was a sitting target for an assassin. He could have been picked off by a shot from any high window. After the carnage following the *coup d'état* there were many who had a score to settle with Louis Napoleon Bonaparte. But he rode on with seeming indifference to danger. This was the legend of which Don Cipriano had spoken to her – a legend come true.

A month later the roles were reversed.

It was at a hunt at Fontainebleau. Eugenie had received a special invitation and Louis Napoleon had mounted her on one of the finest thoroughbreds in the stable. She was wearing a closely buttoned habit, a wide skirt covering grey trousers. Her patent leather boots were high-heeled. Her long plaits were twisted under a felt hat, from which waved an ostrich feather secured by a diamond clasp. The handle of her whip was set with pearls. 'She sat her horse like a knight', despising the saddle ordinarily used by women. She was in her element, back with her old love, and her eyes were shining and she was smiling.[6]

She was the star of the day from the moment they moved away into the forest, her superb Spanish horsemanship and her strength arousing admiration. She was first in at the kill and, when Louis Napoleon galloped up, he paid immediate tribute to her. That evening he sent her a bouquet of flowers. Next day he gave her the horse which she had ridden. He was in love and he made it plain to see. That present set the tongues wagging – 'that devil of a horse', Eugenie was later to say.[7]

The festivities at Fontainebleau lasted for some days. On an afternoon when only the men were hunting, Eugenie, with a party of women guests, waited on a balcony adjoining the Palace chapel to see them come home with their bag. Louis Napoleon called up to them, 'How can I reach you, *mesdames*?' A well known beauty replied, 'You can climb up if I hold out my hand.' Eugenie said: 'As for me, Prince, the only way I perceive is through the chapel.'[8] Her companions took that to have a double meaning – that the way to her bedroom lay through a church.

Another occasion set the seal on the intentions of Louis Napoleon. It was a military review. He rode alone, far out in front, behind him a galaxy of ladies and gentlemen. As was his custom, he never turned his head. It began to pour with rain. As he dismounted at the close of the parade, he saw that only one of the women had braved the downpour – Eugenie.

At a ball at St Cloud Louis Napoleon singled her out, and everyone began asking the same, obvious question – how long would Eugenie resist sleeping with the Prince-President? One lovely lady commented, 'I could have been Empress if *I* had resisted.' The view of the British Ambassador, Lord Cowley, was that 'she has played her game so well that he can get her in no other way but marriage.'[9] No one seemed to appreciate that Eugenie had little wish to sleep with anyone, unless the reason for such action was the procreation of children.

Louis Napoleon was now playing a dangerous game, juggling with the hearts and futures of three women. Lord Malmesbury confirmed that, in November, Elizabeth Howard was still his mistress. He was in love with Eugenie, a lovely prize that he longed for but could not obtain. And he planned that a third woman, the niece of Queen Victoria, should become his Empress. This was as yet secret, though all steps were being taken to find favour at Windsor, including the master stroke of honouring the smooth German mentor of Albert and Victoria, Baron von Stockmar.[10]

First, however, he must await the results of the plebiscite. This was held on 21st November and 7,824,189 Frenchmen voted that the Prince-President should become their Emperor, and only 253,145 that he should not. On 2nd December, the anniversary of Austerlitz, of the coronation of Napoleon I and of the *coup d'état*, the title was bestowed upon Louis Napoleon. The Imperial eagle returned to the flags and the carriage doors and for the first time for fifty years the hymn, '*Domine salvum fac Imperatorem*', was sung in the cathedral of Notre Dame. Ten days later Queen Victoria found upon her desk at Osborne a request from the Emperor of the French, channelled through his ambassador and the Foreign Office, that he be allowed to marry her niece, Princess Adelaide of Hohenlohe-Langenburg. Rarely had she received such a shock and Albert was summoned immediately.

CHAPTER 9

Marriage Market

Ever since the *coup d'état* in 1850 the chief topic of conversation between Queen Victoria and her husband, in the field of international politics, had been the aims of Louis Napoleon. While the Queen regarded him in a not unfriendly light, remembering his support at the time of the Chartist riots, Albert saw him as the acme of sin and danger. In this he was influenced by his uncle, the King of the Belgians.

To King Leopold, now sixty, dried up, with rouged cheeks and pencilled eyebrows, this was a family problem. In the business of 'taking over' thrones, the Coburgs had been the leading operators since Waterloo. They had gained power in Belgium, Portugal and Britain, and had other deals in mind. Now the eagle of the Bonapartes had risen from the ashes and threatened their plans.

As a young and ambitious Prince, Leopold had proved a nuisance to Napoleon I and had been warned to keep out of the way. But he had managed to enter London in the train of the victorious Allied Sovereigns in 1814. There he had made advances to Princess Charlotte, only daughter of the Prince Regent, and two years later he married her. When she died in childbirth, Leopold found himself in possession of a pension of £50,000 a year. Having failed to gain the throne of Greece, he accepted that of Belgium. His next problem was to marry his penniless nephew, the student Prince Albert, to Queen Victoria. This he most successfully did, and a further £30,000 of British taxpayers' money was added to the family income.

Albert did what King Leopold told him to do. By 1850, Queen Victoria was doing what Albert told her to do. The Coburgs were at the helm of Europe. Then came the *coup d'état*.

Leopold loosed off a volley of warning letters to his brother sovereigns, exaggerating the danger of attack by France. He described himself as being 'in the awkward position of persons in hot climates who find themselves in company, for instance in their beds, with a snake; they must not move because that irritates the creature, but they

88

can hardly remain as they are without a fair chance of being bitten'.[1] When Louis Napoleon put out the hand of friendship, Leopold commented – 'his real aim is to place himself above me.'[2] Therein lay the trouble.

The Bonapartes and the Coburgs approached the palaces of power by very different routes. The Bonapartes rode, alone, up the steps to the front door and demanded admission. The Coburgs sneaked in through a side door and took over the best bedroom. While the Coburgs regarded money as a prerequisite of power, the Bonapartes put power first and collected the money as necessary. The Bonapartes believed in achievement, in 'doing things', while the Coburgs preferred to slide into success with the least possible risk and effort. A further reason for Leopold's anger with the Prince-President was that in 1852 the property of his wife's family in France was confiscated, his children thus losing their inheritance.

So it was that, through the insistence of Leopold and Albert, England became convinced that her shores were open to invasion by a new Napoleon. In fact, nothing was further from Louis Napoleon's thoughts. He both liked and admired the country which had given him shelter and he had many friends there. His mistress was English and his cousin was the Duchess of Hamilton. He had even arranged to live in London if the *coup d'état* failed. But Albert and certain politicians opposed to France did not wish to believe that and their call to arms was answered by those die-hards who recalled the threatened invasion by Napoleon I. The memory of that scare lingered on and in many a household recalcitrant children were still being warned, 'Boney will get you if you don't look out.'

Prince Albert's biographer, Sir Theodore Martin, put the position thus:

> In what direction Louis Napoleon might move his forces, who might tell? Switzerland was menaced; the extension of a frontier to the Rhine was darkly hinted at; and Belgium, in alarm at what it had some reason to fear might happen, was strengthening her defences . . . But a move in any of these directions was little likely to be made, for it would have brought against France the united forces of all the great Continental Powers. Was it certain, however, that they would move a step to oppose any attempt upon England? . . . It was under

these circumstances that the country again woke up in its wonted spasmodic way to the fact that the national defences were inadequate. A sudden descent upon our shores might have enabled an invader to inflict serious disaster and still more serious shame. We had been warned of this again and again; but now the danger of an attack must be counted on, if the distrust of the head of the French Government were as well founded as it was widely felt and clamorously proclaimed. A general cry was heard, that the time had come, not merely to augment our naval force, in which we were at this time run very close by the French, but also to strengthen our inner line of defence. A spontaneous movement for the establishment of a force of Volunteers was encouraged by the Government, and ultimately led to what has now become a permanent institution. The Government also resolved to satisfy the prevailing demand for further security by bringing before Parliament a scheme for the re-establishment of a Militia.[3]

Apart from the miscalculation regarding the intentions of Louis Napoleon, the re-awakening process was apposite, for there had been little military advancement, either in weapons or tactics, since Waterloo. Now over-fat young men were lured from office and club and made to 'double' over Chobham heath. Albert went so far as to spend a night in a tent – the nearest that he ever came to the rigours of a soldier's life. But the year passed without sign of aggression by France. When Louis Napoleon became Emperor, Britain was the first to recognise the Imperial title.

At this time Queen Victoria's niece, Adelaide, was staying with her at Osborne. Adelaide's mother was Feodora, daughter of the Duchess of Kent by her first marriage. Despite the difference in their ages, Feodora and Victoria had been close friends during their years together at Kensington Palace and, when Feodora married in 1828 and went to Germany, Victoria missed her sorely. Albert did not like Feodora, showing the same aversion to her as he did towards all those who had held the confidence of his wife in her young days.

The two strongest supporters of the proposed marriage of Louis Napoleon with Princess Adelaide were Morny and Count Walewski, the French Ambassador in London, both illegitimate relations of the Emperor. They saw, and with reason, the prestige and political advantages to be gained. But the proposal both embarrassed and annoyed Queen Victoria. She objected to being placed in a position where a yes or no reply was asked for, and so she tartly informed her Foreign Secretary. She told him that it was solely a question for the girl's parents. But she did add that she considered that the Princess's age and religion weighed against the idea.

Meanwhile, Louis Napoleon had sent an emissary to Langenburg, putting the same proposal to the Princess's father. Prince Hohenlohe replied that he could not dispose of his daughter's hand without her consent, that she was now in England and that he would leave the decision to her.[4] At a meeting between Queen Victoria, Prince Albert and the Foreign Secretary the Queen counselled care, expressing the fear that Adelaide 'would be dazzled if she heard of the offer'.[5] And when she did hear of it, that is exactly what happened.

Adelaide, at sweet seventeen, was gay and pretty but somewhat late in developing physically. Her doctors had given the opinion that she should not marry for two or three years, a point which was seized upon at Windsor. But the thought of escaping the boredom and poverty of Langenburg thrilled her. She was 'dying to be Empress',[6] and her mother knew it. Yet, playing quietly and cagily behind the scenes, the Queen, Prince Albert and King Leopold were determined that the marriage would not take place. The Queen, taking the woman's view point, was thinking of the dangers of an experienced man of forty-four marrying an innocent of seventeen, with probable sexual tragedy; the Coburg men had no intention of allowing a poor, adolescent relation to lord it over them from addresses such as the Tuileries and Versailles.

Walewski set out for Langenburg to interview Prince Hohenlohe. He travelled via Paris. There, to his horror, he learned from Lord Cowley that the Emperor was deeply involved with Eugenie. Calling on his cousin next morning, he was told – '*Mon cher, je suis pris*'. Walewski put his case, the Emperor saw the advantages and agreed that he would do nothing about Eugenie until Princess Adelaide's answer arrived. If the answer was 'Yes', he would make her his Empress. But his heart was elsewhere.

The cause of Napoleon's *volte-face* was to be found in the first imperial party held at Compiègne. It began on 17th December and was due to end on the 21st, but in fact whirled on until the 28th. Four hundred people made the journey to the Palace in the forest. There were one hundred guests, including Lord Cowley and other ambassadors. The Household, stage-managing affairs, was of a like number, and there were two hundred assorted servants. There were shoots and hunts, balls and fêtes. It was the rise of the curtain upon the Second Empire.

There were many on the élite guest list who expected, and hoped, that the pomp and ceremony, the splendour and the etiquette, would prove too strong a test for the adventurous beauty from Spain, and that she would topple. She was the talking point among the women gossiping in the drawing-rooms, among the men chatting after dinner. They were making bets as to when she would surrender. In the event she neither toppled nor surrendered. The end result was that she cemented her position.

Everywhere was the ghost of Empress Marie Louise. Napoleon I had restored Compiègne and taken the Austrian Archduchess there in the flush of his love for her. On the forest side, across the gardens, stretched the mighty avenue which he had cut through the trees to please her. Picture after picture of her looked down from the walls. Her great draped bed stood waiting – waiting for Eugenie, Countess of Teba. There, in the Palace in the forest, she fell in love with a man, a place and a way of life all at one time. As she galloped over the trim green grass and under the ceiling of the naked trees, she was as near to great happiness as she was ever to be. Exploring the narrow streets which tumbled down to the Oise, dancing the night away, entranced by the theatricals, this was dream stuff for any young woman, even one as demanding as Eugenie.

Louis Napoleon was ever by her, ever watching her. Yet a strange change had come over him. In the bigness of it all, he sought out the little things. He picked a single flower for her. He wandered with her through the gardens. He looked after her every comfort. He showed his love in a great many different ways. It was as if the first flame of desire for her had burned out, leaving the after-glow of romance. It was probably his only experience of this indefinable state.

Yet Louis Napoleon was still seeing Elizabeth Howard, calling at her quiet house in the Rue du Cirque. She knew about Eugenie – and suspected the worst. 'But,' she said, 'he suffers from indigestion and I know he will come back.'[7] She would not let him go, although he made matters very plain. She wrote to a friend in England: 'His Majesty was here last night, offering to pay me off: yes, an earldom in my own right, a castle and a decent French husband into the bargain . . . The Lord Almighty spent two hours arguing with me . . . . Later he fell asleep on the crimson sofa and snored while I wept.'[8]

The Compiègne extravaganza had attracted wide attention, not only in France but across the frontiers in Germany, Belgium and Holland. While the nation was prepared to tolerate the peccability of a President, the full-blown love of an Emperor was headline news, pointing the way, as it did, towards matrimony. Thus there broke from the French press a campaign of gossip, scandal and partisanship. Louis Napoleon had early appreciated the danger contained in Manuela's lurid and adventurous career. For twenty-five years her morals had been a talking point in Paris. Now came many new stories – of how she had entertained the customers in her father's wine shop, of her infidelities during her husband's imprisonment, of the scandal which ended her brief period as head of the Household of Queen Isabella, of her reputation of being the property of British Ministers in Madrid, of her country house orgies with young men, and, of course, a great deal about Lord Clarendon, both in Paris and in Madrid.

As is natural on such occasions, opinions were sharply divided as to where lay the future of the Emperor. The younger statesmen and diplomats favoured the choice of Princess Adelaide, and in this they were backed by the British Ambassador, Lord Cowley. A link with Germany could but prove an asset in the future, and the reasons behind their thinking were later to become only too tragically clear.

Many ordinary people in France favoured Eugenie, for a variety of simple reasons – she was not royal – visually, she was a dream Empress – she had already become known for her charitable works.

The older generation, headed by ex-King Jerome, was dead set against Eugenie and would have preferred the Emperor to remain single, thus leaving the succession in the hands of King Jerome's son, Prince Napoleon. Princess Mathilde threw herself at her cousin's feet, begging him to discard the Spaniard.[9] There were those who would have preferred the domestic relationship with Elizabeth Howard to continue on its leisurely way, choosing to believe that 'the English chain' was too strong to be broken.

Under the bombardment of insult and innuendo, Eugenie suffered from increasing strain. Incensed, the Emperor threatened that he would take legal action against the originators and publishers of these stories. So the publishers retreated to Belgium and Germany, printed their fabrications and libels there, and there was very little that even an Emperor could do about that. In the highly emotional and acrimonious atmosphere, Eugenie became a target for personal insult.

The first official reception of the Second Empire was held on New Year's Eve. Eugenie and her mother had been invited to sit at the Emperor's table. As the guests moved in to dinner Eugenie accidentally stepped in front of a certain Madame de Fortoul, who cherished her seniority. In a loud voice Madame de Fortoul informed those around that she was astonished that a young foreigner of questionable origin should attempt to take precedence over her. Eugenie drew back and said, '*Passez, Madame*'. But her cheeks were ivory white and her eyes were flashing anger as she took her place at the table. The Emperor came to her chair and asked her what was the matter. She begged him to take his seat. But he found out afterwards what had happened.[10]

On 2nd January the Emperor received a sad little letter from 'Ada' – Princess Adelaide of Hohenlohe. She said, in dictated words, that she did not feel that she was capable of undertaking the job of Empress.

Once the danger was over, Queen Victoria let loose her feelings in a letter to Princess Feodora:

'. . . . I feel that your dear child is *saved* from *ruin* of every possible *sort*. You know what *he* is, what his moral character is (without thinking him devoid of good qualities and even valuable ones) . . . you know his age, that his health is indifferent, and naturally his wish to marry Ada (is) merely a political one, for he has never seen her . . . I ask you if you can imagine for a moment anything more awful than the fate of that sweet, innocent child . . . a prey to every ill natured remark and observation and to every wicked Counsellor without a female friend in the world!'[11]

Although the Emperor was now free to propose marriage to Eugenie, there were still important preparatory steps to be taken. Austria, Prussia and Russia had not yet accepted the Empire, being unwilling to grant Napoleon the full dignity of title as Emperor. The Ambassadors were, therefore, in the odd position of being accredited to a dead

Republic. On the advice of Morny the Emperor gave ground and on 5th January agreement was reached.

There next came the almost insuperable task of persuading the Ministers and those with influence to accept Eugenie. One minister offered his resignation. Napoleon refused it, telling him to go and see the lady concerned. He did so and returned converted. But many were dead set against the marriage, among them being ex-King Jerome and Drouyn de Lhuys, Minister for Foreign Affairs.

Meantime, Manuela had kept in touch with Lord Clarendon, either directly or through her closest friend, the Marchioness of Santa Cruz. Clarendon was a faithful ally. He it was who arranged that Napoleon and Eugenie should meet, in absolute secrecy, at the apartment of an Englishwoman in the Champs Elysées.[12] Here, undisturbed, they had the chance to get to know one another, in a way that would have been impossible at the Tuileries. Napoleon pulled no punches when explaining to her the difficulties facing an Empress. 'It is only fair that I should set before you the whole truth, and let you know that if the position is very high, it is also very dangerous and insecure.'[13] He warned of assassination, of war and disaffection in the army. It was a challenge which she gladly accepted. This conversation was 'leaked' by Clarendon, with the result that the reputation of Napoleon in important places rose by several notches and the prevalent idea that he was marrying only for sex was scotched.

On 12th January there was a Court Ball. Manuela and Eugenie were escorted by Baron James de Rothschild and his son, who led them to seats against the wall, bowed and retired. Madame de Drouyn de Lhuys was already seated there. She came over to Eugenie and told her that the places were reserved for the wives of Cabinet Ministers. Eugenie rose and whispered to her mother. She too rose to her feet. There they stood, embarrassed, the target of all eyes. The Emperor hurried over and led them to the Imperial dais. He asked Eugenie what had happened but she asked him to wait until later. After recounting what had taken place, she told him that she could stand no more and was off to Italy in the morning. He calmed her by saying that, in the very near future, nobody would dare to insult her again.[14]

Three days later the Minister for the Household arrived at the Montijo home in the Place Vendôme. He bore a formal request to Manuela for her daughter's hand. The request was duly granted. Shortly afterwards another carriage arrived from the Tuileries. It contained the Emperor himself, and he was both angry and bewildered. He announced to Manuela that he had received information that Lord Clarendon was the father of Eugenie. Was it true? It was certainly of vital importance, for Clarendon was a firm friend of Queen Victoria and about to become Secretary of State for Foreign Affairs. In the current spate of rumours and gossip about Manuela de Montijo, there must have been special reason for the Emperor attaching such value to the letter which had reached him. He could have heard the same story all over Paris.

Manuela was up to the situation. '*Sire,*' she said, '*les dates ne correspondent pas.*' Napoleon accepted this and the marriage plans went on.

CHAPTER 10

Notre Dame

Napoleon hated domestic rows. They now loomed up before him like black clouds, threatening to blot out the sunshine of his wedding, for the news of it could not long be withheld from Elizabeth Howard. He therefore devised a ruse by which she would be well out of the way during the vital days ahead.

Elizabeth's former lover, the gambler James Young Fitzroy, had seized the chance of Napoleon's elevation to make discreet demands for money in exchange for certain letters of a compromising nature. These concerned his activities while in England. The Emperor despatched Elizabeth in the care of Mocquard, his secretary and the devoted friend of both of them, to London, with instructions to buy the letters as cheaply as they could.

On the evening of 20th January, 1853, Elizabeth was at the Hotel Frascati at Le Havre, waiting for the boat. She picked up a copy of *Le Moniteur*. In it she read of the forthcoming engagement of Napoleon and Eugenie. Furiously angry, she ordered a special train and returned to Paris. On arrival at her house in the Rue du Cirque she found that the rooms had been searched.[1] Drawers were in chaos and papers had been taken. The Prefect of Police had faithfully carried out his orders to ensure that no incriminating documents remained. There were 'terrible scenes'[2] but Elizabeth realised that Napoleon was fully committed and that there was nothing that she could do now. She accepted that the chapter of her life, featuring the only man whom she had ever really loved, was over.[a]

Not surprisingly, people commented that the Emperor appeared pale and strained, for with one hand he was warding off Elizabeth Howard and with the other repulsing the attacks on Eugenie. On the

(a) Elizabeth Howard was given the title of Comtesse de Beauregard, after the lovely château of that name near Versailles, which she had purchased in September 1852. The Emperor repaid, with interest, the money which she had lent him. In May 1854, in London, she married Charles Trelawney, but the marriage was not a success. She died in 1865. Her portrait hangs at Compiègne.

22nd he faced the Council of State, the Legislative Assembly and deputations of the Senate and, in a long and eloquent speech, put the case for his chosen bride:

> I have preferred a woman whom I love and respect to an unknown one, an alliance with whom might with its advantages have brought the necessity for sacrifices. Without disrespect to anyone, I yield to my inclinations.

He referred to himself as a *parvenu*, saying that the Royal Houses of Europe were clearly unwilling to accept him and that it was better by far to take the woman whom he loved than to return to France with some insignificant little Princess of whom nobody had ever heard. He won the day, but the Royalists were not pleased to hear their ruler refer to himself as a *parvenu*.

The civil wedding was fixed for the evening of Saturday, 29th January, the religious ceremony the following day at Notre Dame. Eugenie and Manuela moved into the Elysée, remaining there in purdah, safe from further insults. But it was a crowded week. There was the trousseau to arrange, the costumiers working overtime. Madame Vignon provided thirty-four dresses and Mlle Palmyre twenty. The *pointe d'Alençon* lace used was valued at 40,000 francs.[3] There were wedding presents to inspect and acknowledge. The City of Paris proposed to give a diamond *parure* valued at 600,000 francs. This Eugenie declined, asking that the money should go to charity. A scheme for founding a school for poor girls was decided upon, and the bride's stock rose overnight. There were newspaper correspondents to receive. There were many many letters to write – this to her sister Paca, Duchess of Alba:

> On the eve of ascending one of the greatest thrones of Europe, I cannot refrain from a certain sense of terror . . . . I thank God who has placed at my side a heart so noble and devoted as that of the Emperor . . . .
>
> I have suffered much in my life. My faith in happiness, so nearly destroyed, now lives again. I was so unaccustomed to be loved, my life was a desert. I lived alone and sometimes when weary of loneliness I tried to seek affection, but when someone cared for me, it proved only to be compassion and I emerged alone and tired.
>
> This man has an irresistible will, strong though not stubborn. It is

capable of sacrifices great or small. He would seek a flower in the depth of a winter night, tearing himself from the warmth and enduring cold and wet to fulfill the least whim or caprice of the woman he loves . . . .[4]

People began arriving in Paris from all over France, for there had not been such a glittering occasion since the days of the First Empire. For many of them, taking advantage of the newly built railways, it was their first sight of the capital. They were curious rather than enthusiastic. In England the wedding was the talk of the day. Queen Victoria wrote to the Princess of Prussia: '*Le grand événement du jour* is the incredible marriage of the Emperor Nap . . . . The future bride is beautiful, clever, very *coquette*, passionate and wild.'[5] The little, and somewhat dowdy, Queen was seeing in Eugenie the qualities which, deep down inside herself, she would have liked to possess. She made certain that she knew all about the wedding from the woman's angle by arranging that Lady Augusta Bruce, lady-in-waiting to her mother, the Duchess of Kent, should send an eye-witness account.

Shortly after eight on the evening of the 29th the Master of Ceremonies and the Spanish Ambassador escorted Eugenie and Manuela from the Elysée to the Tuileries. The bride wore a dress of Alençon lace, her waist clasped by a diamond and sapphire belt which the first Napoleon had presented to Empress Marie Louise, jasmine at her breast. In three stages, her procession made its way to the Salon des Maréchaux. There she took her seat beside the Emperor. The Minister of State put the questions, the responses were made and Napoleon III and the Countess of Teba were man and wife.

There was now placed before them, for signature, the famous register in which Napoleon I had recorded events in the Bonaparte family story, from the adoption of Prince Eugène Beauharnais as his son on 2nd March 1806 to the birth of his only legitimate child, the King of Rome, on 20th March 1811. The guests were intrigued by the behaviour of those who came up to add their names as witnesses. Old King Jerome 'bowed as he passed the Emperor, but took no notice of her'. His son, 'Plon-Plon',[(a)] 'bowed to neither one nor the other'.[6]

(a) Napoleon Joseph Charles Paul, known as Prince Napoleon. 'Plon-Plon' was the nickname bestowed upon him by the army. He disliked Eugenie because, as a girl in Madrid, she had repulsed his amorous advances and because a son born to her would oust him from the cherished position of heir to the throne.

Princess Mathilde, who had an important part to play in the ceremony, had been persuaded to hide her emotions and behave herself, but this did not apply to another of the Emperor's cousins, Mary, Duchess of Hamilton. After the civil ceremony was over, the guests lined up in a long crocodile of pairs to pass before the bride and groom and make their bows. The Austrian Ambassador was coupled with the Duchess of Hamilton, who was in a raging temper. As he took her arm she said: 'You will see the scandal I shall make when we get near my cousin.' Shaken, the Ambassador asked her: 'Have you really made up your mind to do that?' 'Indeed I have,' she replied. 'Then I beg the Duchess to walk on alone,' he said, withdrawing his arm from hers.[7] At which Mary lost her nerve and promised to be good.

Although Eugenie was now married in the eyes of the law, she was not in the eyes of God. After a musical entertainment, she returned with her mother to the Elysée. She rushed off a line to her sister:

> The ceremony was superb but I nearly fainted before entering the *Grande Salle* where we signed. I cannot express all that I suffered during that three quarters of an hour, seated on a throne slightly raised from the dais and facing the crowd of people. I was paler than the jasmine which I wore on my heart . . . . When they address me as 'Majesty' I feel as though we were acting a play . . . .[8]

But there was one humorous diversion. When Eugenie's maid Pepa, a faithful but somewhat rough Spanish woman who had been with her since childhood, attempted to use the address of 'Majesty', she collapsed into fits of laughter.

On Sunday morning, as the bells were ringing out all over Paris, Napoleon arrived for breakfast, thus breaking the customary rule of the wedding day. She put on her gown for him to see and he placed a crown upon her head.[9] At noon Eugenie left for the Tuileries. There she joined the Emperor in the gilded coach which had carried Napoleon I and Josephine to Notre Dame in 1804. The spectacle was stupendous – the decorations in the streets, the troops in their new, full dress uniforms, the long line of carriages, the cuirassiers and carabineers, all enriched by the clamour of the bands and the bells and the guns. Yet the dense crowds were strangely silent, too intent on catching a glimpse of the bride to indulge in patriotic enthusiasm.

And she stole the day. Tribute after tribute came from those who saw her pass. No more beautiful picture graced the nineteenth century. Even her dentist, Dr Evans, accustomed to a more prosaic view, was bowled over as he watched the divinely beautiful bride who sat beside the Emperor like a captive fairy queen, her hair trimmed with orange blossom, a diadem on her head.[10]

The cathedral had been transformed by gangs of artists and craftsmen working night and day. The roof was hung with streamers of all the colours of the rainbow. The pillars were swathed in crimson and blue and decorated with crowns and the initials 'L' and 'E'. Above the high altar, which had been moved to the centre of the church, was a canopy of velvet lined with ermine, suspended on golden cords. Fifteen thousand candles flickered and lustres spanned the aisles from end to end. An orchestra of five hundred replaced the organ.

Back went the procession to the Tuileries, the crowds more enthusiastic now. In the garden of the palace was gathered a multitude of girls, representatives of every village in the environs of Paris. They carried bouquets. In their excitement they mobbed the coach, all attempting to get their bouquets inside. Napoleon and Eugenie disappeared under a hillock of flowers and had to be rescued by the escort. They bolted for the shelter of the palace and a few minutes later appeared, petal strewn, on the balcony.[11]

On the following day Lady Augusta Bruce reported back to Windsor:

> Nothing could be more splendid than the decorations of the Cathedral – velvet and ermine – gold and silver – flags and hangings of all the colours were combined and harmonised with the splendid costumes of the Clergy, the uniforms, civil and military, and the magnificent dresses of the ladies.

But the lady-in-waiting's chief interest lay in the bride:

> It is very difficult to ascertain anything like truth as regards her, but her beauty and engaging manners will, it is thought by many, gain for her, for a time at least, a greater amount of popularity than his friends who now blame the marriage expect. That he is passionately in love with her no one doubts, and his countenance on late occasions, as well as yesterday, wore a radiant and joyous expression very unusual. She, on the contrary, showed a considerable amount

of nervousness at the Civil Marriage, and was as pale as death yesterday . . .

The object of our neighbours seemed to be to scan and criticise the dress of the Bride, and the wonderful penetration and accuracy of their eagle glances was to us something incredible! Certainly, though unable ourselves at such a distance to appreciate the details of her dress or the expression of her countenance, we saw her distinctly enough to be able to say that a more lovely *coup d'oeil* could not be conceived. Her beautifully chiselled features and marble complexion, her nobly *set-on head*, her exquisitely proportioned figure and graceful carriage were most striking, and the whole was like a Poet's Vision! I believe she is equally beautiful when seen close, but at the distance at which we saw her the effect was something more than that of a lovely picture, it was aerial, ideal.

On the classically shaped head she wore a diamond crown or diadem, round her waist a row of magnificent diamonds to correspond, and the same as trimming round the 'basques' of her gown. Then a sort of cloud or mist of transparent lace enveloped her, which had the effect of that for which, when speaking of the hills in Scotland, Princess Hohenlohe could find no English word, '*Duft*.' I hope your Royal Highness will not think me very much carried by what pleases the eye. I felt all the while that one could view the matter but as an outside show; as such, in as far as she was concerned, it was exquisitely beautiful – and I suppose that a sort of national prejudice made me attribute the grace and dignity of the scene, for what there was of either came from her, to the blood of Kirkpatrick!!!![12]

The honeymoon was spent at St Cloud, in a villa in the park. Now it was the custom that, when Napoleon visited this then rustic retreat, all the officials there dined with him. And they had no intention of breaking the rule on this auspicious day. They not only sat down to dinner with the newly weds, but showed no signs of leaving after the meal was over, making speeches and offering congratulations. Napoleon fidgetted and muttered and showed obvious signs of losing his temper. In an aside to Eugenie, he told her to get rid of them. But she, who had only been wife and Empress for a few hours, was defeated as to how to do this. The speeches droned on and the moment for the explosion of the Emperor grew near. She whispered to him: 'Walk to the door – I will follow you.' He pushed back his chair and strode towards the door, Eugenie behind him. It was she who turned and bowed goodnight to the company. By the time that the honeymoon apartments were reached, she was already learning the ways of a wife.[13]

For a few months Napoleon and Eugenie were very much in love. An official entering a room at the Tuileries was surprised to see her sitting upon his knee. In company, when they wished to say private things to one another, they used English, sometimes not realising that there were others there familiar with the language and who were eavesdropping on their endearments. Away from her mother, she was like a girl escaped from school. When the Emperor took her to see the Chamber of Deputies, she addressed an impromptu and impassioned speech to the empty hall. She loved games. A favourite one was 'potting the candles'. After dinner footmen would place heaps of rubber balls on the salon floor and it was the task of the guests to kick these at the many lighted candles until all were extinguished.[14] Eugenie excelled at this palace version of association football. She revelled in the panache but it was noted that, after a time, Napoleon would make excuses to leave. Then, putting on an old jacket, he would get down to work in his study. The eighteen year gap in their ages could not be concealed.

In the weeks following the climax in Notre Dame, sadness came to Manuela. She realised, all too clearly, that she was wanted by neither her daughter nor her daughter's husband. She was, she commented, but a mother-in-law and a foreigner, and *persona non grata* as both. Napoleon did not like her, considered her reputation as an intriguer dangerous, and was determined to get her out of the way. She, in her turn, did not like him and her wide experience of men enabled her to detect his weaknesses. She called him 'Monsieur Isidore' or 'Don Luis'. Eugenie had done her best to be a dutiful daughter but she despised her mother's obsession with worldly values, which she termed the 'vain glories'. And she never forgot that Paca had been the one upon whom the sun shone, and she the whipping boy.

Eugenie advised her mother that it would be better if she returned to Spain. The Emperor took more concrete steps. He bought her off, but, to preserve the decencies, gave her a house so that she might make occasional visits to Paris. Manuela surrendered. Eugenie wrote to Paca:

> Despite our unhappy relationship and the incompatability of our characters, it grieves me to think that she will be lonely and sad. Our house in Madrid is full of memories of me – but from a distance faults may disappear and only the good be remembered.[15]

Yet Manuela still had good friends. When she left for Spain at the end of March, the faithful Mérimée accompanied her as far as Tours. And Clarendon kept in touch by letter, signing himself 'Yours as ever and as always'.[16] He told her that she was wise to return to Madrid, and he was right, for there, as the mother of the Duchess of Alba and the Empress of the French, she was held in high esteem at the court of Isabella.

Eugenie knew full well that her first priority, as Empress, was to bear a child. The people of France expected it. Napoleon longed for it. To secure the succession was the zenith of his ambitions and having to wait for nine months tried his patience. Eugenie played her part well and was quickly pregnant. But that she was not intended by nature to be a fruitful and trouble free mother was early apparent and by mid-March she was obliged to lie up. She was a redhead and no exception to the dangers and hardships which so often come to those with that colouring. The Emperor did not comprehend. His previous experience of fatherhood had come with his peasant mistress during his sojourn in Ham and there had been no like experience on that occasion. He fretted and fussed over his wife, at the expense of the country's business. The British Ambassador complained that he could scarce pay attention to a matter of international importance.

At the end of April Eugenie had a fall and was persuaded to take a long, hot bath to relieve the pain in her aching bones, a proceeding which Queen Victoria was later to tell her was inadvisable while *enceinte*. On the 27th she had a miscarriage. She became seriously ill and was kept in bed for four weeks. She wrote to Paca:

> Who knows what would have been the fate of my child? I should infinitely prefer a crown for my son less resplendent but more secure. Don't think I lack courage. You see my thoughts are not very gay, but remember that I have been lying up for three months and have

pain in all my bones. Today I tried to stand but was too weak from loss of blood.[17]

Napoleon, to his credit, was concerned only with the health of his wife. His disappointment was lost in the relief at her recovery. He told Lord Cowley that it was but a mistake which could be put right, but the Ambassador warned that that might not be the case.[18] The experience both frightened and soured Eugenie. Love, to her, had been a serious, idyllic thing since she had thrown her heart at the Duke of Alba when only in her teens. Her first marital experience had been under the champagne influence of receptions and processions, music and dancing, against the backdrop of the majesty of the new Empire. The pain and the sadness brought with them frigidity, a feeling that sex, for sex itself, was cheap and unworthy. 'Men', she later said, 'are worth nothing at all.'[19]

Napoleon sensed the change. His frequent desires were uncontrollable. He craved for new eyes, new shapes, new experiences. He told his cousin, Mathilde: 'I need my little amusements, but I always return to her with pleasure.'[20] But the indomitable spirit of Eugenie would not permit her to play sweet music on a second violin.

Part III

VICTORIA AND ALBERT

1853-1861

CHAPTER II

To Windsor:

Napoleon had travelled fast since the dramatic days of the *coup d'état* only eighteen months before. He had taken over sole control of France, he had become Emperor, he had married a lovely woman and he had shown that he and his wife were capable of starting a family, tragic though their first attempt had proved.

The next step was to be admitted as a member of the Sovereigns' club of Europe. Improbable as realisation appeared to be in the summer of 1853, he planned a State Visit to Queen Victoria. Maybe he would receive the Garter – that would make him *gentilhomme*. Thereafter he would invite the Queen and her husband to Paris. He remembered the words of his mother that, if one kept saying the same thing often enough, it would eventually come to pass.

Eugenie was also set on the Windsor visit and she played her part. During her early married life she made a number of visits *incognito* to Britain, travelling as Madame de Guzman. In those days it was easier to cross the Channel unnoticed, especially if one was a fine lady who kept to her cabin and had a reserved compartment on the railway. At the Tuileries it was said that Her Majesty was visiting her Scottish relations and taking a short rest, but in the event she was also staying at Watford, at the house of a man who knew her identity but kept his silence. There she was called upon by none other than Lord Clarendon, the Foreign Secretary and her mentor, whose stately home, The Grove, was nearby.[1]

In the autumn of 1853 stories appeared in the Paris newspapers that the Emperor and Empress would soon be paying a State Visit to England. When the foundations of the idea had been firmly laid, the Minister of State, Achille Fould, tackled the British Ambassador, Lord Cowley, on the subject. Lord Cowley had heard nothing from London about such a visit and accordingly asked Lord Clarendon for guidance. Lord Clarendon wrote to the Queen. She saw straight through the Emperor's ruse and replied:

> The Queen hastens to answer Lord Clarendon's letter and wishes him to inform Lord Cowley that there never was the slightest idea of *inviting* the Emperor of the French and that Lord Cowley should take care that it should be clearly understood that there was and would be no intention of the kind, so that there should be no doubt on the subject. The Queen feels sure that the Emperor has had these reports put in himself.[2]

Undismayed, Napoleon returned to the matrimonial line of attack. He suggested that his cousin, Prince Napoleon, alias 'Plon-Plon', should wed the Queen's cousin, Princess Mary of Cambridge. Now the marriage of twenty-year-old Mary was already causing the Queen some anxiety. She was a flirt and Princess Christian of Denmark commented that if she had such a coquette for a daughter, she would box her ears.[3] But the Princess, who was already developing features which were later to lead to her being dubbed 'Fat Mary', was very particular in her requirements for a husband. On being acquainted with the aspirations of the French Prince, she stamped upon the idea with heavy foot. Lord Palmerston could not understand this, saying that the Frenchman was at any rate better than a German princeling.[4]

Despite his elaborate planning, Napoleon was still not one step nearer to Windsor. Then an event in far off Crimea gave him the chance for which he sought. The Russians, who had long cast covetous eyes on Constantinople, pressed their claims to protect the Christians in the Turkish empire with such ferocity that in October Turkey declared war. The British public was solidly in favour of going to the rescue of the Turkish ally.

The Emperor of the French promptly offered to join his army with that of Britain and the King of Sardinia followed suit, provided that Britain would straightaway attack Russia. Lord Aberdeen, the Prime Minister, held back, hoping that a way could be found to avoid

Emperor Napoleon
III. From the
painting by
Winterhalter

Empress Eugenie.
From the painting
by Winterhalter

Eugenie and Napoleon III being received by Queen Victoria
and Prince Albert at Windsor Castle, 1855

Queen Victoria.
From the painting
by Winterhalter

Prince Albert.
From a miniature
by Robert
Thorburn ARA,
engraved by Francis

hostilities. Lord Palmerston, eager for a fight, resigned from the Home Office on a minor point of reform. Public outcry was so loud and threatening that Aberdeen was forced to recall him to avoid the fall of the Government. There had to be a scapegoat for the tardiness in declaring war and it was on Prince Albert that the blame fell. He was labelled a Russian spy and the rumour spread that he was to be imprisoned in the Tower of London. The pressure built up and there was no containing it. By March Britain and France found themselves in alliance against Russia.

The relationship between the Tuileries and Windsor changed overnight, a change greeted with reluctance by both Queen Victoria and Albert, and certain senior soldiers. By tradition, France was regarded as Britain's enemy – one general, Lord Raglan, referred to the Russians as 'the French' throughout the duration of the Crimean War. But an alliance was an alliance, and some sign of goodwill and comradeship must be shown. Accordingly, on 12th May, the Queen attended a *bal costumé* at the French Embassy at Albert Gate. But she retained her insularity and individualism, as she alone of the guests appeared in ordinary evening dress.

The problem of personal contact with Napoleon worried Albert considerably. Here was a man who had had two illegitimate children during imprisonment and who had lived openly with an English publican's daughter while President of France. In addition, he both smoked and gambled. First approach and exploration, the Prince came to the conclusion, must be made by a member of the royal circle whose hands were already stained by the dye of sin. There were two obvious candidates – George, Duke of Cambridge, the Queen's cousin, who lived with an actress and had three bastards, and his own brother, Ernest, Duke of Coburg, a syphilitic and one of the biggest rapscallions in Europe. There was no chance of their linen being further soiled.

Ernest was invited to stay at the Tuileries and he thoroughly enjoyed himself – it was the kind of life to which he would have liked to become accustomed. The Emperor said the 'nicest things' about his family and Ernest passed on to his brother the Empress's deep wish to meet the royal children.[5] Napoleon, like Disraeli, had decided that flattery was the oil which eased the opening of the Windsor doors.

George, Duke of Cambridge, stayed for a week in Paris in April, on his leisurely way to the war in the east. He was accompanied by an impressive military staff but there also travelled with him, in a separate compartment, his beloved Louisa,[a] one of his sons and Louisa's sister Georgina. The Duke stayed with Lord Cowley at the Embassy, the ladies and the boy at the Hotel de Londres. There now came for George the problem of dividing his hours, and his attentions, between the Emperor, the Ambassador and Louisa, and there simply were not enough hours in the day.

Napoleon was determined to impress the Queen's cousin. Apart from numerous military inspections, there was a reception at the Tuileries, a visit to the Opéra Comique, a Great Review on the Champs de Mars, a trip along the new Rue de Rivoli, an afternoon at St Cloud and a walk with Eugenie round the gardens, and a gala performance at the Palais Royal Theatre.[6] Lord Cowley was somewhat disturbed by the little time his guest spent under his roof. Some days the Duke visited his wife before breakfast, and at other times late at night, when Georgina's presence was a little frustrating, for as Louisa later complained, it made it 'hard to have a cuddle'.[7]

Ernest and George having survived their meetings with the 'Beelzebub of the Boulevards' and made favourable reports on him, Prince Albert now decided that he must meet Napoleon himself and make a final check before exposing his wife to contamination. The *rendez-vous* was to be Boulogne.

On the evening of 3rd September 1854 *Victoria and Albert* left the Solent, the Queen following for a while in her smaller yacht, *Fairy*. The royal yacht sent up a goodnight kiss of blue lights. *Fairy* answered, went about and headed for the Isle of Wight. Albert went to his cabin and commented that the bed 'had a very blank and desolate look'.[8] There was a certain amount of naval bad temper on deck next morning, for the escort of ships of war was nowhere in sight and the royal yacht was obliged to enter Boulogne harbour unescorted. The Emperor was waiting on the quay and Lord Cowley, who was with him, reported that it was the first time that he had ever seen him suffering from nerves.

The two men got along surprisingly well together. Their ways of life were poles apart and yet they shared the common ground of

(a) Louisa Fairbrother, whom he had married in secret. She was known as Mrs Fitz-George.

intelligence and common sense. Albert approved of Napoleon's German accent and his happy reminiscences of boyhood in Bavaria, but disapproved of his addiction to smoking. Napoleon, for his part, was risking no criticism and put it on record that he had never met anyone with such a various and profound knowledge and that 'he had never learned so much in a short time'.[9] For Albert, it proved a hard five days and nights, for the Emperor had him up at six in the morning and kept him busy with inspections and military manoeuvres until late in the evening. In between there were long discussions on warlike and political matters, conducted in thick clouds of tobacco smoke. Albert's bed was too short, 'the counterpane too heavy, the pillows of feathers and the heat frightful'.[10] But by the 9th he was back at Osborne and cosy with Victoria.

Napoleon had, of course, broached the question of his visiting England and had received a cautious, but optimistic, reply. The Queen, encouraged by her husband's reports, suggested mid-November. The wily Frenchman switched his tactics and replied that a later date would suit him better. The angry Queen suspected a trap and that he was trying to make out that he was doing a favour by coming. She told Lord Clarendon: 'The Queen would wish that no anxiety should be shown to obtain the visit . . . . His reception here ought to be a boon to him and not a boon to us.'

Napoleon's next card was an announcement that it was his intention to travel out to the Crimea and there command the troops in person. This galvanised Europe like an electric shock. The Queen regarded with horror the thought of a Frenchman commanding British troops. The politicians were fearful as to what would happen in France while he was away. The French army was adamant that this was a soldier's war and that Napoleon's brief training in Switzerland did not allow him the status of a commander. For many the thought of another Bonaparte loose in Europe at the head of an army was too terrible to contemplate. Clarendon was sent over to reason but Napoleon would not abandon his dream. There was, however, one method of delaying this catastrophic step and that was to invite the Emperor and Empress to visit Windsor. A return visit would follow and then the summer would be over. The Queen hoped that Albert's logic and persuasive powers would put an end to the hare-brained scheme.

Early on the morning of 16th April 1855 Prince Albert was on the landing stage at Dover, waiting to receive the Emperor and Empress. Triumphal arches had been erected, red carpets laid. But a fog came in from the Channel and doused their splendour. Dover became a ghost town as visibility shrunk to a few yards. Four hours passed and no news, except for a false alarm, came from the sea. Suddenly the yacht *Pélican* materialised out of the grey blanket, the Emperor and Empress at the rail. He was in general's uniform, she in a tartan dress with a plaid ribbon in her hat – the true Kirkpatrick. She looked pale and tired and Albert took her arm and led her to the Lord Warden hotel for refreshment. Then off they went in the special train. A second ship, carrying staff and luggage, had not yet docked, but the Queen was waiting at Windsor and crowds were lining London's streets from the Bricklayers' Arms station at Southwalk to Paddington: further delay was out of the question.[11]

It was growing dark when the pony carriages came smartly up the hill to Windsor Castle. The Queen was in something of a tizzy – 'I cannot say what indescribable emotions filled me.' The Emperor received two salutes, on either cheek, from her. 'I next embraced the very gentle, graceful and evidently very nervous Empress.'[12] Eugenie at first refused to lead the way up the Grand Stairs but gave way under persuasion.

It was already time to dress for dinner. Crisis followed crisis. Her hairdresser, Felix, precious and petulant, had not arrived. He was, in fact, at Charing Cross, threatening suicide if someone did not quickly transport him to Paddington. This fate was avoided but he reached the Castle too late to be of practical assistance.[13] In addition, Eugenie was told that her dressing case and the trunk containing her dresses were also missing. One of her ladies came to her rescue, lent her a simple dress and put chrysanthemums, from a vase, in her hair. The Queen thought that she looked lovely.

Three nights were spent at Windsor and two in London. The main events at the Castle were a review, the investiture of the Garter and a ball. As the Queen danced with her guest, she thought to herself: 'Really, to think of a grand-daughter of George III dancing with the nephew of our great enemy, the Emperor Napoleon, now my most firm ally, in the *Waterloo Gallery* is incredible!' As the Emperor received the Garter, a spectator remarked that he had never before seen such a look of triumph on a man's face. As he left the room he whispered to the Queen: '*Enfin je suis gentilhomme*'.[14] While in London the Emperor and Empress drove in state from the Palace to the Guildhall to lunch with the Lord Mayor and City dignitaries: attended the opera, boxes for the occasion fetching as much as a hundred pounds; and visited the Crystal Palace, which had been moved to Sydenham the previous year.

The State visit proved a resounding success on all counts. The public was obviously glad and excited to be able to pay tribute to allies in the war. The great crowds roared their applause at the Emperor and were intrigued by the Empress. A much needed feeling of unity was created between the two nations, a feeling which was to survive the test of the years. Charles Greville wrote on 20th April:

> The fineness of the weather brought out the whole population of London, as usual kept in excellent order by a few policemen . . . It was a beautiful sight last night when the Royal and Imperial party went to the Opera in state; the streets lit by gas and the houses illuminated and light as day . . . I am glad that the success of the visit has been so great, and the contentment of all the parties concerned so complete, but it is well that all will be over tomorrow, for such excitement and enthusiasm could not last much longer, and the inconvenience of being beset by crowds and the streets obstructed, is getting tiresome.

For each of the four chief participants, those five days were among the most important of their lives. For Victoria, they were undoubtedly among the most happy, to be rivalled only by her expeditions in Scotland. Napoleon held the key role. The eldest of the quartet by a considerable margin, and by far the most experienced, he played his part to perfection – he even convinced Lord Aberdeen that he was not an enemy of England. His manners were above reproach, he said the right things to the right people and he gave the right presents to the right people. He injected a shot of panache into a Court which was indubitably staid. He made love to Victoria in a sophisticated, somewhat daring, way and, as Lord Clarendon noted, she was 'mightily tickled by it, for she had never been made love to in her life, and never had conversed with a man of the world on a footing of equality; and as his love-making was of a character to flatter her vanity without alarming her virtue and modesty, she enjoyed the novelty of it without scruple or fear.'[15]

Albert, at first none too certain of his ground, was delighted to talk to a man older than himself who listened to what he had to say, reasoned with him logically, and even flattered him. Albert had few men friends who could share his interests. Napoleon did his best. Music he could not converse upon but he trudged around the Windsor farms and approved of what he saw, although he queried the policy of gaining ground by grubbing out hedges as this deprived the birds of their shelter.[16]

But it was the hours spent with Eugenie that the Prince treasured most. With her, he was as near in love with a woman, apart from his wife, as he was ever to be. Victoria noticed at once and was glad. When they had first married, she was forever keeping a sharp eye on him, suspecting that, in the way of men, he might slip off with a saucy lady-in-waiting, but, as the years passed and no aberrations blotted the copybook, she had become somewhat puzzled. She now wrote: 'Altogether I am delighted to see how much he likes and admires her, as it is so seldom I see him do so with any woman.'[17] Elegant, cultured, somewhat shy and turning to him for guidance, Eugenie appeared to him as the star of an operetta. It was quite unnecessary for him to assure Baron von Stockmar that 'Our relationship rests upon an honourable moral basis'. She would not have it otherwise, even if he had wished it so. She brought out the gallant in him, a side which seldom showed. When she complained of tiredness on a tour of the Crystal Palace, he summoned a bath chair. When she admired it, he bought it for her on the spot. And for a Coburg to part with cash was a very rare occasion.

For Victoria it was not only a happy interlude but one of vital importance to a sovereign. She learned the lesson that personal conversation between principals on the one hand and the advice of family and ministers on the other, could lead to very different conclusions. Talking with the Emperor, she realised that his supposed plan for the invasion of Belgium was rubbish. When alone with him, it was like having Lord Melbourne beside her once again, pouring out his wisdom, his fun and his mature judgment. The truth was also there, though unperceived, that Albert alone was insufficient for her. He was younger, he was not widely travelled and he had never faced up to hardship or danger. Although hard working and academically brilliant, he was only a student Prince, had ever leaned on elders for advice and was wed to Coburg and German aims in general.

Victoria was a straightforward, obvious person. One could tell at a glance whether she liked or disliked, whether she was happy or sad. She needed a master. In Napoleon she found one. 'That he *is* a very extraordinary man, with great qualities, there can be *no* doubt – I might almost say a mysterious man. He is evidently possessed of *indomitable courage, unflinching firmness of purpose, self-reliance* and *great secrecy* . . . at the same time he is endowed with wonderful *self-control*, great *calmness*, even *gentleness*, and with a *power of fascination* . . . .'[18] And with a sense of humour also. As the royal party was preparing to leave for the opera, he knocked his coffee all over his spotless and impressive cocked hat. He roared with laughter and set off everyone else.

To Eugenie, the last of the quartet and the youngest, this was her 'coming-out' ball in international politics. The experience made her into an Empress. She was, to her delight, treated as an equal at Windsor and, if she was equal there, she was equal anywhere. She gained confidence, not only in herself but also in her husband. She had high standards and he attained them. She learned of the rules for a Queen from her hostess and how to sit down without checking that there was a chair under her. She established herself as the fashion plate of Europe and set the trend for the crinoline and the wide brimmed hat. Victoria made notes of every dress that she wore. One evening she whispered to one of her ladies: '*N'est-elle pas delicieuse?*'[19] The royal children adored her.

When, on the Saturday, her guests had left, there was an emptiness in the Queen's life, a true sign of happiness that was over. She wanted none of the future, just a re-play of the past. Just to forget the despatch boxes and the war position and to go over and over in her mind the happenings of the past few days. 'We could only talk, not do anything.' However difficult relations between the two countries might become in future years, Napoleon and Eugenie must have known that, if ever their world was to clatter round their ears, Victoria of England would give them refuge.

There were two widely varying by-products of the visit. The first came in a letter from the Emperor, saying that he had now changed his mind and decided that he would not go to the Crimea. The second was a bill for £846. 6. 8. from the Lord Warden Hotel, Dover, for accommodating the Prince and his suite for one night and for refreshing the Emperor and Empress on their arrival. Furnished apartments, £207 12.6. ... additional furniture installed, £520. 19. 8. ... flowers, £103. 10. 0. ... flags and ornamental inkstand, £14. 4. 6. ...[20]

Albert was not amused.

CHAPTER 12

Victoria for the Continent

At noon on Saturday, 18th August 1855, Emperor Napoleon rode up the hill to the north of Boulogne, pausing at the crest to look out over the English Channel towards the white cliffs of Dover. It was along this road that he had marched early on an August morning fifteen years before when the ghostly shape of the *Edinburgh Castle* lay off Wimereux.

It was boiling hot. Soon, through the heat haze, he picked out plumes of smoke and the outlines of craft approaching the shore. The new royal yacht, *Victoria and Albert*, was bringing the Queen and her husband to France. He was waiting at the quayside as the yacht came in at twenty minutes past one. It was an historic moment, for not since Henry VI had been crowned King of France in Notre Dame in 1431 had an English Sovereign made the journey to Paris.

The Emperor and Empress had been thinking of the visit ever since they had said goodbye to the Queen at Buckingham Palace in April. Napoleon was determined to outshine the British programme and he urged Baron Georges Haussmann to hustle on with the plan for converting Paris into a worthy and beautiful imperial capital. This was done with such effect that even that superb organiser and designer, Prince Albert, was impressed. After he had seen the progress he told King Leopold:

> Paris is signally beautified by the Rue de Rivoli, the Boulevard de Strasbourg, the completion of the Louvre, the great open square in front of the Hotel de Ville, the clearing away of all the small houses which surrounded Notre Dame, by the fine Napoleon barracks, the completion of the Palais de Justice, and restoration of the Sainte Chapelle, and especially by the laying out of the ornamental grounds in the Bois de Boulogne, which really may be said to vie with the

finest English parks. How all this could have been done in so short a time no one comprehends.[1][(a)]

A high spot of the royal programme was to be a visit to the Universal Exhibition, by this time in full sway. With its site of twenty-four acres and twenty thousand exhibitors, Napoleon was looking forward to favourable comparison with the Great International Exhibition held in Hyde Park in 1851.

Eugenie was busy with the problems of a hostess – interior decoration, staffing, costumes. The guests were to stay at the Palace of St Cloud and the apartments which they were to occupy were transformed. Redecorated in white and gold, they emerged as an imitation of the Queen's private suite at Buckingham Palace. So fastidious was the Empress that the legs of a priceless table were cut down to suit the convenience of the five-foot Queen.

Eugenie was somewhat worried as to the clothes that would be worn by her female visitors. She had seen in England that Victoria's dress sense was practically non-existent and she did not wish the smart Parisians to mock and scorn. Now the Queen had a French *coiffeur* and it was arranged that, when he next visited Windsor, he took with him some of the latest Paris fashions. He was showing them to the Queen when Prince Albert walked in. His comment was brief. 'That,' he said, 'you shall not wear'. There was also the problem of Vicky, Princess Royal, who, with Bertie, Prince of Wales, was to accompany her parents on the trip. Eugenie considered that the staid, Germanic dresses which the fourteen year old girl had worn in England would never do for France. But how to tell her mother without giving offence? An idea came to her. She obtained Vicky's measurements,

(a) Napoleon, with the aid of Baron Haussmann, from 1853 – 1870 created Paris as we know it today. The railway stations, which became the gates of the city, were provided with wide streets giving access to them. An intersection of roads was made between the boulevards of Sebastopol, Saint Michel and Strasbourg and the Rue de Rivoli, and the intersection at the Place de la Republique was created. The Opéra and Etoile became traffic centres. Wide streets were laid along the left bank of the Seine and squares were laid out on the British model. The river was spanned with new bridges, including the Ponts National, de Solferino and Alma. The Halles Centrales were constructed and public buildings took the place of the houses of the Cité. For recreation, the Parisians were provided with the Bois de Boulogne and the Bois de Vincennes and the Parcs des Buttes Chaumont, de Montsouris and Monceau. Water supplies were brought in and sewerage arrangements modernised. By 1860 Paris had spread as far as its old fortifications and boulevards were laid into the countryside beyond.

had a 'body' made of her life-size and dressed it as she thought that a girl should be dressed. The 'doll' was sent to England as a memento of the English visit. The Queen may not have taken the hint, but money was always close to her thoughts. Here was a chance of dressing Vicky for free. So off came the clothes from the doll and on they went to the Princess Royal.[2]

Victoria was also in a state of considerable excitement. Her experience of such occasions had been limited – a few days with old King Louis Philippe at the Château d'Eu, a State reception at Cologne and Bonn as the guest of the King of Prussia. She was doubtful how she would stand up to an arduous programme in the heat of Paris. She was worried about the precedence that would be granted to her husband. She fretted about her wardrobe, being fully aware of Eugenie's superior dress sense. The problem of how many children to take with her was settled by an outbreak of scarlet fever among the younger ones. That left the two eldest. This, she thought was sufficient. She considered that she might look somewhat ridiculous parading at the head of her entire brood.

Then, in June, the news came that Eugenie was pregnant. The doctors discovered only just in time. If their opinion had been delayed, she would never have been able to bear children. She was rushed off to Eaux Bonnes in the Pyrenees and there underwent painful treatment. She had already had two miscarriages and the next four months were vital.

Victoria was delighted and as proud as if she were herself the father. The two had had long talks on maternal matters in the spring and here was an immediate and satisfactory result. Eugenie acknowledged the worth of the advice and later said: '*Telle était ma conversation avec la Reine et onze mois après en résulta le Prince Imperial.*' The older woman, with the experience of eight births behind her, continued to pour out her wisdom – no hot baths, no temper or worrying and particularly no over-exertion during the State Visit. 'Do please remember my plans and don't weaken yourself too much: above all, go out as much as you can in the air without tiring yourself.'[3]

The Empress returned to Paris a few days before the visit was due to begin but was too weak to undertake the rail journey to meet the Queen.

In the early afternoon of that August day there were scenes of near panic at the harbour of Boulogne. The arrival of a boat is ever apt to fire the Gallic emotions and this auspicious occasion proved too much for unrehearsed officials; the presence of forty thousand troops added to the air of general excitement. 'The confusion about luggage and attendance was quite *beyond description*,' reported Lady Bruce. Cries of 'Idiot' and 'Imbecile' echoed along the quay and platform as ladies-in-waiting struggled to keep check on their possessions.

The train pulled out late and became later and later as the journey progressed. Abbeville . . . Amiens . . . Clérmont . . . at every station there were *préfets* with speeches, girls with posies, bands and stands. The compartments were as hot and stuffy as a greenhouse. Being unprovided with catering facilities or toilets, the multitude of those in attendance made quick dashes for sustenance and relief. Such delays the Queen referred to, unfittingly, as 'stoppages'. As the evening drew on, the Emperor became increasingly impatient, for sixty thousand troops and half a million Parisians were lining the streets of the capital and he had planned for a daylight drive.

At Pontoise the train was shunted. The public were allowed on to the platforms and seats were provided, at a price which it had been forecast no one would pay. In the event all were taken. Madame Maria Deraismes, who was there, reported:

> The Queen was stared at as if she were a curious creature in a show. The spectators were mostly provincials, and said aloud exactly what they thought. 'What a little bit of a woman!' cried a notary's wife to her husband at some distance from her. 'She must be a good family woman,' shouted some other bourgeoise. Another exclaimed: '*Elle est agréable; mais pour être belle – ma foi, non.*' The windows of the State carriage were open, and the poor Queen could hear all that was said about her. Apparently the Emperor heard, for he looked concerned, and tried to prevent her listening by talking almost into her ear. Her Majesty was not merely red, but purple, from the broiling heat. Her light blue eyes stood out . . . .[4]

It was twilight as the train pulled into the illuminated and beautifully decorated *Gare du chemin de fer de Strasbourg* and the Queen stepped out to greet the dignitaries and the Bonaparte family. She was abominably dressed. She wore a plain straw bonnet and carried a parasol of glaring green. On her massive handbag was embroidered a white poodle – she pointed out proudly that it had been worked by one of her daughters. Yet it was to be her evening. The weather was perfect, the crowds were gay and they roared their approval all along the sand-covered route from the station to the Palace of St Cloud. People said that not even when the great Napoleon returned after his victory at Austerlitz had there been a roar like this. The Emperor and the Queen sensed the magic of that unforgettable evening and thereafter walked hand in hand, tirelessly, confidently, through the spectacular programme ahead. Princess Lieven summed up the scene thus in a private letter:

La visite de la Reine a été une perfection de tout point sauf le retard du premier jour – Pour tout le reste, curiosité, bienviellance dans le public, bonne réception partout, fêtes magnifiques, tenu superbe, bonne humeur en haut, en bas – la Reine ravie, émerveillée, enchantée de son hôte, témoignant son plaisir de tout – On l'a trouvée parfaitement gracieuse, digne, toujours reine, toujours droite, toujours charmante – voilà la vérité vraie, car c'est tout le monde qui le redit. Le Prince Albert beau et raide, moins avenant qu'elle – la Princesse Royale, pas jolie, mais spirituelle en train extrèmement agréable – le Prince de Galles, très gentil et avec un air de ce qu'il sera un jour. L'Empereur n'a pas quitté la Reine d'un instant, galant, empressé, l'amusant, l'intéressant et lui plaisant superlativement – la plus grande intimité avec l'Impératrice, celle-ci décidement grosse. Belle comme le jour à la magnifique fête de Versailles – on dit que tout était féerique – Je n'ai rien vu – rien pu rêver ou penser ... Votre Reine a plu à tout le monde et toute cette affaire a été admirable. Paris pavoisé et en gala jusqu'à la fin.[5]

Eugenie avoided the more arduous engagements and did not dance at the balls although she managed to remain the *belle*. When driving out with the Queen, cushions were laid on the carriage floor so that she could lie down if she became tired. She 'received' in her bedroom and the English ladies in attendance who visited her there complained that her sole topic of conversation was the hazards of pregnancy.

This reduction of a quartet to a trio came somewhat hard upon Albert. It was obviously a case of two's company and three none as Victoria and Napoleon went sightseeing and chatted together from breakfast time until midnight. As a result, he sallied off on his own, exploring the mechanical and scientific wonders of the *Exposition* and enjoying cultural experiences, in the spheres of the arts and the theatre, which would frankly have bored his wife and the Emperor. But the frayed edges showed and on one occasion, when Victoria and Napoleon had arranged to rendezvous with him at a certain place at a certain time, and were late, there were clear signs of petulance. As Lucy Cohen said: 'His is such a false position that one does not feel much astonished at his being stiff, and rather pompous and sour . . . I had rather be a shoeblack!'[6]

There was also trouble over Albert's status. Old Jerome, who for a time had held the paper title of King of Westphalia, decided that he could not allow the Queen's princeling husband to take precedence over him. Accordingly he retired to Le Havre. Out of curiosity, he came to Paris for a day to pay his respects to the Queen but, even so, he demanded that the Emperor pay his travelling expenses. And there were problems with the ex-King's children, Princess Mathilde and Prince Napoleon. Mathilde was living in open sin, and lurid sin at that, and people wondered how the strait-laced Victoria would greet her. The Queen advanced and kissed her on both cheeks, which surprised many people. Such a sinner would not have even received an icy glance at Windsor, should she have managed to gain entrance. If there was a snag in the nine-day wonder visit it lay in Prince Napoleon – 'Plon-Plon'. In appearance he resembled the villain in a third rate repertory company and Lord Clarendon referred to him as 'the Assassin'. In her diary the Queen made frequent reference to this unpleasant Prince, 'whose manner is rude and disagreeable in the highest degree. *Il me fait peur*, and has a diabolical expression . . . .'[7] He seems to take pleasure in saying something disagreeable and biting, particularly to the Emperor, and with a smile which is quite satanic.'[8]

The wonder of the visit to fairyland was the Queen's energy. Lord Clarendon commented that 'no Royal Person ever yet known or to be known in history comes up to her in *indefatigability*.'[9] One sweltering day she walked for an hour in the grounds of St Cloud, made a conducted tour of the Tuileries, spent three and a half hours at the Louvre and then danced through a ball in the evening. It was the Louvre marathon which floored her followers. Ruthlessly she marched on through gallery after gallery, now slow, now fast, firing her questions and acknowledging the answers. Even the Emperor lagged behind, showing great distress on the last league. One member of the French entourage was very fat and his uniform was tight. Sometimes he had to trot to keep up. He whispered in Clarendon's ear: '*Je donnerais tout – tout – la Vénus de Milo ci incluse – POUR UN VERRE DE LIMON-ADE.*'[10]

The pace told also on Lord Clarendon, who was both Minister-in-waiting and Foreign Secretary. Not only had he to be present at all functions but also to cope with Foreign Office business. Five hours of sleep was the maximum that he could manage. But he did have one evening off and called upon Manuela de Montijo in her comfortable house in the Champs Elysées. She received him with delight. She had grown stout but was still full of fun. She reminisced about the days when he had been plain George Villiers and teased him about his present high position. She told him how, two years before, the Emperor had demanded of her whether or no he was the father of Eugenie and of how she had replied, '*Sire, les dates ne correspondent pas.*'[11]

Clarendon's wife, Kathy, was not in Paris for the Queen's visit. It was said that it might have been awkward for her as her husband was Minister-in-waiting and therefore not able to escort her to functions. But there were other reasons, such as the curiosity of gossiping Parisians. Clarendon was cornered by Eugenie and asked the whereabouts of his wife. When she learned that she was not coming, she was a '*leetle* bit put out'.

After his evening with Manuela, Clarendon did a strange thing. He wrote to Kathy and told her of the Emperor's question. Kathy thought it all most odd.[12]

The Paris interlude moved towards its close. Into the roseate past went the fête at Versailles when the *Grandes Eaux* played, the lunch at the Trianon, the hunt in the Forêt de St Germain, the ball at the Hôtel de Ville. The climax came at Les Invalides. The Emperor, torch in hand, led the Queen through the late evening light to the chapel where lay the coffin of Napoleon I, his hat and sword at its foot. The kilted Prince of Wales knelt before it. There was silence. The flickering torches held by veterans of the First Empire threw strange shadows from crypt to dome. Then a muted organ played 'God Save the Queen' and, as they came away, a thunderstorm broke over Paris.

On the 27th came the goodbyes. Victoria gave her last maternal instructions to Eugenie – 'such a dear, sweet, engaging, and distinguished being, a fairylike *Erscheinung*,[(a)] unlike anyone I ever saw.'[13] Vicky, who had developed a girlish 'crush' for the Empress, burst into floods of tears. Bertie asked if he could stay behind in Paris, adding that he would not be missed at home.

At Boulogne Napoleon boarded the *Victoria and Albert* and went a short way out to sea with his departing guests. It was after midnight before he climbed down to the boat waiting alongside. The Queen wrote:

> We followed him to the ladder, and here I once more squeezed his hand and embraced him, saying, *'Encore une fois, adieu, Sire!'* We looked over the side of the ship and watched them getting into the barge. The Emperor called out, *'Adieu, Madame; au revoir '* to which I replied, *'Je l'espère bien.'* We heard the splash of the oars and saw the barge, lit by the moon . . . . Then we sent up endless rockets.[14]

A permanent alliance between France and Britain seemed assured. Yet the Queen noted that, in reminiscing with her husband, her enthusiasm and optimism were not fully shared by him.

Two events tarnished the shine on the loving cup. The first came on 8th September when Sebastopol fell, making it clear that the Crimean war was moving towards its close. The military honours went to the French and Napoleon, short of money and anxious to exploit his success, wished to bring hostilities to an end quickly. Lord Palmerston preferred to wait until there was a more favourable showing by British arms.

The second came on 29th September. On that day, at Balmoral, Prince Frederick William, nephew of the King of Prussia, proposed to fourteen year old Vicky, Princess Royal. This was a Coburg plan, fostered by King Leopold of the Belgians, part of the strategy to create a liberal minded, unified Germany in league with Britain. Utter nonsense was talked by Prince Albert – 'The young people are ardently in love . . . Abundance of tears were shed . . . Deep visible revolutions in the emotional natures of the two young people and of the mother were taking place . . .'[15] The girl who but a few days before had been enveloped by a 'crush' for the Empress Eugenie, was now inveigled by her father into saying that she had always been in love with 'Fritz'.

An attempt was made to keep the engagement secret but the news

(a) Vision

leaked out. It was unpopular both in France and England. The press, and in particular *The Times*, raved in anger and forecast marital and international disaster. During the engagement period Prince Frederick William visited Paris. After his departure, the Empress wrote:

> The Prince is tall and handsome, a head taller than the Emperor, slight and fair, with a straw-coloured moustache. He displays a chivalrous courtesy, and there is something of the Hamlet about him. They are an imposing race, these Germans; Louis calls them the race of the future. *Bah! nous n'en sommes pas encore là!* [16]

And she scowled towards the Rhine.

CHAPTER 13

Bombs from Birmingham

The Empress was kept busy during her pregnancy. There were other State visits. King Victor Emmanuel arrived from Sardinia. He was bluff and lewd and upset Eugenie by remarking that he had heard that the ladies of Paris wore no knickers, which was a most convenient arrangement. With the end of the Crimean War, delegations from many nations descended upon Paris in February for the peace conference and each was treated to a dinner at the Tuileries. Eugenie complained to her sister of the hardships of being permanently on parade when in her condition. 'It is extremely annoying to live in public and never have the right to be ill when unfortunately one is subject to the same maladies as everybody else.'[1] She made her last appearance on 9th March.

The governesses and the nurses took station and prepared for action. Among them was a stalwart Englishwoman, Miss Shaw. The wetnurse was a jolly peasant from Burgundy who wore a red skirt, a black bodice and clasps of gold. Queen Victoria sent over the Empress's old friend Lady Ely, with instructions to assist as necessary and report in detail. Lord Clarendon, attending the Congress, was able to keep in close touch with the condition of the young woman for whom he felt so special an affection. Manuela and the Duke and Duchess of Alba were in the Champs Elysées. The people of Paris presented an ornate, but entirely impracticable, cradle. The *layette* was on view to the public. It filled three large rooms and the queue to see it was so long that the traffic in the street outside had to be diverted.

Labour began on Friday the 14th. Napoleon was distraught. He could not bear to hear her call out in her agony. Here was contrast with his uncle who, when Marie Louise was in a like condition, noticed that the doctors were suffering from nerves and bade them to think of their patient as if she was a laundress. On the present occasion the doctors were instructed 'to use any palliative or sedative which modern science

had devised even if they ran clean contrary to ecclesiastical prescrip-
tions'.²

Saturday was a nightmare. On occasion Eugenie had to be taken from
the bed and supported in a standing position. She asked for still another
specialist to be called in, who told the Emperor, bluntly, that the most
violent methods would have to be used and that he must choose
between the life of his wife or the child. Unhesitatingly Napoleon said
that Eugenie must come first. Hour after hour he walked around the
waiting-rooms, sometimes holding his head in his hands, sometimes
crying unashamedly. For long periods he stood by the window drum-
ming his fingers on the panes. His ordeal was aggravated by the presence of Plon-Plon, waiting with other members of the family behind
the half opened door. Plon-Plon was in the worst of tempers. If a boy
was to be safely born, he would lose his heirdom. Monocled, male-
volent, he sent a chill through those fighting for a life. The long delay
caused rumours to start in England that a supposititious child was being
obtained. Lady Ely, who was by the bedside constantly, was able to
give the lie to that.³

Midnight of Saturday chimed and Sunday began. 'At last the decisive
moment appeared to have arrived, and, according to ancient tradition,
and to late enactment, the Minister of State and the Keeper of the
Seals, with Prince Napoleon, Prince Charles Bonaparte, and Prince
Lucien Murat, entered the Empress's room. Their entry gave her a
nervous shock and, when Prince Napoleon fixed his monocle, the
course of nature, to the violent torture of the poor woman, was again
suspended.'⁴ Mother and child were now in utmost danger and the
accoucheurs applied their instruments. At quarter past three on that
Sunday morning 'the Child of France' was born, a healthy and a heavy
boy. Napoleon was beyond clear thought. Soon he stood by the
bedside and a voice asked from the pillows, 'Is it a boy?' 'No,' he
replied. 'Is it a girl?' 'No,' he replied. A pause, and then the voice from
the pillow, sharper now, demanded, 'Well, what on earth is it?' Then
it was that the Emperor realised that his ordeal was over and he ran
from the room and kissed the first five people whom he met.

The first shadow in the life of the Prince Imperial came during the
witnessing of the *acte de naissance*. Plon-Plon refused to sign. Princess
Mathilde turned on him in fury, telling him that she had waited about
long enough and asking him if he thought that, by not signing, he

could put the baby back. So he signed but with such ill grace that he made a great blot on the paper.[5] Within a few hours of his birth the baby was baptised privately, the Pope being his godfather. The names given were Napoleon Eugène Louis Jean Joseph. The Emperor and the Empress became godfather and godmother to all children born legitimately on that Sunday, 16th March 1856. Lord Clarendon called to present the congratulations of the Queen. He reported to London: 'The Emperor is enchanted with his son, dying for peace, does not care sixpence for the terms.'[a]

The Empress's ordeal left her very weak and it was not until May that she was able to walk without support. The public baptism was therefore put off until 14th June. That perfect summer day was one of the most glorious in the story of the Second Empire. Napoleon had determined that it would be. Notre Dame was unbelievably beautiful and the ceremonial impressive. Only the baby, who howled throughout the proceedings, did not appreciate it. The crowds, celebrating not only the birth of an heir but also the coming of peace, were enthusiastic. Paris was lit up as it had never been before. The theatres were open free and rockets went up from the Place de la Concorde. Napoleon told his wife that the little boy had brought more good will than a coronation.

But tragedy lay close behind the scenes. Although the imperial couple had been married for little more than three years, the health and physical strength of both of them had deteriorated to a surprising degree. Eugenie, who in the autumn of 1852 had had steel in her arms and legs, could manage any horse and be first in at the kill in the hunts at Compiègne and Fontainebleau, was now a weakling, hardly able to hold her baby. Such had been the price of sex. She wrote to Paca, sadly comparing the wreck she was now with the tomboy that she had been in her teens. The doctors told her that if she was to attempt to have another child, she ran the real risk of death.

In May she was examined by Dr William Fergusson,[b] called in from London by Dr Conneau, who remained the Emperor's personal physician. Dr Fergusson reported to Queen Victoria that, although there was nothing radically wrong with the Empress's health, she

(a) The formal treaty of peace was signed on 30th March, thus bringing the Crimean War officially to an end.
(b) Professor of surgery in King's College. Created a baronet in 1866.

would take a long time to recover and would be subject to fits of depression. In effect the message was clear – Eugenie's life as a physical wife was ended.

Dr Fergusson also examined Napoleon. Among the failings that he unearthed were 'neuralgia, sciatica, dyspepsia, fatigue, irritability, insomnia, contraction of the fingers, loss of appetite and decline in sexual potency'.[6] His premature birth, childhood weaknesses and his incarceration in the damp of Ham had taken their toll. He was forty-eight. In the case of a man with normal health and occupation, such a deterioration would not have been expected for another four or five years, and even then to a less obvious extent. Certainly overwork and anxiety had contributed, but the major cause was apparently his over-indulgence in sex.

Napoleon I had suffered from such a problem. Frank Richardson, M.D., in his *Napoleon: Bisexual Emperor*, gave his reason for believing that 'his affairs with his mistresses may not have been very passionate on his part, or very satisfying to them, in that he was not physically equipped to be the great lover which he liked the world to believe he was. It was not only true sexual satisfaction which eluded him, but love, which is far more important.'[7] He went on to quote the views of other authorities:

> Dr Leonard Guthrie, who in 1913 made the earliest study of the effect on Napoleon of hypopituitarism (deficiency of pituitary gland secretion) considered that his sexual impulses were very variable, often strong but waning quickly; and that he had been incapable of lasting affection for a woman. A later medical biographer, Raoul Brice, was of the opinion that 'most of his mistresses were momentary episodes'.[8]

It was love that was lacking in Napoleon III – it was often noted that there was no real warmth in his embraces. He could become accustomed to a woman, be happy and contented in her company, as he had been with *la belle Sabotière* and Elizabeth Howard. But there was little sadness at parting for there had been no real love on his part. Eugenie was in a different class. She had resisted him. He had wanted to fill the vacant post of Empress and she was the loveliest woman that he had ever met, but he would have taken Princess Adelaide if she had said yes. He was faithful to Eugenie for only six months. The other women in his life up to 1856 were too transient to merit mention – as in the case of Napoleon I they were but momentary episodes.

It is possible that Napoleon III was subject to internal pressure on his sexual glands – he was to die of a stone in his bladder. He was thus being encouraged to waste energy that should have been channelled into sustaining his physical strength and general health. The theory that he was merely proving that 'he was a man' may have some bearing, but it was not necessary to continue proving this night after night.

This was all most disconcerting to Eugenie, who knew as much about sex as she did about driving a railway engine. As often occurs with the daughters of experienced mothers, she had shied away from the physical details. Love to her meant romance, beauty, admiration, belief, legend. If bodily happiness was to come to her, let a roseate mist shield her from the intimate happenings. Yet she was robbed of sex before she had indulged sufficiently to satisfy her body, leaving her convinced that men meant 'absolutely nothing', as she put it.

The result was a hotchpotch of strange reactions. She would, for example, make remarks and tell stories, *risqué* but never coarse, which shocked her husband. She became obsessed with 'beautiful' men. She spotted one as she drove out in the park – next day he became a royal groom. She tried to seduce a giant sentry from his duty. Even with all her loveliness and teasing, she could not make him flinch or move his eyes. In temper she smacked his face. Next day she sent him the equivalent of £500. He returned it, saying that the slap was an honour. She encouraged an Austrian 'lady-killer' at a *bal masqué*. She told him that she would meet him by the lake next afternoon and would identify herself by brushing her fingers across her lips. Waiting there for his unknown date, the Austrian saw the Empress's carriage approaching. Smiling, she drew her fingers across her lips. There were other signs of upset, including the throwing of kisses to girls.[9] But faced with the close proximity of passionate emotion, she froze. A young man of the Household fell blindly in love with her. Standing close beside her in the course of his duty, he whispered, 'I love you'. Eugenie told the Emperor and the poor young man disappeared over night.

Although, under Eugenie's guidance, Napoleon followed the rehabilitation programme laid down by Dr Fergusson, the plans of the Scottish surgeon went agley owing to the arrival in Paris of the most beautiful girl in Europe. She was a spy and in her handbag were instructions from Cavour,[(a)] Prime Minister of Piedmont, to seduce the Emperor at any cost and by any means – all in the interests of a Franco-Italian alliance and the unification of Italy.

Virginie Oldoini was born in Florence on 22nd March 1837. She was the daughter of the Marchese Filippo Oldoini, at one time tutor to the young Prince Louis Napoleon, and she was a cousin of Cavour. She was a forward child and fully developed by the time she was twelve. In 1855 she married Conte Francesco di Castiglione, a good-looking young man in the household of King Victor Emmanuel. He was a model and obliging husband, seeing nothing, hearing nothing. In any case his duties kept him much in Piedmont and Sardinia.

Virginie Castiglione was provided with a code-book so that she might send home messages in cipher. Her role was authenticated by a message from Cavour to his Foreign Minister in Turin: '*La belle Comtesse est enrollée dans la diplomatie Piémontaise. Je l'ai invitée à conquéter, et s'il le faut, à séduire l'Empereur.*'[10] His personal instructions to her read: 'Succeed, my cousin, by any methods you like. Only succeed!'[11] As part of her 'training' Virginie spent the last night before her departure for France in the bed of King Victor Emmanuel. She passed the test.

In her old age Lady Holland, hostess supreme, looking back over forty years of entertaining at the top level, said that the only beautiful woman that she could recall 'as being absolutely faultless, alike in figure and feature, from the crown of her head to the sole of her foot', was *la belle* Castiglione.[12] Unfortunately there were two qualities missing in her make-up, and those were brains and mercy. She was ambitious, proud, cunning, pitiless and mercenary – one of her prizes for doing the job was to be that her brother would receive a senior post in the embassy at St Petersburg. When she discovered that the cost of living in Paris exceeded the amount that Cavour allowed her, she accepted an

(a) Count Camillo Cavour was one of the makers of modern Italy. In 1847 he joined the movement which was to eventually result in the independence and unification of Italy. For the next fourteen years he was editor of *Il Risorgimento* and held a number of government posts, ending as Prime Minister. He co-operated with the Allies in the Crimean War and then negotiated with the Emperor of the French for the expulsion of the Austrians from northern Italy. This resulted in the successful war of 1859. Thereafter he encouraged Garibaldi in the expedition which liberated Sicily and Southern Italy. He saw the Parliament of 1861 summoned and Victor Emmanuel declared King of Italy, and died the same year.

offer of a sum, said to be £20,000, from an English mi'lord for one night of love. She did not appear in public for three days after the event but, when the couple were next seen together, there was an air of mutual respect and they sat well away from one another.

Virginie rocked Paris society, somewhat effete, somewhat bored with the same old round of illicit love. She was powerful and she was outrageous. She was a pioneer of the 'see through' top. Under classical excuse, she arrived at a ball naked from the waist up, parts of her breast being covered by pendants suspended from extended earrings. The Empress sent her home and the girl pouted. Undaunted, she returned with a dress cut up the full length of the side. As she danced, the silhouette of her was visible, high and round fore and aft, and long of leg. She arrived at a reception in a dress covered with queens of hearts. This time the Empress commented, acidly, that surely one of the hearts 'was rather too low'.[13] She was unquenchable. She would sit in the ball room, languid, unspeaking, until the Emperor entered. Then, in a second, she would become electrified, eyes flashing, laughing. As she made her way towards him, men, and even women, would climb on to chairs to watch what exhibition she would make. Poor Napoleon had no chance. Soon *la belle* Castiglione was being treated *en princesse*, spending weekends in the villa in the park at St Cloud, walking the dark paths in evenings at Compiègne.

In January 1857 the British Embassy passed word back to London that the Emperor was visiting the Contessa di Castiglione every night. In April his ardour was cooled by a very icy bucket of water. As he came out of her house in the Avenue Montaigne in the early hours of the morning, he was attacked by three men and only the quickness and courage of his coachman saved him.[14] The police discovered that they were Italian trouble-makers and this pointed to the involvement of Virginie Castiglione. She was curtly informed that her presence in Paris was no longer desirable.

Napoleon was not for long lonely in his nights. His next choice came from his family circle – Marianne, the wife of Comte Alexandre Walewski, son of Napoleon I by Marie Walewska. Marianne Ricci was his second wife[(a)] and, like her predecessor as mistress, came from Florence. She was cultured, politically minded, well mannered and

(a) Comte Walewski's first wife was Catherine, daughter of Lord Sandwich. She died in 1834.

polished. Bismarck put it on record that he had found in France only two amusing women, Comtesse Walewska and the Empress.[15] When in 1855 Walewski retired as Ambassador in London and he and his wife had farewell audience at Windsor, Queen Victoria wrote in her diary: 'She is such a charming person. She will be an immense loss.' As mistress of the Emperor she was tact itself and Lord Clarendon noted: 'The uninitiated would not think there was anything between the Empr: & Mdme: W: as all the *convenances* are rigidly observed.'[16]

Eugenie did not appear to mind her husband's new aberration. Perhaps this was in part relief, for she had loathed Virginie Castiglione, who had been rude and unnecessarily hurtful, and had behaved scandalously. She realised that Napoleon must have 'amusements' which she could not supply and at least now he was in safe hands. 'With the exception of Madame Walewski,' wrote Lord Malmesbury, 'the ladies who surround the Empress are decidely vulgar.'[17] Unfortunately the political views of the two women were far apart, for example in their ideas on the treatment of Italian and Spanish questions, and it was suspected that Marianne's liaison with the Emperor was in part to keep safe her husband's job, as Comte Alexandre was somewhat lacking in the qualities necessary for a Foreign Minister. But Eugenie overlooked this and when tongues wagged and Marianne came to her and begged not to be invited to the Tuileries until matters quietened down, Eugenie just hugged her and thereafter treated her with re-doubled affection.[18] It was indeed a strange relationship.

Although she was as yet unaware of this affair Queen Victoria began to feel annoyance with the Emperor at about this time. He was apparently becoming pro-Russian. He was interfering in Balkan affairs. Worst of all, he was building a modern navy. The correspondence between Windsor and the Tuileries continued, but it was now to the Empress that the Queen addressed her letters. The advice given before the birth of the Prince Imperial linked them together. In addition, Eugenie was growing up politically, leaving behind the image of the shy bride concerned with little more than her clothes.

Victoria found her views sound, sounder in fact than those of her husband. But she did not make sufficient allowance for changed circumstances. When Napoleon had visited her he was but an upstart Emperor, understandably honoured and impressed by the call to visit Windsor. Now he was the most powerful ruler in Europe.

The Queen's obvious concern in her letters to Eugenie, regarding the deteriorating relations between France and Britain, was passed on to the Emperor. He decided that something must be done and he invited himself to Osborne. He wished, he said, 'to prevent by personal communication with the Queen, his Royal Highness and Her Majesty's Government the dissidences and *mésintelligences* which the Emperor thinks will arise from want of such communications.'[19]

The imperial couple disembarked from the *Reine Hortense* at the private landing-place on the Osborne beach on the morning of 6th August 1857. Their party included Ambassador Persigny, Foreign Minister Walewski and his wife Marianne.[a] It was a cosy little stay, spent for the most part in the policies of Osborne House. The Emperor was a relaxed guest and never wore uniform. At the end of the four days he remarked that, if he were to stay on the Isle of Wight much longer, he would forget that such a place as France existed. He and his advisers had long talks with Prince Albert and Lords Palmerston and Clarendon and at their close the Foreign Secretary commented: 'A very black cloud hung over the alliance when the Emperor came here; but all was sunshine before he departed.'[20] Yet Clarendon knew full well that the Prince, despite his outward show, held the Emperor in deep distrust. It was a bias with which he had ever to contend.

Yet for the Empress the Prince held very different views, playing the gallant as he had never done before and would never do again. The Queen was full of praise and confidences, the royal children adored her. Host and hostess even went so far as to tell the Emperor that he would be well advised to take heed of her political ideas. To which the Foreign Secretary, former close friend of her mother, listened with deep gratification.

The *Reine Hortense* sailed away; hands waved, scarves fluttered, last goodbyes went out over the water and the band played the theme song[b] of the Second Empire so fittingly composed by Queen Hortense herself. Napoleon's bread and butter letter was a masterpiece:

(a) As yet the Queen was unaware of the relationship between the Emperor and Marianne. Later the knowledge that she had entertained a 'mistress', was to add to her anger that the Emperor, with whom she had squeezed hands, should have taken an ex-Ambassadress as his lover. It touched her status and affronted her possessive feelings towards the Emperor.

(b) '*Partant pour la Syrie*'

Madam and very dear sister,

   We left Osborne so touched by the kind reception of your Majesty and of Prince Albert, we are so struck with admiration for the spectacle of all the virtues which is presented by the Royal family of England, that it is difficult for me to find words adequate to express all the sentiments of devotion and regard which we feel towards your Majesty.

   It is so sweet to us to think that, apart from political interests, your Majesty and your Majesty's family entertain some affection for us . . . I believe that after passing a few days in your Majesty's society, one becomes better; just as when one has learned to appreciate the various knowledge and the exalted judgment of the Prince, one goes away from him more advanced in one's ideas, and more disposed to do good . . .

   Adieu, Madam. Heaven grant that two years may not again elapse before we have the pleasure of finding ourselves near you, for the hope of seeing you again is the only thing to console us for this painful parting.[21]

But the warmth of happy memories lasted only until frozen by the ice of winter.

   Half past eight on the evening of 14th January 1858. The Emperor and Empress were driving to a gala performance at the Opéra. One act of *Guillaume Tell* was to be followed by the ballet of *Gustave III* and *Maria Stuarda* with Ristori.[22] Eugenie was in white. With them in the carriage was General Roguet, aide-de-camp. There was an escort of Lancers of the Guard.

   The Opera House[(a)] stood in the Rue Lepelletier. By it was a narrow alley known as the Passage Noir, which led through to the Boulevard des Italiens. In its shadow lurked Italian conspirator, Felice Orsini, and three accomplices.

   As the carriage slowed before the Opéra steps, an explosion rocked the street. Seconds later came another . . . and then a third. The gas lights on the theatre went out. The awning over the door crashed down. Glass from broken windows fell like hail. Horses bolted, or screamed in agony. In the absolute darkness a thousand people stumbled,

(a) Work on the present Opera House began in 1861.

ran, shouted, fell, lay still. In all one hundred and fifty six were wounded by the conspirators bombs, of whom twelve died.

Lanterns came from the theatre. Eugenie opened the carriage door and faced an assassin. The police pounced. Her dress was streaked with red, splattered by blood from a wound in General Roguet's neck. By a miracle, neither she nor the Emperor were seriously hurt. She had a cut from a glass splinter close to her eye. His nose was gashed and there was a hole in his hat.[23]

The theatre manager ran to the carriage and offered his arm to the Empress. 'No,' she told him. 'I will get out alone. Let us show the assassins that we have more courage than them.'[24] Napoleon wished to stay and speak to the wounded. '*Pas si bête,*' she snapped. '*Assez de farces comme ça.*'[25] She was ice-cold; he moved as if in a trance – demoralised. She led him to the front of the Imperial box. They bowed. The audience went mad. Soon the curtain rose and the show began.

It was discovered that the conspirators had come from England and that the bombs had been made in Birmingham. The French army boiled with patriotic fervour. In London Ambassador Persigny screamed at Lord Malmesbury – '*C'est la guerre, c'est la guerre.*'[26]

CHAPTER 14

Into Battle

The explosions of Orsini's bombs rocked Europe. Amongst other damage, they upset Anglo-French relations. The threats and the insults of the French militarists enraged public opinion in Britain and led to the downfall of the Government. Lords Palmerston and Clarendon gave places to Conservative Lords Derby and Malmesbury. But both the Queen and her Ministers wished to retain the French alliance and a helpful step in this direction was the replacement, as Ambassador, of the fiery Persigny by General Pélissier, a hero of the Crimean War whom Napoleon had created Duc de Malakoff. He was fat and genial, much liked at Court and a favourite both of the royal children and the children of London's streets. The heat came off and Napoleon invited the Queen and the Prince to meet him at Cherbourg early in August.

They went, but in an atmosphere very changed from that in which they had sailed to France in 1855. The thoughts of Queen Victoria and Prince Albert were strictly German-slanted now, for in January their eldest daughter, Princess Royal, Princess Victoria, had married Prince Frederick William of Prussia and she was already pregnant. Germany was to be next on their visiting list. Berlin had become their Mecca and Albert was pouring out his advice and wisdom both to the Heir to the Prussian Throne and to his daughter, seemingly unaware that the views of Coburg were unwanted. The point was being made very clear to the poor Princess Royal and her nerves suffered so severely that she all but lost her own life and that of her child.

Prince Albert's fears centered about the increased French navy and new fortifications at Cherbourg, ignoring the point that Napoleon would hardly have invited him to see his new vessels and inspect the fortifications if he had had any intention of using them against Britain. The visit turned out to be a display of naval might, the fleet escorting the *Victoria and Albert* and the French warships and gun emplacements all banging away to see which could make the most noise.

The programme got away to a bad start when Queen Victoria

refused to kiss Madame Walewska, as she now knew all about Marianne's relationship with the Emperor. As a result the Walewskis decided to boycott the official dinner given on board the flagship *Bretagne*.[1] This incident may have contributed to Napoleon's ill humour. He asked his guests, sarcastically, if the British still expected an invasion. He complained about the press attacks upon him. While the Queen found the Empress as responsive and friendly as before, she could do nothing with the Emperor. She described him as being 'rather *boutonné* and silent and not ready to talk'.[2] Prince Albert absorbed the detail of the naval might and announced that it made his blood boil. Unconcerned, the Emperor politely waved goodbye and continued with his plans for making war, but not a war directly involving British interests.

Since boyhood he had had two dreams – to found a Second Empire and to free Italy. Nearly thirty years had passed since he had joined the Italian revolutionaries, seen his brother die, and escaped the Austrians by disguising himself as the footman of Queen Hortense. He had not forgotten. But, strangely enough, it was the bomb outrage and Orsini's plea to him, before execution, to free Italy, that convinced him that he must go to war. Also he felt that, if his Empire were to survive, he must provide a victory for celebration and a territorial gain. He must act before he grew too old – or before another disgruntled Italian made an attempt on his life. He had survived two such attempts, and next time might be lucky for the assassins.

But the stage had to be set and that presented many problems. Although the army was ready and eager to fight, the mass of the French people were dead set against war. The financiers, busy with building programmes and fearing for the value of their railway shares, viewed any such project with horror. Equally important, Eugenie would not tolerate any aggressive step which might annoy or weaken the Pope.

Italy was a jigsaw puzzle of eight states. In the south Naples and Sicily formed the Kingdom of the Two Sicilies. To the north of them lay the Papal States, ruled over by the Pope. Then came the Grandduchy of Tuscany and the small states of Lucca, Parma and Modena. Sardinia and Piedmont were under the rule of King Victor Emmanuel. Finally, Lombardy and Venetia were part of the Austrian Empire. It was against Austria that Napoleon directed his threat. He was back now with his favourite pastime of planning and scheming just as he had planned and schemed before Strasbourg and Boulogne, before his escape from Ham and before the *coup d'état*. He was pokerfaced and very skilful. He met Cavour in secret at Plombières in the Vosges and they had finished their talks before Europe discovered where they were. He agreed to send an army to Piedmont and to attack the Austrians on condition that Savoy and Nice were ceded to him. He made another stipulation, that his cousin Plon-Plon should be allowed to marry Princess Clotilde, daughter of King Victor Emmanuel. That Prince Napoleon Jerome was thirty-six and sexually lurid and most experienced, while Clotilde was barely sixteen, ugly, spotty and very pious, did not enter into the matter. The point was that the Bonaparte family would be allied to an ancient royal house. Plon-Plon welcomed the idea and was married next year.

Napoleon strengthened his forces and began to play martial tunes to excite the Gallic emotions. He stressed the tyrannical behaviour of the Austrians. He spoke of duty and great adventure. He sold his military expedition as if it was to be a package tour to Italy. He was extremely rude to the Austrian Ambassador. All that he prayed for now was that Emperor Francis Joseph of Austria would give him grounds to attack. And that Francis Joseph, misguidedly and stubbornly, did. In April 1859 Austria sent a peremptory demand to Piedmont that she should disband her forces within three days, on pain of invasion. The threat inflamed French public opinion and on the 29th war was declared.

On 10th May the Emperor left for the front to take command of his army. There was Mass at the Tuileries and then out he drove into a crowd wild with emotion, part religious, part nationalistic. He might have been setting out on a religious crusade. Chaplets rained upon him. Old soldiers threw their medals at his feet. The Empress, who had been appointed Regent, was beside him and drove with him as far as Montereau.[3]

On 4th June he sat on his horse by a bridge at Magenta, watching his 54,000 men struggling with the Austrians, who outnumbered them. They fought without allies, for the troops of Piedmont, who had promised support, had not shown up. This was Napoleon's testing hour. Would he match up to the example of the Great Emperor, whose ghost sat in the saddle beside him? He watched his Imperial Guard cut to pieces. His face remained expressionless. He smoked cigarette after cigarette, throwing each away half finished and lighting up another. It was a close run thing. At one time the Austrians were on the point of victory. When excited staff officers reported back to him, asking for orders and begging for reinforcements, Napoleon snapped out, 'Hold on'. There were no reinforcements. It was not until the evening that Magenta was captured. Then, and only then, did the Emperor collapse on to a chair, overcome and appalled by the slaughter which he had witnessed. He still sat there when King Victor Emmanuel arrived full of apologies for missing the action. He received a brusque reply.[4] In Paris the guns of Les Invalides told of the victory, bands marched through the illuminated streets and the Empress drove to Notre Dame for the *Te Deum*.

Emperor Francis Joseph now took command of his troops. Near Solferino he faced Napoleon in command of the French and King Victor Emmanuel with the Piedmontese and Sardinians. Seldom before, and never again, were three rulers to face one another on the field of battle. A letter arrived for Napoleon from Eugenie. She told him that the Prussians were mobilising on the Rhine to aid the Austrians. She urged him to make peace or return troops to France. The news galvanised him. He summoned up a power and vitality that he had never shown before, lending determination to those about him.

At first light on 24th June the 150,000 men of France, Sardinia and Piedmont moved on a twenty-five mile front from Lake Garda to Castel Goffredo. At seven Napoleon climbed the high tower of the church at Castiglione and ordered the advance on Solferino, clear on a hill. The French Guards stormed the village and won it, but at fearful cost. It was sweltering hot. In the afternoon the Austrians counter-attacked but the French held firm. At four o'clock a violent thunder-storm swept over the battle-field and, taking advantage of the driving rain and the poor visibility, the Austrians slunk away.

Tired out and sickened, Napoleon rode back to his headquarters, past the harvest-heaps of dead, to the sad tune of the cries of the wounded. He telegraphed to Eugenie: 'Great battle, great victory.' Then he sat as if in a trance, unheeding of the conversation of the officers about him. At last he rose and dismissed them. 'Gentlemen, the day is over.'[5]

Next morning he went out on to the battlefield once more. He was a lonely man, for his favourite horse, Philip, which he had taken with him to Windsor in 1855, had been killed. The Austrians had lost 22,000 men, the Allies, 17,000 and the slender ambulance service simply could not cope. Many of the wounded lay for three days where they had fallen while Lombard peasants robbed them of their boots and possessions.[6] Napoleon saw the festering wounds and winced at the moaning and the cries for water. He had had his bellyful of war and turned away.

Now the great divide between himself and Napoleon Bonaparte showed clearly. The old Emperor had been 'little moved by the sacrifice of millions of his men to his megalomania, and even seemed to derive some reinforcement of his sense of power by viewing the bodies of men who had died doing his bidding.'[7] After Eylau he had turned over the corpses of his dead soldiers with his foot. 'Small change! Small change!' he had said. 'A night of Paris will soon adjust these losses.'[8] Napoleon III was an humane man, more a statesman and a planner than a soldier. He saw on that day of Solferino that modern weapons had converted war into a form of mass murder, robbing it of the glory and adventure which had cloaked it in the past. The Austrians had retreated behind their fortifications and he was determined to have no repeat of such slaughter.

There was another observer on the battlefield whose mind was much disturbed and who was thinking on the same lines as the victorious Emperor. He was a young Swiss stretcher-bearer and his name was Henri Dunant. He wrote of his experiences in the bloody aftermath of Solferino in a booklet[(a)] which shocked Europe. Dunant said that he prayed that he might live to see 'the leaders of the military art of different nationalities agree upon some sacred international principle, sanctioned by convention, which, once signed and ratified, would serve as the basis for the creation of societies for the aid of the wounded in the different European countries.' His appeal quickly found its echo. Backed by the personal influence of the Emperor Napoleon, an international conference was held in Geneva in 1864. The outcome was the Geneva Convention. It was decided that there should be general respect for the wounded and that the symbol of their protection was to be a white flag bearing a red cross. The Red Cross was born.

On 11th July the Emperors of France and Austria met at Villafranca and made their peace. By its terms Lombardy was united with Piedmont but Venetia remained under Austrian rule. Napoleon had boasted that he would free Italy from the Alps to the Adriatic and Cavour, who

(a) *Un souvenir de Solferino.*

had not been consulted, raged in fury, insulted King Victor Emmanuel and resigned – in the event only temporarily – from office.

Napoleon had proved himself as a military leader but the threat of Prussia from the north and the appalling losses suffered by his forces left him no alternative but to compromise. After quieting his nerves with a fishing expedition to Lake Garda, he returned home. He had only been away for nine weeks but the tension and the effort had played havoc with his health. He needed peace and he found it, with his wife and child, at St Cloud.

On 14th August the troops came marching home and Paris was ready for them. No one who witnessed the spectacle was ever to forget. Thirty-five years afterwards Dr Evans wrote:

> I remember, as if it were yesterday, the 14th of August, 1859 . . . the flags and the banners in the Rue de la Paix . . . the triumphal arches; the immense ornamental columns surmounted by colossal Victories holding in their outstretched hands golden wreaths or crowns of laurel; the rich draperies spread from balcony to balcony across the facades of the buildings that front upon the Place Vendôme; the great tribunes to the right and the left, rising tier upon tier, and filled with thousands of people; and the gallery built over the entrance of the Ministry of Justice, where, under a magnificent canopy of crimson velvet, studded with golden bees and fringed with gold, the Empress sat . . . .[9]

'A magnificent spectacle,' commented Benjamin Disraeli, 'which has only cost 100,000 lives and 50 millions of pounds sterling!'[10]

The Emperor came in at the column's head. He was mounted on a charger which he had bought from a Piccadilly horse-dealer for five hundred guineas.[11] He rode alone, as was his wont, his face expressionless, his horsemanship superb. He never feared the risk that he took on this, his favourite act. If a well aimed shot came from a high window, he would fall, clean, unknowing, into the pages of history, joining the great ones in the cloisters of their fame. It was devilish devices such as the bomb that he feared, weapons *sans merci* which brought death, torment and mental anguish to the innocent.

In the Place Vendôme he rode to the foot of the column raised to the memory of the Great Emperor. He sat motionless on his horse as the regiments marched past and the crowds sang out their names. It was not only the fit who marched, but also, it seemed, the wounded and the dead. Casualties unable to walk rode by in ambulances. The gaps in the ranks showed where dead comrades would have marched if they had survived the fields of Magenta and Solferino.[12]

As a great body of cavalry poured from the Rue de la Paix into the Place Vendôme, Napoleon played his ace of trumps. An equerry, carrying the three year old Prince Imperial, stepped out and placed the boy on the pommel of his father's saddle. He was dressed in the blue and red uniform of the *Grenadiers de la Garde*. It was his first public appearance and it seemed that the cheers would have no end.[13]

The Imperial family left for a seaside holiday at Biarritz – 'our Osborne', Napoleon called it. It was time to take stock and do the sums. On the credit side, he had proved himself as a military commander and his wife had earned high praise for her role as Regent. He had given France true reason for great celebration. There was territorial gain for, although Italy still laboured in her troubled fight for unity, within a few months Savoy and Nice moved under the Imperial cloak. On the debit side were the heavy casualty list and the drain on the country's finances. Relations with neighbouring countries had also been upset. Italy, expecting more favourable results from the campaign, was ungrateful for what had been done, forgetting that French troops had borne the brunt of the fighting. Austria had been humbled. In Prussia Prince William, who had taken over power from the incapable King Frederick William IV, was saying little but had, by mobilisation, indicated his intentions. In Britain good feeling towards the Emperor Napoleon had waned and suspicions regarding his future designs stirred military enthusiasm throughout the country. In May 1859 a volunteer force was formed by royal command and Queen Victoria backed it with all her Hanoverian zeal.

Forgotten now were the peaceful summer days which she passed at St Cloud. In May 1860 she wrote to King Leopold: 'France must needs disturb every quarter of the globe, and try to make mischief and set every one by the ears. Of course this will end some day in a general crusade against the universal disturber of the world.'[14]

CHAPTER 15

Last Meetings

In the early August evenings of 1860 the Empress was often to be seen driving in the Bois de Boulogne. Beside her in the carriage, half lying, propped up by cushions, was a pale and beautiful woman, near to death. Her sister Paca, Duchess of Alba, had suffered from cancer of the breast and now a rare disease of the spine was eating away her life. She and her three children were being cared for by her mother, Manuela, at the newly opened Hôtel d'Albe in the Champs Elysées, built for her by the Empress.[1]

Satisfied that Paca was in good hands, Eugenie left St Cloud with the Emperor on the 23rd at the start of one of their longest and most exciting tours, a tour that was to begin as a triumphal march and end in utter tragedy. Their first destination was Savoy, where the population was delighted with the union with France and determined to show it.

Travelling via Dijon and Lyons, they came to the land of snow-capped mountains and dancing rivers and cowbells tinkling in the quaint village streets. Eugenie wrote to Paca: 'Impossible to describe the enthusiasm, which bordered on the delirious.'[2] At Chamonix she climbed to the Montanvert on a donkey. She made an excursion to the Mer de Glace and set a fashion with her short skirt and the green veil she wore to protect her eyes from the sun.[3] It was at Annecy that the high spot came, an experience that she was to describe, long after, as among the four happiest in her life.[4]

One of France's loveliest jewels, the lake lay still on a perfect summer's evening. Its surface was a mirror, reflecting the light of a sky full of stars, of fires which burned on the peaks, of thousands of torches held by sightseers who ringed the shore, of flares and rockets flashing their welcome. The Emperor and Empress moved out upon it in a large Venetian gondola draped in purple, with twenty men at the oars. They sat on thrones on a raised platform. Around the gondola was a flotilla of smaller boats, festooned with coloured lanterns.

The music of the bands came across the water and echoed in the hills.

Eugenie wore a low cut dress. Her perfect neck sparkled with diamonds. There was a diadem on her head. Across her shoulders she had thrown a scarlet burnous fringed with gold. Intoxicated with the scene and the sounds around her, she stood up on the dais and the cry went up from shore to shore, '*Vive l'Impératrice*'.[5] With a half smile, Napoleon looked up at her and said: 'You look like a Doge's wife.' The two were closest to one another when the crowds were roaring. In describing this to Paca, Eugenie added: 'For two pins I would have thrown my ring into the lake, as the Doge did when he presided over the wedding of Venice to the Adriatic.'[6]

They went on their way and the applause went with them, to Avignon and Arles and the coast. At Marseilles they boarded the Imperial yacht and sailed for Corsica. It was the first time that either of them had been to the old home of the Bonapartes and it was in the nature of a pilgrimage. In Ajaccio they visited the house in the Place Letizia, full of memories of *Madame Mère*,[7] mother of Napoleon I, and placed flowers on her grave.

There was an ulterior motive for the Emperor being away from Paris at this time. He wished to be remote from critical happenings taking place in Italy. In May Garibaldi and his Thousand had conquered Sicily and Garibaldi had become Dictator. Wishing for a free hand, he refused to agree to the annexation of Sicily to Victor Emmanuel's kingdom of Piedmont. However it was essential to the King and Cavour that Garibaldi's military adventure should be for the benefit of a unified Italy rather than for personal aggrandizement, and that no attack on the Papal States should call in the big Powers to their defence. On 8th August Garibaldi crossed the Straits of Messina with twenty thousand men and headed for Naples. King Francis II of the Two Sicilies fled and Victor Emmanuel and Cavour decided that they must occupy Umbria and the Marches and bar the road of the Red Shirts to Rome. Napoleon was consulted and he warned that he would take action if there was military interference with the Papal States. He then went on with his tour, leaving his Foreign Minister, Thouvenel, somewhat in the dark. Nevertheless Victor Emmanuel used the excuse of certain hostile movements by the Pope to deploy his own troops, and the Papal forces, under command of the French General, Lamoricière, were routed at Castelfidardo. So it came about that Victor Emmanuel and Garibaldi met and entered Naples together. The first steps towards the unification of Italy had been taken.

The rout at Castelfidardo, and the lack of firm action by her husband, deeply upset a daughter of the Church as devout as the Empress Eugenie. However she was unaware of these events which unfolded as she was sailing the Mediterranean and sightseeing in Algeria, and the shock for her lay ahead.

Eugenie loved Algeria and the men of Algeria worshipped her. To them she was a radiant goddess. The Chiefs came in to pay homage and the horsemen raced upon the plain. As General Fleury, who was in the Imperial party, wrote: 'The woman was uppermost in her and she found this homage all the more pleasant for being so artless and unexpected.' Yet there was sadness for her, for she had had no news of her ailing sister. It was not until they landed in France on 21st September that Napoleon told her the truth – Paca was dead. She had died five days before, as Eugenie danced at a ball. The funeral had already been held.

Napoleon had made one of the biggest miscalculations of his life. As he broke the news to her, she felt a wave of hatred for him. For the sake of his personal glory on this triumphal tour, he had robbed her of the chance of being by the deathbed of the sister whom she loved dearly, of saying the last goodbye and praying for her soul. Her fury at the rout of the Pope's forces poured out. Accusations regarding his unfaithfulness and cruelty followed in a bitter flow. She had always been somewhat afraid of his expressionless demeanour, but no longer now. She knew that he dreaded domestic rows more than anything. So she screamed and she accused.

By the time they reached St Cloud, the coffin of Paca had been moved from the Madeleine to the church at Rueil near Malmaison, lying between the memorials to the Empress Josephine and Queen Hortense. Each day Eugenie prayed beside it and, when the time came for the body to be moved to Madrid, she wrote: '*En voyant emporter le corps de ma soeur, il me semblait qu'on arrachait mon âme.*'[8]

She realised now that she must get away from her husband for a while, see new places, give herself a chance to recover from the morbid obsession with death which possessed her. She planned in secret. Incognita, she would visit England and Scotland. She would speak with Lord Clarendon, ever a tower of strength and wisdom. She would stay with her friend, her husband's cousin, the Duchess of Hamilton, formerly Princess Mary of Baden. Perhaps she would pay a courtesy visit to Queen Victoria. But there was one reason which overrode all others. For some time she had had pains in her back and she feared that she was suffering from the disease which had killed Paca. So she planned to visit Dr Simpson[a] in Edinburgh.

She told the Emperor little of her plans – simply that she was going. She took two ladies and two gentlemen with her and assumed the name of the Comtesse de Pierrefonds. On 14th November the Emperor saw her off at the Gare du Nord. She did not realise then what a stir her trip would make. In her early married days she had made several such excursions and little notice had been taken. But then Napoleon had been but an Emperor in name – now he was the most powerful, and the most watched, man in Europe. Before she could move about unrecognised – after the exchange of visits with Queen Victoria, she was known throughout Britain.

A statement was put out through French diplomatic channels that, owing to the effect on the Empress of the death of her sister, the doctors had counselled a change of air and that she was visiting Scotland in the strictest incognita.[9] Soon after she had left, Napoleon received a message from the Duchess of Hamilton inviting Eugenie to stay. He replied: 'The Empress is seriously unwell, especially mentally. She has left for Scotland, I doubt if she can go to Hamilton.'[10] A strange reply indeed. Mystery was rife and rumours raced through every court in Europe. It was said that the Emperor and Empress were about to separate, that she was furious about some new woman in his life, that she was suffering from a fatal illness. Old King Leopold of the Belgians put his long nose in and added this theory that 'there seems to be a difference of opinion with her master on the subject of the Pope.'[11] Prince Albert informed his Prussian in-laws: 'The Empress of the French has burst upon this country like a bomb. The secret history of her visit is unknown to us. I will not bore you with mere guesses; thousands are in circulation.'[12]

The Empress and party reached London Bridge station late in the evening and set off in a cab to find accommodation, unaware that the

(a) Sir James J. Simpson invented the uterine sound and was the first to apply anaesthesia by ether to midwifery practice.

new Lord Mayor was giving a big reception at the Guildhall and that London was full. Four hotels turned them away, but the fifth, owned by Mr Claridge, was able to take them in. When Napoleon heard that his wife had been circulating London late at night in a 'growler' looking for a bed, he rocked with laughter.

Now a new game began – spot the Empress. Reporters besieged Claridges but, on being received by the ladies in attendance, were informed that she had been 'chopping'. Which was true as she had slipped out on foot to visit such high class establishments as William Hanson, the jeweller, who knew full well how to do their business behind closed doors. She sent a note to the Queen, saying that she hoped that they would be able to meet on her return from the north. It is clear that she also saw Lord Clarendon, for he was the only person who could throw light on her visit or unravel what he termed 'the Eugenian mind'.

The Imperial party travelled, via York, to Edinburgh, arriving on the 17th and putting up at the Douglas Hotel. The Scots were standing no such nonsense as incognita and the City authorities presented her with an address. *The Scotsman* pointed out that 'since hapless Mary, Queen of Scots, landed at Leith three hundred years ago, no royal lady of France has, till yesterday, visited the Scottish capital.' Eugenie went to Holyrood Palace to see the relics of that unhappy Queen. She also called upon Dr Simpson and received a clean bill of health. She explored Melrose, Abbotsford and Dalkeith and on the 23rd reached the Birnam Hotel at Dunkeld.[13]

Meantime the Queen was trying to keep tabs on the visitor. On the 21st she wrote to her eldest daughter in Germany: 'The poor Empress Eugenie is said to be very ill and in a morbid state of mind. She is going about in Edinburgh and no one knows where she is going to next!'[14] But her ever vigilant spy, Lady Augusta Bruce, picked up the trail:

Fancy the joy of the D. of Atholl meeting Her driving to Blair from Dunkeld at 3 p.m. – jumping into the carriage – getting there in the dark – shewing her into the housemaid's room, the only fire there was – the house all dismantled – by tallow candle light – tea and chops at the Hotel and back to dinner at the Hotel at 11 p.m. Next day he took her to the *Kirk* and afterwards to call on Lady

James (Murray). The Duchess, who is in waiting, grieved that he did not take her in by the window, so Lady J. in her alarm might have jumped out at the door![15]

Now completely under the spell of Scotland she sauntered on, to Perth and Stirling and Taymouth Castle, by the shores of Lochs Katrine and Lomond to Glasgow, by which time she had star rating. When she arrived at Motherwell on her way to stay with the Duke and Duchess of Hamilton, the station was solid with people and there were dense crowds all the way to Hamilton Palace and in the park. 'It seemed as if the whole country had collected to stare, not at any grand procession or military display, but simply at a graceful lady, in deep mourning, who wore such a thick veil that not a feature was discernible.'[16] On her way south she received an Address at Manchester, was mobbed at Leamington, and then disappeared for a while. She surfaced at Claridges on 2nd December.

Two days later a special train took her to Windsor for lunch. The Queen wrote to Germany:

> Such a contrast to '55! A wet dark day – no demonstrations beyond Papa's going down to the station to bring her up and our being all at the door to receive her. She was in deep mourning – lovely and charming – but so sad – She cried in speaking of her shattered nerves (she could neither sleep nor eat till she came here). She never mentioned the Emperor but once and that once *de presenter ses compliments* and never went near politics.[17]

The visit did not please the Empress. It was altogether too stiff and formal, so she confided to Lord Clarendon. His opinion was: 'I am sure The Queen *intended* to be civil but she doesn't understand scrambles and larks and hack cabs which give her vague impressions of impropriety and curdle the blood in the Consort's veins.'[18] Word must have leaked through to the Queen for, when a few days later, she and the Prince were in London for the Cattle Show, they called in at Claridges to see the Empress.[19] This meeting, although rather a 'lark' for Albert, proved most successful. Eugenie, who had dispensed with her veil, was in good spirits and chatted away with Victoria about shops, and Madame Tussaud's, and the British Museum. It was the last time Eugenie was to see Albert, for at the end of the following year he died.

On the evening of the 12th December Mr Claridge himself escorted the Empress to the station. Next day the Emperor came as far as Amiens to meet her. He had been punished and was contrite. Conjugal relationship, albeit of a frigid nature, was resumed. There was one difference. She was the master now.

Part IV

TOWARDS THE ABYSS

1861-1870

CHAPTER 16

Bismarck and Marguerite

The death of Prince Albert on 14th December 1861 was to alter the course of affairs for Napoleon and Eugenie. It was as if the wind had changed that tragic night at Windsor. The change came, not because the Coburg princeling had particular power in Europe, but because of a statement made by Queen Victoria shortly after his death: '. . . *his* wishes, *his* plans about everything, *his* views about *every* thing are to be *my* law.'[1]

'*His* views about everything' included the following: that his son and heir was 'the most thorough and cunning lazybones[2] and a sexual menace; and that the Emperor of the French was a conspirator, a spendthrift, a philanderer and a 'walking lie'.[3] His last fusillade of abuse of Napoleon was fired off as late as 22nd November. 'Papa,' the Queen told her eldest daughter, 'had the worst opinion of him, which was never removed.' To quote Harold Kurtz: 'Prince Albert . . . had indeed raised Prussian goodness and Napoleonic evilness to the status of primary political dogmas, and for many years after his death his distracted widow conceived it as her mission to follow him with undeviating obedience in this as in other respects.'[4]

Among the mental legacies inherited by Victoria from her husband was an obsession with the Germanic. Albert's love and loyalty for his fatherland were always clear – he had said openly, 'I shall never cease to be a true German,'[5] which had caused Lord Clarendon to comment that, under such circumstances, he could not declare that he was guiding the Queen on *British* interests.[6] Yet, by early 1862, the Queen was writing to Berlin that her soul craved for everything German. Another legacy was Albert's animosity to the Catholic Church – 'dear Papa had such a horror of the priestly dominion.' She poured derision on 'the bowings, scrapings and confessions'.[7] As Eugenie was at the same time threatening her husband that, if he interfered with papal powers, she would leave him and take up residence with Pope Pius – 'who, after all, is the godfather of my son' – it was clear that there was a great divide between the Queen of England and the Empress of the French. Yet it was the Empress's letter of condolence which touched the Queen most deeply, for Eugenie was still grieving over her sister's death and was able to give an understanding which others were unable to do.

Directed by such prejudices, guided as if by orders from a spirit world, Victoria stepped back into a black-edged gloom, away from the eyes of men. Sitting alone there, weeping, clad in thick skirt, shawl and mourning cap, she bore no likeness to the gay, untiring little Queen who had danced with Napoleon at Versailles seven years before. Soon she was listening only to the sound of but one voice, that of a simple Scottish ghillie who shielded her through the day and through the night. His name was John Brown. He considered that strangers began at Carter Bar and 'unspeakables' at Calais.

Meanwhile invasion scares swept through the country and it was rumoured that flat-bottomed boats were being massed on the French coast. It was all a hoax, said Richard Cobden, and the hoax originated at Windsor.[8] Victoria was unapproachable, self-imprisoned and consumed by her husband's feud against France, and there was nothing that Napoleon could do about it. It was his personal magnetism which had brought about the *entente cordiale* of 1855. He had shown then, and again in 1857, that he could court and sway Victoria. Now he was not to see her again until, ill and broken, he sought sanctuary as an exile. Within a short time the *rapport* between Britain and France was ruptured.

The Prince Consort's views on the threat from France had been more exaggerated than those of his two chief advisers, King Leopold of the Belgians, 'the Nestor of Europe', and Baron Stockmar, the 'think-tank' of the Coburgs. His obsession had been a constant handicap to Lords Cowley and Clarendon. Could the answer lie in a word which lies beyond the orbit of official history, the word 'jealousy'?

Physically, Albert was a weak man. Mentally, he was a solipsist, encouraged as such by his brilliant mind. One thing that he could, and would, not tolerate was another person having a greater power over his wife than that held by himself. He backed those with whom she was on bad terms, such as Sir Robert Peel and her mother, the Duchess of Kent. He ousted, or ruined, those who held her ear and trust, those unfortunates including Lord Melbourne, her old governess, Baroness Lehzen, and her half-sister, Princess Feodora. He showed no more mercy towards them than he did for the deer which he shot down when trapped in a stockade.

Napoleon had shown, quite clearly, that he could woo Victoria. Victoria had shown, quite clearly, that she liked it. Inexperienced in the ways of men, she had perhaps reacted too obviously to the wiles of an experienced womaniser. Albert had attempted to counter-attack by displaying, for the one and only time in his life, an attraction for a lovely woman, the Empress. If he had hoped that this would cause Victoria to be jealous, his hopes were to be confounded. She welcomed the signs, only hoping that a *soupçon* of the Gay Lothario might find its way into her bedroom. Then, on the return visit to Paris, Eugenie was pregnant and the charade could not be played. Hence Albert's tantrum when Victoria and Napoleon, off on their own, kept him waiting at a *rendez-vous*. The Emperor had repeated his performance at Osborne but blotted his copy-book when he slipped with Madame Walewska. But Albert never forgave those who crossed him and in death passed on his hates to his widow. Now, in her long and weary winter without him, the Queen betrayed her old French friend, as, in the aftermath, she had betrayed Lord Melbourne. *Albert über alles.* So small a thing – one man's jealousy. Yet it must take its place along-side finance and lust for power and territorial gain as a force which assists in the turning of the tides of nations.

The snapping of the link with Windsor came at a most unfortunate time for Napoleon, for now more than ever he needed the friendship and support of the British Queen. The whistle had blown for half time for his Empire. As he rested for a while, he hoped for a less arduous second half. He had brought off his *coups*, done his fighting, seen the blood and heard the cheering. Ageing, he wished to play more slowly now. He wished to concentrate on the life of Julius Caesar which he was writing – he wanted to potter about the gardens of Malmaison and, peaceful with the ghost of grandma Josephine, plan the flowers and the shrubs. He had mellowed. 'I am a socialist,' he said. 'The only Bonapartist is Persigny, and he is mad.'⁹ The panache had gone and he had lost touch with the gay adventurer who had been his comrade at Strasbourg and Boulogne.

He was also, of his own free will, releasing the firm grip which, since 1851, he had held on the affairs of France. While the Empress was on her mystery tour of Scotland, he had produced his famous Decree of 23rd November. This was the first step towards the founding of the Liberal Empire. The Decree gave the Legislative Body the right to discuss speeches from the Throne and the opportunity of proposing amendments to laws. Small as the concession was, it appeared radical at the time.

As the energies of the Emperor decreased, those of the Empress increased. This was how he wished it to be, as if to make amends for his failings and infidelities. She had shown herself to be efficient and restrained during the Regency and from now on she invariably took her place at ministerial Councils, presiding over them if her husband was ill or away on duty. This did not please all Ministers, who feared the effect of her influence. 'Persigny was deeply hostile to her; Prince Napoleon detested her; Morny distrusted her. Yet she held her own, and little by little asserted more and more her own enterprise and her own decisions.'¹⁰

There was talk of her mental unbalance and criticism of her 'incessant championship' of the Pope. There had been signs of such unbalance after the birth of the Prince Imperial. Then Eugenie had fallen under the influence of Daniel Dunglas Home, a young Scottish medium whom Robert Browning had labelled 'Mr Sludge the Medium'. She had described to her sister a *séance* held on the anniversary of the death of Don Cipriano:

As we sat round the table a hand never ceased to press mine or to pull my dress in order to make me give it. Surprised by such importunity, I said to it: So you love me? The response was a very distinct pressure of my hand. Have I known you? Yes. Tell me your name on earth. Spelling the letters came the reply: Today is the anniversary of my death. Those present asked me who it was, and I replied: My father. Then the hand pressed mine with great affection and allowed me to press his. Then it made with a finger three signs of the cross on my hand and disappeared for ever.[11]

Walewski, then Foreign Minister, considered Home to be a fraud and suspected that he was an Italian spy. Napoleon, on the other hand, was intrigued and eager to discover the truth. One evening he asked Home to produce Emperor Napoleon I and King Louis Philippe. The medium requested those present to stand round a table. After a short while the Emperor received a hefty kick up the backside. He was never able to decide whether he had been attacked by the Great Emperor or the Citizen King. Shortly afterwards Home made the mistake of forecasting that the Prince Imperial would never reign. He was expelled from France.

But the experiences with Home had come as Eugenie was recovering from a birth which had all but cost her life and when she was facing the hard truth that her marital role was over. Now she had come to terms with that truth. There were still worries over her husband's aberrations, but they did not hurt so much. Her bigger worry now was his health, and this was the main reason why she must learn to play the part of professional Empress.

Napoleon was suffering from a disease of the kidneys, resulting in the stone in the bladder,[12] (which was not diagnosed until three years later). The illness was changing his character. He would sit for hours, silent, engrossed in his thoughts. He was losing the common touch. Often he was in pain but refused to admit it. He was a bad patient, leaving treatment until too late and then demanding immediate relief and adjuring his doctors to silence. Eugenie could find out little. In any case, certainly in the early stages, she could have been of little help. In-experienced in medical matters, she was a believer in the theory that the strength of the spirit should overcome the weakness of the flesh. Strength of spirit would most certainly have had beneficial effect if it had been applied to the eschewance of women, but could help little with the cure of diseased kidneys.

In the early summer of 1862 another cloud appeared on the horizon. Prince Otto von Bismarck was appointed Ambassador for Prussia in Paris. He arrived without his wife, and his first action was to sack the Embassy cook for fiddling the accounts. While taking his meals in cafés, he received an invitation from the Emperor to join his wife and himself at Biarritz. He wandered through France and lay in the sun by the Atlantic.

Bismarck had been to France for the Peace Conference of 1856 and the following year paid an unofficial visit. A bull of a man, with wide brow, protruding eyes and a moustache like downturned horns, he stood out in contrast to most of those found at the Court of the Second Empire. Known when young as 'the Mad Bismarck' on account of his wild escapades, he was partial to the ladies. Waltzing at the Tuileries in his White Cuirassier uniform,[13] he set one female heart a-flutter. Eugenie thought that this was very funny.

She arranged with Mérimée to make a plaster cast of Bismarck's head. This was placed on the pillow of the lady in question and the likeness to a sleeping figure was completed with the aid of a bolster. Eugenie put the finishing touch by wrapping a handkerchief round the head to represent a nightcap. She and the Emperor hid in the passage while the rest of the company, in the secret, retired to their rooms. The victim did likewise. Seeing, in the candlelight, Bismarck lying in her bed, she ran screaming into the corridor, only to hear peals of laughter from Eugenie. Meantime a footman, having entered the room in the course of his duties, had also been fooled, had retired with apologies and had spread the news 'downstairs' that the Prussian statesman was in a lady's bed.[14]

Bismarck was slow to sum up Napoleon, a man older than himself and far more experienced, who knew every card in the poker game of politics. Later he was to admit that he had overrated his intellect and underrated his heart.[15] But the Prussian had little time for kind hearts. Eugenie impressed him from the first time he met her, and his respect continued despite all the disasters and sadnesses that the years poured out. It was not only her beauty, he said, there was something beyond that. That 'something' was strength – the strong calling to the strong. He told Jules Favre that he had never in his life been so dazzled by feminine loveliness as when he saw the Empress receive King William of Prussia in the grand vestibule at Compiègne Palace.[16] He feared falling under the spell of her charm – 'When she practised this power on me, I always felt that I must be more than usual on the *qui vive*.'[17] He was especially vulnerable as his own wife was hideous. Described by Queen Victoria as 'a rather masculine and not very sympathetic lady',[18] Fürstin

Napoleon III *(right)* riding with the Tsar
during the Paris Exhibition
in 1867. From the painting by Ch. Porion

The Imperial Hunt in the Forêt de St. Germain, 1855

Above left: Empress Eugenie. From the painting by Winterhalter
Above right: Napoleon III. From a drawing by Edouard Detaille
Below left: The Prince Napoleon (Plon-Plon). From a photograph by Roger Fenton
Below right: Madame de Castiglione

von Bismarck had terrific feet, said to be the largest ever to make imprint west of the Rhine, and these filled Eugenie's *petites mesdames* with hypnotic horror.

Eugenie early appreciated the danger of Bismarck, saying in 1859, 'If he barks, then surely he must bite.' Yet she had a liking and respect for him and never blamed him for her tragedies as bitterly as she might have done.

Now, in the summer of 1862 Bismarck intended to stay for only three days at Biarritz, but he was there for three weeks. He saw no papers, forgot about politics – he was human for the last time. It is difficult to recognise the Iron Chancellor. He wrote: 'I am nothing but sea-salt and sunshine . . . I stayed over half an hour in the water, and feel there as if I could fly, except that I have no wings. After dinner we went for a ride along the sands. The moon was shining and the tide had ebbed.'[19]

He later commented that in France he had met two amusing women but not one man. The first of the women was the Empress Eugenie, and the second was Princess Orloff, wife of a Russian diplomat. Bismarck wrote: 'Out of sight of every one, lying between two rocks on which heather is blooming, I look at the sea, which is green and white in foam and sunshine. Beside me is the most charming of women . . . gay, clever, amiable, pretty and young.'[20] The Princess played the piano to him as he sat by an open window looking out over the moonlit sea. It was his last romance.

There was much French fun that summer. Watching Madame Rimsky-Korsakoff was a feature of the day. She was not pretty but her figure was divine, and she knew it. She wore a bathing dress made of light material designed to cling to her shape. As she stepped out from her cabin the word ran along the beach. When she returned, 'focussed by a hundred fieldglasses, she looked as if she had just stepped out of a bath'.[21] The Empress put a stop to that.

In September Bismarck was recalled to Berlin. King William of Prussia had been involved in violent conflict with his Parliament on the question of army reforms. A believer in the divine right of Kings, he contemplated abdicating in favour of his son, Frederick William. The Minister for War, von Roon, persuaded him to carry on the struggle and to appoint Bismarck Minister-President. So the age of 'blood and iron' began.

After Napoleon's affair with Madame Walewska had ended in 1860 and thereafter he relied upon his 'Minister for Pleasure', M. Bacciochi, to produce feminine amusement as required. All proved of a temporary nature. On two occasions, after indulgence in this fashion, the Emperor was found, prostrate and unconscious in a fainting fit, upon the floor. But in 1863 he showed signs of recovering his strength and it was then that a strumpet extraordinary crossed his path. Or maybe she was placed upon it, her orders and her payment coming from Germany.

The Emperor was taking an afternoon drive in the Bois. A storm blew up. He saw a young woman sheltering from the rain under a tree. He stopped the carriage and threw her a rug. Next day she arrived at the Tuileries, plus rug, and insisted upon seeing her benefactor. He saw her. She conquered.[22]

Her name was Justine Marie Leboeuf, but she had adopted the more attractive label of Marguerite Bellanger. She was twenty-five. A *femme de chambre* in a Boulogne hotel, she had run away to Paris with a commercial treveller.[23] Abandoned, she had joined a circus and become a bare-back rider and acrobatic dancer. From the prone position, she could leap to her feet in a flash. It was said that, on request, she would walk into the Emperor's presence on her hands. She was a tall girl, but thick and strong about the hips and legs. She had progressed to small parts on the stage, but in the main relied for her livelihood on the officers of the Ecole Militaire. They called her '*Margot la Rigoleuse*'.[24] She was a *grisette* rather than a *cocotte*, lacking the polish of a *demi-mondaine*. There was no mistaking the message in her candid eyes and on her sensual mouth. She was an exaggerated version of *la Belle Sabotière* – Napoleon had come full circle. He was besotted. He set her up in an apartment at Fontainebleau.[25] He gave her superlative horses. He bought her a house at Passy. He lavished money on her. Caesar, commented Prosper Mérimée, has found Cleopatra.

The Bellanger affair was unfortunate on three main counts. It debased the international status of the Second Empire. It hastened the collapse of Napoleon's health. And it infuriated Eugenie. So acrimonious did the relationship become that rumours began that there might be a separation. A number of people about the Court heard them quarrelling, among them statesman Emile Ollivier, who was horrified.[26] Eugenie confided in the Walewskis: 'Do not suppose that I have not always been aware of this man's infidelities. I have tried everything,

I have even tried to make him jealous. It was vain, but now that he has sunk down to this *crapule*, I can stand it not longer.'[27] The sad truth was that she was not in a position to make him jealous. It was not that she was lacking in admirers – she had a troop of them, including Graf von der Goltz, the Prussian Ambassador, and they all adored her. She knew that they loved her and she returned the feeling with sisterly affection, respecting their confidences, caring for them when they were ill. But these admirers caused the Emperor no jealousy. Only if his wife had behaved with them as his mistresses behaved with him, would his temper have flared. That, physically and morally, was out of the question. There was much in common between Eugenie's case and that of Alexandra of Denmark, Princess of Wales. As Eugenie had her Goltz, so 'Alix' had her Oliver Montagu. Both women had to learn to withstand the insulting stares of their husband's mistresses. And the parallel extended to other spheres. Alexandra and Eugenie shared much – brilliant dress sense, love of horses, deep religious beliefs, concern with the sick and the needy, mistrust of Germany – two lovely women forced to surrender pride of place to lechery masquerading as 'amusement'.

The strain told on the Empress's health. She lost her appetite and could not sleep. She began to cough. When in the summer of 1864, she learned that Napoleon was taking Marguerite to stay at his creeper-clad villa at Vichy, she decided to follow her doctor's advice and seek a cure at a German spa. She took the waters at Schwalbach.[(a)] She travelled incognito as the Comtesse de Pierrefonds and was accompanied by only a small party of ladies and gentlemen. Within days her health improved.

She was great fun to travel with and, like Queen Victoria, she took the greatest interest in all that she saw. She laughed – at the food and a German attempt at *poulet rôti* which smelled so vile that it had to be rushed away – at the luck of one of her ladies who experimented with gambling at the Kurhaus at Wiesbaden, staked one louis and was handed thirty-six – at the spring which was said to contain the gift of eternal youth – at the night scare when a supposed attack by an intruder turned out to be one of her gentlemen shouting in a nightmare.[28]

Eugenie had looked forward to privacy while on her rest cure but

(a) In the Duchy of Nassau, then governed by Duke Adolphus of Nassau.

this was not to be. Early one morning the King William of Prussia arrived bearing a large bouquet of red roses. He stayed for the day. He was sixty-six and a ladies' man, and had been entertained at Compiègne. But his call was not altogether social – owing to Prussian aggression in the Duchies of Schleswig and Holstein, bordering Denmark, he wished to keep in the good books of the French. Next the Emperor Alexander II of Russia, who was staying at Darmstadt, paid a courtesy visit. And the Grand Duke of Baden, with his Napoleonic connection, insisted that she be his guest. Every time she moved, the train was decorated, the bands played, the crowds gathered.[29] It boosted her ego. She was a much stronger and more determined woman when she returned to Paris in October.

There Marguerite Bellanger was vaunting her power. It was not coincidence that, everytime Eugenie took an afternoon drive *à la daumont*, she was passed, and repassed, by the flashy carriage of her husband's mistress. It was both a defiance and a challenge. And the artificial marguerites decorating her hat left no doubt as to her identity.

The challenge was shortly to be taken up. Napoleon was brought back from Marguerite's house in Passy in a state of collapse and Eugenie knew that, if she did not act, France would lose her Emperor. She must face the woman. She whispered of her plan to Lord Cowley, who passed the news on to Lord Clarendon. The Ambassador's view was that he had never heard of such imprudence and put it down to 'Spanish blood and Spanish jealousy'.[30] Undeterred, Eugenie recruited the assistance of M. Mocquard, brother of the Emperor's secretary who had cared for Elizabeth Howard. She hired a cab and the two drove to 27, Rue des Vignes, Passy. Striding in, the Empress opened up with a burst of accusations. Marguerite, accustomed to coping with barracking in the theatre, gave back as good as she received. 'If he comes,' she said, 'it is because you bore him and annoy him.'[31]

The noise increased and proved altogether too much for the nerves of M. Mocquard. He stepped back, closed the door and retreated to a safe distance. Soon the clash of angry voices subsided. He waited a while. Curious, apprehensive of what had happened, he crept back along the passage. Cautiously he opened the door a few inches. There came to him the sound of laughter. Peeping into the room he saw the Empress and Marguerite Bellanger sitting beside one another on the sofa. They were chatting together as if they were old friends.[32] The

Empress arose, embraced Marguerite and took her leave, a suprised M. Mocquard trotting at her heels.

Thus ended the love affairs of Napoleon III. There were to be tales of other amorous adventures but they were insignificant. Eugenie knew well how to cope now. And as for Marguerite, she was well provided for. She had a château at Villeneuve-sous-Dammartin and property in Paris and Touraine. She married a Prussian named Kulbach.[33]

It was another Prussian who next claimed the attention of Napoleon and Eugenie.

Bismarck had become obsessed with the aggrandizement of Prussia. He wanted a unified Germany. But not the unified, liberal-minded state of which Prince Albert had dreamed; a state of culture and industry, of trade fairs and concerts and bands playing in the parks on Sunday afternoons. Bismarck was set on a German nation dominated by Prussia; a nation which would dominate first Europe, and then the world.

After two years in office, Bismarck wanted a war, not a full-blown affair but an exaggerated military exercise, in which he could let his troops taste of blood and victory, in which he could test new weapons, in which he could gain experience of the new and vital element in warfare – the railways. He decided to take over the Duchies of Schleswig and Holstein, buffer states between Germany and Denmark. In his crystal ball he saw the Kiel Canal, and great warships passing from North Sea to the Baltic. He enlisted the help of Austria, declared war on Denmark, and won an easy victory.

Bismarck now became a changed man, a point noted by foreign diplomats. The former attractive qualities disappeared. He strutted and he shouted. He lost respect for national leaders. With the might behind him, he had full confidence in his own cunning. Weakness and ill health became points to be exploited, lies became good statesmanship, to win became all.

This was the moment when Napoleon might have opposed Prussia and, if he had, he would have had the backing of Eugenie. But Napoleon was ill and his troops were scattered in Rome, Algiers and Mexico. He tried to retain his position as the arbiter of Europe through statesmanship not war, and he concentrated on driving a wedge between Prussia and Austria. To an extent he succeeded, but delay of the day of reckoning was his only prize. It was to Britain that he should have looked for the answer to the threat rising like a mist about him. But there Queen Victoria, who should have been talking face to face with the Emperor whom she had liked and understood so well, was sitting in the gloom listening to the sepulchral voice of Albert repeating on the well worn record that everything that Prussia did was right.

If the Queen and her Ministers had talked with the Emperor at this time, perhaps the German Empire would never have been born. Thirty years later Lord Rendel was chatting with Mr Gladstone:

Mr G. told me as a fact not enough known ... that the Third Napoleon had in 1864 missed an opportunity which, turned to account by France, would probably have altered the whole course of subsequent history. Lord Palmerston, without the consent of the Cabinet and without, indeed, any consultation with it, made, towards the end of the Session, in and through him, a statement that if Denmark chose to stand firm in the Augustenberg affair and resist the dictation of Germany, Denmark would not find itself alone. Denmark naturally interpreted this declaration as a pledge of British aid, and on finding it a broken reed greatly resented the betrayal. When it came to the point, it was clear that England could not undertake to protect Denmark single-handed against Prussia, Austria and the Bund, and so it was necessary at the last to throw over Palmerston and Denmark.

But meanwhile the Government made proposals to France for a joint assistance of Denmark, and undertook, if France would go in with England, to aid Denmark with all its force by sea and land. Napoleon was foolish enough to decline the proposition, on the ground that the interests involved for France were much inferior to those of England, which might look after its own affairs. So Denmark went to the wall, and the first aggressive steps in the series of movements by Prussia towards the creation of the German Empire and the reduction of French pretension was secured at a time when Louis Napoleon might easily have nipped the Bismarck programme in the bud.[34]

Bismarck appeared at Biarritz again in the autumn of 1865. Not for him, now, idle hours staring out to sea, forgetful of politics. He strode beside his host across the sands, talking, talking, talking, expounding on his dreams for Europe and how both could benefit. 'Is he mad?' Napoleon asked Mérimée. 'He keeps offering me things that are not his to give.' The Prussian was certainly not mad – he was just making certain that the Emperor would not interfere with his next military adventure.

The Seven Weeks War began in June 1866. Prussia, allied with Italy, attacked Austria, backed by the countries of Southern Germany. France, anti-Prussian in sentiment, remained neutral. Napoleon made a secret, last minute agreement with Austria regarding the ceding of Venetia, but insisted that he wished to keep his hands free. In the event he was in no position to wage war. Queen Victoria, awake now to the menace abroad in Prussia, had offered to mediate but received a rebuff from Bismarck, who accused her of meddling for 'selfish domestic reasons'.[35] This was apposite, for one of her sons-in-law, Crown Prince Frederick William, was commanding for the Prussians, another, Prince Louis of Hesse, married to Princess Alice, was commanding on the other side. Her cousin was King of Hanover and her brother-in-law, Duke Ernest of Coburg, backed the Austrians.

On the 16th Princess Marie of Battenberg wrote in her diary: 'A sad day, full of fear! News came the Prussians have occupied Hanover, Saxony, Kurhesse, Nassau and Oberhesse.'[36] Thus, in a most unexpected way, came the unification of Northern Germany. On 3rd July the blood-red name of Königgratz was written into history. For eight hours the two main armies, each nearly a quarter of a million strong, duelled for the mastery of Germany. When evening came to the village of Sadowa, the Austrians had suffered 45,000 casualties, the Prussians less than 10,000. The Needle Gun[a] had won the day and the slaughter was terrific.

It was not only the Austrians who were vanquished at Sadowa, but the French also. Napoleon had lost his power in Europe. His offers to mediate were brushed aside. Even King Victor Emmanuel ignored him now. He knew full well that, with his forces deployed and the feeling of the people against war, he could not face a show-down with Bismarck. He did not realise that, if he had quickly despatched a force to the scarcely guarded banks of the Rhine, the Southern States might well have joined with him and the Prussian forces been obliged to retreat

(a) A breech-loading rifle, invented by gunsmith Johann von Dreyse (1787–1867).

towards Berlin. Yet that fear hung heavily over Bismarck's head-quarters.

Eugenie saw this. She realised that, if a stand was not made now, the Prussian steam roller would flatten France and end both the Empire and the prospects of her son. The Minister for War told a Council at St Cloud on 5th July that '80,000 men could be concentrated on the Rhine immediately, and 250,000 in twenty days'.[37] Eugenie made eloquent appeal for the attack to start. Perhaps under her spell, Napoleon agreed to mobilisation plans, but overnight he changed his mind and the decisions were never published. To Austrian emissaries he kept repeating, 'I am not equipped for war.' Eugenie wrote to Prince Metternich, Austrian Ambassador to France: 'My word has no more weight. I am almost alone in my opinion. Today's danger is exaggerated the better to hide tomorrow's . . . . If you could give them a good drubbing!'[38]

The truth was that Napoleon, in his weakened health, could not absorb the shock of Sadowa. He had foreseen a long war, a war which would sap the strength of equally matched contestants, leaving him, at its conclusion, the power to be reckoned with. The Needle Gun had upset that dream. Eugenie noted that he was irresolute and exhausted, scarcely eating or sleeping. By the end of the month he was seriously ill. Eugenie contemplated taking over as Regent and told the Austrian Ambassador: 'We are moving towards our fall, and the best thing would be if the Emperor suddenly disappeared, at least for a time.'[39]

Certainly she was the power now and everywhere she travelled through France, to inspect hospitals and attend local celebrations, she was received with acclaim. She despatched her husband to his villa at Vichy and there, bedridden, it seemed that he was losing his grip on life. In September, however, he joined his wife and son at Biarritz and made a miraculous recovery. Playing on the sands with the boy and his dogs was the best medicine that he could have had.

That autumn, in London, Bismarck casually informed Disraeli that, had he known in July that Napoleon had only 140,000 men, he would have marched into France.

CHAPTER 17

The Princes

During the 1860's two princes were to afford Eugenie particular pleasure. Her son, the Prince Imperial, whose company at Biarritz had been such a tonic to the Emperor was one. The other was Prince Richard Metternich.

Richard Metternich was the son of the great Austrian Chancellor and he was thirty when he took over from Count Hübner as Ambassador to the Tuileries in 1859, the year in which his father died. He was broad and tall and handsome, with long, fair whiskers, and he dressed well. He was gallant with women and reticent with men.[1] He was a born musician and had the waltzes of Strauss and Lanner at his fingertips. Evenings at the Tuileries were often boring, but not when he sat down at the grand piano in the Salon d'Apollon.[2] He was also an enthusiast for charades and on wet afternoons when the Court was at Compiègne, he would say, 'What shall we do, or get up charades.'[3]

Richard, somewhat spoiled and indolent, was not in the same class as his father. He had no chance to be, for the role of Ambassador had changed radically in a short space of time. A quarter of a century earlier a country's representative had been cut off from his capital, communications being so slow that it was his responsibility to make instant decisions. By 1860 the electric telegraph clicked and expresses ran through the night. But Richard's star shone brightly on account of his relationship with the Empress.

With her sympathies ranged on the side of Austria, Eugenie found in the Austrian Ambassador a perfect foil and a very necessary safety valve. Through the tense years of the 1860s she would run to him 'rather to discharge the electricity of an amazing mind than to seek his prudent counsel'.[4] Their letters to one another, and their numerous and outspoken conversations, 'form one of the most bizarre and fascinating chapters of European diplomatic history'.[5] Napoleon did not mind – he was only too happy that his wife's electrical discharge should earth elsewhere. In any case, through the liaison, information came to him which might otherwise have been withheld. Although Eugenie treated Prince Richard shamefully, on one occasion hunting him out of bed in the early hours to urge him to take action on some point which worried her,[6] the two were close friends. It was fitting that, as the curtain fell dramatically on her years as active Empress, it was his solid form and his steady eyes which gave her comfort.

Richard's wife, Pauline, was eight years his junior and she was his niece, a relationship which did not upset their family life. Opinions upon her were sharply divided. Some liked her and some did not, but all admitted that she was dynamic, *une grande dame* and had exquisite taste in dress. According to fancy, she was known as '*Notre Dame de Vienne*' or '*La Reine Peste*'. A man who knew her well thus described her:

> She was hideously ugly – yellow skin, pop eyes, thick lips (she called herself the '*Singe à la Mode*', and the name was appropriate and stuck to her), looking somewhat like a white 'Topsy' – but very clever and with the audacity of Old Nick himself. She had, like the Empress, that really rare gift of the '*sentiment de la toilette*' to a degree approaching genius, and could wear the most amazing dresses . . . It was she who discovered, at Gagelins in the Rue de Richelieu, that young Englishman from Lincolnshire, Worth, took him up and made his fortune . . . She sent for Theresa[(a)] to teach her how to sing her songs, '*La Femme à Barbe*' and the rest, and use the vile gestures that she, Theresa, used and eventually did the whole thing better than Theresa. She did, in fact, all kinds of funny things that would have hopelessly polluted most women, but Pauline Metternich – yellow skin, pop eyes and all – remained always and for ever and through it all *grande dame quand même*.[7]

Pauline's father was Count Moritz Sandor, a famous Hungarian horseman who had so many falls on his head that in old age he became mentally unbalanced. Her mother was her husband's sister. Pauline had endless physical energy and could not tolerate doing nothing or being bored. Thus she was a much better Ambassadress at times of crisis and adversity than when international affairs were settled and peaceful. Life at the Tuileries was monotonous; as one of the ladies-in-waiting said, 'We dress, we chatter, we undress'. Eugenie's ladies were not

(a) A great music-hall star, the Marie Lloyd of Paris.

inspiring and she needed someone in the social round to lead and stimulate. Pauline filled the bill exactly.

One night Eugenie and Pauline both dressed up as men and went for a ride round Paris on the top of a horse bus. Pauline designed a dress for Eugenie which necessitated the wearing of tights, but Napoleon discovered this in time.[8] She, and Worth, however, did persuade Eugenie to abandon the crinoline.[9] When asked how she dared to be so familiar with the Empress, Pauline replied that she was not a real Empress, like Elizabeth in Vienna. When Eugenie's young son, the Prince Imperial, was being petulant and troublesome, she smacked his face, a traumatic experience which he never forgot.[10] One evening, bored stiff, she ordered a bowl of flour to be brought in. Placing one of her rings on top, she induced the company to attempt to pick it up with their lips without getting flour on the tips of their noses.[11]

She drank and she smoked cigars. She showed her legs and she made outrageous remarks. At a diplomatic party she said loudly to a friend whom she passed on the stairs, 'Don't go in there. It stinks of Excellencies.' When she was old and saw the foxtrot being danced, she remarked: 'When I was young we used to do that sort of thing in bed.'[12]

Pauline was the only woman around the Court who could compete with Eugenie in physical exercise. At Biarritz long walks and rides were the order of the day, and Eugenie would swim in any weather. Under such strain her suite and guests soon wilted. She decided that, for a change, she would take them out in her small yacht, the *Seagull*. Pauline asked her: 'Might that prove even more trying for them?' Eugenie was surprised that anyone should be upset by the sea and the innocents piled aboard in their best holiday regalia. A storm blew up and soon she was the only one standing. Unperturbed, she handed round basins to prostrate figures. It was after two in the morning before the *Seagull* could land them at Biarritz. Only then was the Empress frightened, for there stood Napoleon, and he dressed her down good and proper as white faced, desolate figures crept ashore.[13]

The other prince in Eugenie's life, her son, was a delightful boy. He inherited the best traits in the characters of his father and his mother. If he was spoiled, what else could be the fate of an only child upon whom so much depended.

He had deep blue eyes and bright brown hair. He was known as

Loulou. It was by this name that Napoleon spoke of him about the Palace, while Eugenie used the more formal, the Prince Imperial. Napoleon had been accustomed to having boys around him – his two sons by *la Belle Sabotière* and Elizabeth Howard's son by Major Martin. Starved of marital love, he craved for the love of Loulou. Eugenie, on the other hand, was totally inexperienced with children. She therefore looked back to the days of her own childhood for guidance and recalled her hard and adventurous times with Don Cipriano, when she and Paca had followed him, bare-back, on their ponies across the Spanish countryside. She perceived the boy's destiny more clearly than her husband, and was haunted by the knowledge that no heir born to the throne of France had lived to ascend it since the days of Louis XIV.

When Loulou was old enough to respond and have reactions, it was noticed that there was a permanent look of boredom and lethargy in his eyes. A doctor gave his opinion that the child was bored stiff, that his days were so ordered that there was no light and shade, no fun and no difficulties. If he felt like a drink, one appeared. If he wanted to use the chamber pot, it was immediately produced. Every moment of his life was ordered and there were no babyhood excitements. Eugenie did her best to correct this. From the age of two, if he fell, he was left to get up by himself. If he lost his ball, he was told to find it. French mothers considered this to be inhuman.

Miss Shaw, the large and smiling head nurse who had been recommended by Queen Victoria, was the cornerstone in his life. She spoke a curious mixture of French and English and resisted furiously all attempts by indigenous helpers – aristocratic governesses, under-nurses, teachers and physical training instructors – to usurp one iota of her power.[14] She slept in an alcove in the Prince's room. She was the ultimate authority on everything. She paid little attention to the remedies and diets recommended by the doctors. If her charge was off colour, she fed him on fried bacon.

Loulou began his riding lessons at the age of six months, being tied to a safety saddle. His mount was Balmoral, a Shetland pony presented by Queen Victoria.[15] He progressed to a larger and more lively animal named Bouton d'Or.[16] When riding at St Cloud, the Empress came across her four year old son being led on Bouton, escorted by Miss Shaw and others. Outraged at the sight of such mollycoddling, she hit the pony across the rump with her whip, whereat Bouton accelerated away, pursued by grooms. 'Oh, Your Majesty,' said Miss Shaw firmly, 'you should not have done that. You have only *one*, you know.'[17]

Loulou adored dogs. He had a large one called Nero, who was most possessive. In the evenings, when he came downstairs to see his parents, the boy sat with his books on a sofa and it was the custom of the dog to jump up beside him and go to sleep. One evening Napoleon was too quick for the dog and occupied the chosen place beside his son, explaining something in the book. Nero jumped over the back of the sofa and sat, bolt upright, between the two. Then, very carefully, he began to push and twist, enlarging the space between father and son. When the Emperor was nearing the sofa's end, the dog curled up and went to sleep.[18] A visitor from England regarded the imperial defeat with amazement.

The creed which was drilled into the Prince from the moment he could speak was that a Napoleon was never afraid, that bravery was everything. When a doctor carried out a minor operation, and Loulou winced, the doctor asked, 'Did I hurt you?' 'No,' was the reply. 'But you startled me.' It was the sea that upset the record of heroism. When he was still very young, Loulou, according to the rough custom of the time, was thrown head first into the waves at Biarritz. The noise on his re-emergence was horrific and he was captured after a wild burst of speed towards the hinterland. At last some sort of order was restored and his mother enquired why, if he was not frightened of cannon fire, he was frightened of the summer sea. Teeth still chattering like castanets Loulou considered the problem for a time and then announced; 'I am in command of the soldiers, but I am not in command of the sea.' He was never known to show fear again.[19]

To the Prince, from the beginning, the army was everything. As a baby, he did not wave to those he recognised from his pram, but treated them to a military salute. In 1860 he was incorporated among *les enfants de troupe* of the Grenadiers of the Guard. That same year he gave the toast at a regimental dinner and, mounted on Bouton d'Or, followed his father at military reviews. Then drilling began and he learned the goose-step, bayonet exercise and fencing. He was exceedingly proud of his uniform and wore it whenever he was allowed. He carried the rank of corporal and the badges of that rank appeared on his tunic. It was soon discovered that by far the most effective means of inflicting punishment upon him was to deprive him of those badges of rank. On the occasions when his epaulettes were unsewn, he cried, and only then. The news that he had been reduced to the ranks for cheeking his mother reached the Press and Private Napoleon shuffled very self-consciously around the Bois de Boulogne.[20]

His cross was loneliness, the lot of the only child. His parents did all they could to offset this and companions came to the Palace to share his lessons and his games, chief among them being Louis Conneau, the Doctor's son, and the sons of Generals Fleury and Espinasse.[21] But in the evening they returned to their homes, leaving loneliness behind them. Although Napoleon and Eugenie avoided the mistake of Albert and Victoria, who isolated their children from others, at Buckingham Palace there were no less than nine occupants of the nurseries and schoolrooms, and there was always someone to confide in and whisper to. Loulou had only Miss Shaw. The visitor to Compiègne today will be shown a delicate table scarred by the cuts of a penknife. Across the polished surface can be discerned the signature of the Prince Imperial. One wet afternoon when there was no one to play with he had relieved his boredom by carving his name.

To counter the emptiness of his evenings, Napoleon and Eugenie allowed the boy to stay up much longer than was advisable. He would wander about among the guests at the Tuileries, joining in their conversation, or, ignoring them, play at being his hero, the Great Napoleon, a footstool for a horse. His father who, as he grew older, preferred to be quiet, put up with the racket without a word of admonition. 'It is impossible to bring the boy up properly,' complained his mother.[22] She did her best. A visitor brought Loulou a vast box of chocolates. She told him to hand them round to the company before sampling one himself. But temptation overcame him and half way round the circuit he popped one into his mouth. In a moment she had him by the back of the neck and extracted it from his mouth.

It would have been best for him to go to school, like his father. But there were difficulties in the way of this. As the heir to the Empire, he was in a unique position. Republican feeling was growing in France and he might have been subjected to unpleasant experiences. Moreover, though he excelled in sculpture and drawing, he was backward in most subjects, and it was not fitting for a Napoleon to be anything but first. Then there was his health to consider. He was slight and prone to ills, as indeed his father had been. When he was nine he contracted measles. During convalescence he caught a chill and complete collapse followed. It was several months before he fully recovered.

The following year, while showing off in front of his mother on the trapeze, hanging by his feet, he fell and hurt his hip. An abscess developed and a serious operation was necessary. His only worry was that he would have a scar on his back. People might think that he had been wounded while running away from the field of battle.[23]

The illness of the Prince Imperial caused endless rumours to spread throughout France, rumours which were eagerly seized upon by those who wished the Empire to give place to a Republic. He was said to suffer from every disease which had ever appeared in a reigning house, from scrofula to haemophilia. He was degenerate, the stories ran, and would never be fitted to reign. Fortunately the boy was protected from such malicious gossip.

There was, however, one shadow in his young life, that of Prince Napoleon. The unpleasant Plon-Plon never recovered from the shock of being ousted from the heirdom to the Empire and could hardly be persuaded even to attend the baptism. When he so far unbent as to take the baby on his knee, he saw that the Empress and Miss Shaw were watching him anxiously. 'Do you think that I am going to give him arsenic?' he asked. He always referred to the Prince as 'that poor little brat' and when he became ill, remarked, 'What did I tell you?'

Loulou was given orders to be most polite to his cousin. On an occasion when the two found themselves alone on their way through the Tuileries to the dining *salon*, he stepped back and gave way to the elder Prince at the first doorway. Plon-Plon snapped out, '*Passez*'. At the second he tried again to give way, only to be told gruffly, '*Passez donc*'. At the third attempt, at the entrance to the *salon*, he received a hearty push which sent him spinning and sliding across the polished floor. As the dinner guests stared in amazement, Loulou, white faced, recovered his balance, ran to his father's side and held his hand.[24]

Being so much with his parents, the Prince Imperial came to know them very well, their weaknesses and their strengths. His father was more like a kindly elder brother – they would scheme together how to outwit the tutors and avoid a lesson. Loulou soon learned that his mother's bark was worse than her bite. Her concern when he was ill was indicative of the deep, all-enveloping love which she held for him.

171

When she had evening engagements, she would always come to see him at work on his 'prep' before leaving. She would drift into his room, a vision of loveliness, the lamp light sparkling on her jewels, her wide skirt rustling, her scent wafting about him. 'Good night, Louis darling,' she would say and kiss him. 'Do not get up.' As soon as he was old enough to wear long breeches, she had dropped Loulou for Louis.

One day he showed her that he had her measure and left her speechless. It was Loulou's delight to escape from the eagle eyes of Miss Shaw and his tutors and play with the children of the soldiers stationed for guard duty at the Tuileries and St Cloud. From them he picked up expressions seldom uttered in Palace corridors. Eugenie heard him use an epithet common among the military, and reprimanded him. 'Mama,' he replied, 'you speak French very well, but you are a foreigner and do not know the finer points of the language.'[25]

He played his ace of pranks on the occasion of the visit of Archduke Maximilian of Austria and his wife, Charlotte, in March 1864. It was an event of importance, for the future of Mexico hung in the balance. The Emperor and the Empress and a concourse of Ministers and notables awaited their arrival at the Tuileries.

Now Loulou had a donkey, a particular friend and a companion for his ponies. Not being included in the official reception committee, he waited, astride the donkey, out of sight round a corner in the courtyard. The carriages arrived, the guests stepped down. As they made their way towards the entrance and their advancing host and hostess, Loulou moved out in front of them, riding his donkey up the steps.

Miss Shaw, who had been invited to watch the reception, screamed. Prosper Mérimée and the Emperor went into the attack, attempting to grasp the boy. The donkey, taking exception to this onslaught, increased his speed upwards. The two men collided and fell. On went the donkey, Loulou, triumphant, still upon its back. Reaching the summit it trotted off out of sight down a corridor, the Archduke, in fits of laughter, in pursuit.—

Everyone was talking, gesticulating. The Empress comforted the disconsolate Miss Shaw. Napoleon and Mérimée picked themselves up and tidied their clothes. Then, at the head of the staircase appeared the donkey, led by Loulou with the Archduke riding. Grinning widely, Maximilian dismounted and an attempt at reception procedure began.

Loulou pulled long strings of spaghetti from his inside pocket and began to feed the donkey. Oblivious of the excitement, the donkey munched fast. 'I hope,' said the Emperor to his son, 'that you have left some for our lunch.'[26]

CHAPTER 18

The Poisoned Cup

A young married couple, of particular interest to Napoleon and Eugenie during the 1860's were the Archduke Maximilian and the Archduchess Charlotte of Austria, who became the Emperor and Empress of Mexico and whom we have just met in the encounter with the Prince Imperial and the donkey.

They were to suffer a tragic fate and their tragedy was a political disaster for Napoleon and Eugenie. Maximilian was the younger brother of Emperor Francis Joseph of Austria. Some said that he was the son of Napoleon II and there was certainly much in common with that son of the first Emperor, who died so young. Queen Victoria, who was quick to spot the weaknesses in a man, noted the lack of firmness in his mouth and chin.[1]

In 1857 Maximilian had married Charlotte of Belgium. Her father was King Leopold, uncle of Queen Victoria, and a Coburg. Her mother, Queen Louise, was a daughter of wily King Louis Philippe. The mixture provided a spirited and ambitious young lady well endowed with business acumen.

In 1859 Maximilian was approached by Mexican exiles with the suggestion that he should be a candidate for Emperor of their homeland. Mexico was certainly in need of stable control and at the end of 1861 England, France and Spain sent a joint expedition there to settle grievances, to secure the interest on bonds which the Government had suspended, and to ensure better treatment for their nationals.

By the spring of 1862 England and Spain had obtained the guarantees which they required and their forces sailed for home.

But the French, having made exaggerated demands for recompense, stayed on. It was clear that Napoleon had other objects in view. Although basically interested in finance and raw materials, he was once again chasing a nationalistic ideal, while Eugenie had the romantic dream of building a Catholic Empire in the Western World and thus gaining the approbation o the Pope. So began the fiasco of building an

Empire thousands of miles away, on the frail foundations of a divided people whose problems were little understood. After a defeat at Puebla, which upset feelings at home, Napoleon sent out an expeditionary force of 30,000 men, and this at a time when Bismarck was rattling the sword in Berlin.

In October 1863 Maximilian was offered the throne of Mexico. Owing to the necessity of renouncing his imperial rights in Austria, he was chary of accepting. But his ambitious wife had visions of the glories of the House of Habsburg and, in her shrewdness, made provisions which she deemed would guarantee their future. It was soon after the visit to Napoleon, Eugenie and the Prince Imperial at Tuileries, in March 1864, that the decision was taken and in June the new Emperor and Empress entered Mexico City.

Both Napoleon and Charlotte had misjudged the leadership qualities of Maximilian. His primary concern was with the importance of being a Habsburg and with being accorded the correct Court procedure. He was widely extravagant. His modern thinking was unwanted. Poor judgment and vacillation marred his rule from the start. He upset conservatives, liberals and clericals.

With the aid of the French troops he reduced Mexico to subjection, but he was entirely dependent on Napoleon and was at loggerheads with his military commanders. In December 1865 the United States, having settled their Civil War, demanded that the French troops in Mexico be withdrawn, and the hard-pressed Emperor had no choice but to accede. Whereupon the republicans set about a campaign of reconquest. Maximilian despatched his wife to Europe to implore help from Napoleon and the Pope.

It was on 8th August 1866 – a date which she was ever to remember – that Eugenie received a telegram announcing that Charlotte had landed at St Nazaire.[2] The previous day Napoleon had returned from Vichy and he was so sick, dejected and shocked by the battle of Sadowa that she had put him straight to bed. Bismarck was threatening invasion, her husband was of little support and she dreaded the thought of coping with the irate and desperate Empress of Mexico.

Charlotte put up at the Grand Hotel. There, on the afternoon of the 10th, Eugenie called upon her. She found a woman very different from the one she had entertained only two years before. She did all that she could to keep the conversation on a casual basis, but Charlotte would not have it. Dressed in mourning black,[3] pale of face, she demanded to see the Emperor. Eugenie explained that he was unwell. Charlotte had no intention of being robbed of the audience which she had travelled so far to seek. If she was refused, she said, *'Je ferai irruption dans son cabinet.'*[4] Next day she drove to St Cloud.

Again Eugenie tried to smooth the troubled waters. She arranged that the Prince Imperial, wearing the chain of the Mexican Order of the Eagle, should meet her carriage, resurrecting the memory of the adventure with the donkey. The boy took her by the hand, led her up the steps and into the presence of the Emperor. But there was no escape. For two hours Charlotte 'argued, entreated, supplicated, shed tears of anguish, and finally burst out into imprecations.'[5] She waved one of Napoleon's letters in his face – *'Vous pouvez être sûr que mon appui ne vous manquera jamais . . . dans l'accomplissement de votre tâche.'*[6] The Emperor looked towards his wife for support and tears ran down his cheeks. All he could say was that France could not spare another man or another sou.

Charlotte was attended by two Mexican ladies of honour – 'very ugly, black, short and ungraceful'. One of them asked that a glass of sherbert should be sent into the Mexican Empress, as she was accustomed to taking one at this hour. The drink was accordingly produced. But Charlotte looked at it with surprise and suspicion and was with difficulty persuaded to drink it.[7] The fear that she was being poisoned lurked in her mind.

An interview with the Ministers for Finance and War, Fould and Randon, followed. Charlotte did not mince her words. 'Whose are the pockets', she cried, 'which are being filled with gold to Mexico's hurt?'[8] She made the accusation that there had been a conspiracy in Paris to ruin her husband. This was too much for Fould, who lost his temper. As Empress and Minister railed at one another, Eugenie staged a diversion. She broke into floods of tears and then pretended to faint.

Napoleon realised that, ill or not, he must settle the matter. On the 13th he called upon Charlotte at the Grand Hotel. He told her that she must not indulge in illusions. She snapped back: 'Your Majesty is directly concerned in this affair and should also not indulge in any.'[9] He kissed her hand and, as he bowed himself out, he told her that a special train had been arranged to take her to the French frontier on her way to Italy. Charlotte sat down and wrote to her husband: 'I have thundered at them and torn off their masks. Nothing so unpleasant has happened to them in their lives.'[10]

After a stay at her husband's castle of Miramar near Trieste, at the end of September Charlotte travelled to Rome. On the morning of the 27th she had audience of the Pope. After learning that he could do nothing for her, and in any case disapproved of Maximilian's liberal measures, her mind gave way and the obsession that she was being poisoned overcame her. She would not eat and her only drinks came from public fountains, by scooping water up in her hand. Next day she returned to the Vatican. Her eyes were wild and her clothes in disarray. She forced her way through to the Pope's quarters, her heart-rending screams overcoming those who tried to stop her. All Pius's efforts to calm her proved in vain. She cried out that she was being poisoned and that he must arrest her suite. She refused to leave the precincts and in the evening a bed was made up for her in the library. Still she would not eat.

In an attempt to divert her attention, the Mother Superior of the Convent of St Vincent persuaded her to visit a children's orphanage. There, in the kitchen, she saw a stew cooking on the stove. Crazed with hunger, she plunged in her hand and seized a piece of meat. She suffered severe burns and fainted and the opportunity was seized upon to return her to her hotel. She recovered consciousness on the way and was carried, kicking and screaming, to her room. Thereafter she was escorted back to Miramar.[11]

On 16th October Queen Victoria wrote to her daughter in Berlin: '. . . What can have given rise to all this? It is said that she is afraid of being poisoned, that she went unannounced to the Pope and ate her dinner dipping her bread into his soup plate, that she insisted on sleeping in the Vatican. That at Miramar she ran furiously up and down the garden, that men keepers had to be fetched out of a lunatic asylum to take care of her . . .'[12]

What indeed? Charlotte was only twenty-six and it seems strange that a woman of that age, known to be strong minded, should collapse completely. She had been just two years in Mexico and there met little but unfriendliness. There were thwarted ambitions, certainly, but she was young. As for fears of her husband's safety, it was in his power to withdraw, a step which was being urged upon him. As for the future, he, as the brother of the Emperor of Austria, and she, as the daughter of the King of the Belgians and an heiress, would have had to face no hardships.

The possibility, indeed the probability, exists, that Charlotte was correct in her belief that she was being poisoned and that small quantities of loco weed[a] were being added to her drinks. Her behaviour was indicative that this was so.

Charlotte slipped into the mental twilight which was to last sixty years until her death at the Château de Bouchout, near Brussels, in 1927. She was never to see her husband again.

(a) Loco, or Crazy, weeds, species of *Astragalus* and *Oxytropis*, are found in the arid plains from Canada to Mexico. Loco is from the Spanish, meaning crazy. Symptoms produced by consumption of the weed are those of a disordered nervous system.

CHAPTER 19

Vanity Fair

As in a sandwich, between the decline and actual fall of his Empire, Napoleon provided, both for history and for the people of his times, the justification of his work and of his struggles. It was the Paris Exhibition of 1867. It was superb. It was indeed a World's Fair. Here was an assertion of France's hegemony in the arts and sciences, industry and commerce, armaments and medicine, and the bright light reflected on to the small and weakening figure of Emperor Napoleon III. It was his answer.

There were 52,000 exhibitors and visitors could stare at scenes as diverse as a model of a Siamese elephant, Krupp's Great Gun, a truck for 'Conveying Lengthy Goods on Railways with Sharp Curves', a 'Speculum for Obtaining a View of the Larynx' and a machine which, when fed with rabbit skins, turned out felt hats ready for wear. A replica of the interior of the Palace of the Bay of Tunis became a mecca for the curious. There were fashion displays from India and Japan and there were queues to sample the restful movement of a patent rocking chair from the United States. Refreshments were available at Chinese, Spanish and Swedish cafés.[1] Tourists by their thousands came from America and the cross-Channel packets from Dover were heavily booked. So great was the interest in Britain that the *Illustrated London News* carried weekly descriptive supplements for circulation to schools and universities. For many of the visitors it was their first sight of the wide boulevards which had been created by Baron Haussmann. He had also been behind the planning for the Exhibition and its opening was his finest hour.

Invitations were despatched to no less than eighty Sovereigns, Rulers and leading Royalties. Only Queen Victoria and the Pope declined. Napoleon met all these guests at the railway station, their arrivals being staggered throughout the summer months. 'The season,' wrote Prosper Mérimée, 'is prolific in princes and arch-dukes.' The crowds flocked to see the Tsar Alexander of Russia, the Sultan of Turkey, the Khedive of Egypt and the brother of the Mikado of Japan. Kings and Queens were commonplace and grand-dukes two a franc.

Queen Victoria was not enthusiastic about the Paris jamboree. Firstly, it took her mind back to Prince Albert's Great Exhibition of 1851, and she would have no comparisons with that. Secondly, it smacked of gaiety and licentiousness and she was in no mood for frolics. Thirdly, some of the visiting potentates had travelled long distances and wished to take the opportunity of meeting the Queen of England. She dreaded the thought of such invasions, saying that she was too unwell and lonely, and in any case could not afford to entertain. She detailed the Prince of Wales to represent her at the Exhibition but gave him strict orders that he must return at once if any Eastern gentlemen – Oriental Brothers, she called them – headed towards Windsor.

Forty-eight now, putting on weight, with a complexion spoiled by lack of attention, a permanent mask of misery on her down-turned face, dowdy in her drab coloured skirts and widow's cap, she indeed bore little resemblance to Britannia. But, mindful of her manners, she could not ignore the invitation of the Emperor and Empress and accordingly asked them to visit her at Osborne. Napoleon declined, on the grounds of his many engagements, but Eugenie slipped over on the *Reine Hortense* for two days.

Seven years had passed since the two women had met. In 1860 it had been Eugenie who was sad, grieving over her sister's death and her husband's infidelities. Now it was Victoria who moped. And there were so many subjects which had to be avoided or only touched upon with care – Mexico, the Pope, Prussian aims and the personal behaviour of Napoleon.

The visit began badly. As the Queen, her family and Household waited to receive the Empress at the front door, she alighted at a side door and came upon the party from the rear. 'You can imagine our horror from highest to lowest,' commented the Queen. This was certainly no way to greet the wife of a reigning sovereign. The excitements in the programme prepared by the Queen for the following day were a morning visit to the Church of St Mildred's and an afternoon drive to the Swiss Cottage and Newport. The only light relief for Eugenie came when a piper marched round the table at lunch and dinner.[2] After the guest had departed next morning, the Queen wrote in her diary: 'Great relief that the visit was over.'[3]

Eugenie went back to the bright lights which twinkled nightly in Paris until the early hours. It was all dancing, love, laughter and fat cigars. Haussmann gave a ball at the Hôtel de Ville for eight thousand guests, and the bill was £30,000.[4] The Empress gave one at Versailles. The Metternichs roofed over their garden and invited the élite. There, that night, a tune was played in Paris for the first time. It was called *The Blue Danube* and Strauss himself conducted.[5] The dance floor was empty, for every one was so entranced that they could do nothing but listen. At the theatres it was Offenbach all the way. His stars, Theresa and Hortense Schneider, were the toasts of Paris. The Khedive of Egypt fell desperately in love with Hortense.[6]

Yet such a scene was set for drama, with Paris choc-a-block with Heads of State and the vast crowds giving cover for malcontents. The explosion, which many feared, came on 6th June.

It was the day of the great review at Longchamps, when 30,000 picked French troops paraded before the Tsar of Russia and the King of Prussia.

It was the last pageant of the Empire, and it passed with a gleam of helmets and the flicker of sunlight on fixed bayonets. The shakoes of the infantry went by and the green *Chasseurs* and the great drum-majors and the little *vivandières* in their bright petticoats. There was a great stream of red and blue as the Zouaves swung past, and then the cavalry went jingling by – the *Guides* in green and gold, the Lancers in their *schapskas* with a flutter of pennons, and the tall helmets of the heavy cavalry . . .[7]

On the way back Napoleon drove in a carriage with Tsar Alexander. Eugenie followed in another with King William. A Polish exile forced his way through the crowd and fired at the Russian Emperor. The leader of the escort saw the man take aim. He dashed forward and the bullet killed his horse. Napoleon stood up and assured those around him that no one had been hurt. Then, turning to Tsar Alexander, he embraced him and said, 'Now we have been under fire together.'[8]

That night Eugenie, white as ivory, stood beside Tsar Alexander at a ball. Thereafter, she would not leave him, riding beside him in his carriage. It was said that it was her administrations which persuaded the Russians not to return home immediately.[9] Tsar Alexander was not only politically the most important guest in Paris that summer, he was also a financial asset, for he spent no less than three million francs at the Exhibition.[10]

Drama came also to the greatest day of the Exhibition, the distribution of prizes in the *Palais de l'Industrie* in the Champs Elysées on 1st July. During the early hours Napoleon and Eugenie were awakened by a messenger from the Foreign Office. A cypher message had come in containing the news that the Emperor Maximilian of Mexico had been executed at Querétaro by the Mexican republican army.

The decision had to be made – should the prize-giving be cancelled? Napoleon decided to take the risk that the news was false and ordered that the show should go on. Eugenie rose early and, dressed all in black, went to the church of St Roch to pray.[11]

The long procession left the Tuileries, the Emperor and Empress riding in the red and gold glass coach which had carried them on their wedding day. At the *Palais de l'Industrie* 20,000 people were waiting and, as the Imperial party entered and took their seats on the dais, an orchestra of 1,200 struck up a hymn by Rossini.[12] Before the hymn was over an equerry stepped on to the dais and handed a message to the Emperor. Inscrutable as always, he wrote a few lines on the message and handed it back. The equerry made his way to the Austrian Ambassador, whereat Prince and Princess Metternich and their staff withdrew. The message confirmed that Emperor Maximilian had been shot and the news had appeared in the Belgian press.

The sun beat down on the roof of the Palais and the heat within was almost unbearable. The glare from the mirrors, the uniforms and the jewels was brilliant enough to hurt the eyes. One by one the prize winners stepped up the dais to receive their ribbons – 900 medals in all were distributed, of which Britain received 88 gold and 325 silver.[13] Eugenie swayed under the ordeal. Once back at the Tuileries, she fell to the floor in a faint.

The Exhibition churned on, the balloons went up, the bands played, the fireworks cracked, for the crowds were bent on enjoying themselves and were little concerned about a tragedy in far off Mexico. Spotting personalities was the game of the day and none was more sought after than Bismarck. He, with General von Moltke, had arrived in attendance upon the King of Prussia – in theory, that was, for in practice the two soldiers were sizing up the French troops, the French defences and the French arms. For them, the music of the Exhibition was the overture to war.

It is difficult to understand why Paris made such a fuss of Bismarck. Since Sadowa he had been a threat to the security of France and he had the reputation of being an ogre. Certainly a glimpse of the Junker colossus, clad in the white uniform of the Cuirassiers of the Guard,[14] his long sword clanking, the wide eagle on his helmet, was enough to provide a memento of the Exhibition. Yet there was more to it than that. There were cries of '*Vive Bismarck*' as he drove along the streets. When this was pointed out to him, he replied: 'Oh, no. They only shouted "*V'là Bismarck*". I heard them perfectly. But still I was flattered.'[15] Perhaps some people thought that, if they were kind to him, he would come to love France. Certainly he showed signs of friendliness. He sauntered along the boulevards, stopping at a pavement café for a drink. He made calls on all the right people. He went frequently to the Variétées, to admire Hortense and to guffaw at the Offenbach wit.[16]

The couturiers and manufacturers of fabrics were quick to climb on to the Bismarck bandwaggon. They gave him a colour – brown – and it became a vogue which lasted until long after the Prussians had returned to Berlin. It began as a plain Havannah brown, known simply as 'Bismarck'. It became darker, *Bismarck malade*, and then switched to lighter tints, *Bismarck content* and *Bismarck en colère*, and reached its peak with *Bismarck glacé* and *Bismarck scintillant*. 'And it was Bismarck of one shade or another everywhere; there were Bismarck silks, satins and velvets, woollen stuffs and cotton fabrics, Bismarck boots, Bismarck gloves, Bismarck parasols, and Bismarck bonnets.'[17] The bonnets were, of course, made of Bismarck straw and trimmed with Bismarck lace. The end of the nonsense came with the Bismarck chignon, compelling ladies to have their hair dyed to the Bismarck tint in fashion at the moment.

When the spate of visiting royalties subsided in August, Napoleon and Eugenie arranged to visit Emperor Francis Joseph and Empress Elizabeth of Austria. Owing to the death of his brother, Maximilian, Francis Joseph had cancelled his trip to the Paris Exhibition, but Napoleon dearly wished him to see it before it closed in October. The two Emperors had not met since the day that they had made peace at

Villafranca after the battles of Magenta and Solferino. There were
subjects for conversation which called for tactful handling, not least the
withdrawal of French support for Maximilian. Yet the future held a
common threat which must override disagreements and tragedies of
the past. That threat was Prussia.

For Parisian society the interest in the visit lay in the question of how
Empress Elizabeth would get on with Empress Eugenie. It was thought
that there would be a clash between the 'real' Empress, daughter of the
royal house of Wittelsbach of Bavaria who did not appreciate being an
Empress, and the 'parvenu' Empress, who most certainly did. As for
Eugenie, she dreaded the meeting. She told Prince Metternich: 'It
will be the most painful thing in the world, to find myself face to face
with a brother and a mother[a] to whose grief I have contributed by my
insistence upon the expedition to Mexico. If I had already known the
Emperor, the Empress, and the Archduchess Sophie, I should long since
have thrown myself into their arms to show what I feel, though that
they can hardly doubt. But since I do not know them, I am afraid that
I may seem too cold or too tragic.'[18]

The Imperial train travelled through Bavaria and reached Salzburg
on the afternoon of the 18th. Owing to Court mourning for Maximilian, there was little display but great fires were burning on the peaks
all around.[19] Napoleon was at his most tactful and it was soon clear that
he and his host were on the best of terms. The wives were even more
so, an unexpected turn of events as Elizabeth had only with difficulty
been persuaded to appear. Yet the two women had much in common.
They both loved horses. As a child, Elizabeth's eccentric father had
taken her on riding expeditions, visiting the peasants in their huts and
living rough, in the same manner as Don Cipriano had hardened his
two daughters in the countryside around Madrid. Another common
ground was that both had sexual problems with their husbands.
Standing side by side, they made a picture of beauty which men were
long to remember. Yet in one physical feature the French Empress
outshone the Austrian – the hands. Eugenie's were slender and white
and beautifully formed. Elizabeth's were long, the tips of her fingers
were flat and her nails were ugly. The difference pointed to contrast in
character.[20]

(a) Archduchess Sophie, mother of Emperor Maximilian.

On the 23rd the visit ended, Emperor Francis Joseph promising that he would visit the Exhibition before it closed. This in due course he did, though Elizabeth, by then pregnant, excused herself.

From her seculsion at Balmoral Queen Victoria noted the perambulations, visitations and receptions of the French couple with interest and perhaps a touch of envy. It was she who had made them respectable on the European scene and yet she alone among the Sovereigns had received no plaudits from the Exhibition stage. Even the weak King of Spain had received a bigger press than her representative, the Prince of Wales.

The Queen had her problems. Six years had passed since the death of Albert and the agony of her sorrow had eased, although she still feared facing public occasions without him. During the first three years of widowhood she had plagued her married daughters to spend more time with her. In self-defence, they had arranged for her favourite ghillie, John Brown, to be in permanent attendance upon her. Thereafter the position was reversed and the daughters found difficulty in obtaining invitations to visit Windsor and Osborne.

In her loneliness the Queen had developed the power of 'oneness', as Sir Henry Ponsonby, her private secretary, called it. Plainly, that meant making herself felt to the exclusion of all others. She was already an expert in 'one-upmanship'. Combining the two qualities, she decided to make impact upon the Continent of Europe, and France in particular. The means was to be a holiday in democratic Switzerland. She sent an equerry to Lucerne, to report upon the scenery and to enquire about accommodation. She sent for her Controller of European Travel and ordered him to arrange transport. He contacted Paris and was offered the loan of Napoleon's Imperial train.

In August of 1868 she crossed to Cherbourg in the Royal Yacht, with strong naval escort. Her retinue numbered over a hundred – ladies-in-waiting, equerries, doctors, governesses for the younger children, coachmen, grooms, detectives, dressers. With her went her ponies and carriage, her dogs, her armchair, and, of course, her bed. At Cherbourg a 'flying bridge' had been constructed to give her direct access from yacht to train. This consisted of no less than ten coaches and baggage waggons. H.M. took over the luxurious drawing-room and sleeping cars previously only used by Napoleon and Eugenie. The journey to

Paris lasted all night as the Queen stipulated a speed limit of twenty-five m.p.h.

Lord Lyons, who had succeeded Lord Cowley as Ambassador, received her at the *Chemin de Fer de l'Ouest* and conducted her to the Embassy. In the afternoon the Empress paid her a courtesy call. In the evening the Imperial train continued on its journey to Switzerland.[21]

On the return journey Queen Victoria was undoubtedly rude. Although the Emperor and Empress were in the environs of Paris, she made no attempt to return Eugenie's courtesy call. Instead she drove out to St Cloud and walked in the park and gardens, but did not enter the Palace. Disraeli commented to Lord Cairns:

> There was a sort of Fenian outrage in Paris. One O'Brien shook his stick at Princess Louise and shouted, '*A bas les Anglais*'.[a] I fear between ourselves the greater outrage was that our dear Peeress did not return the visit of the Empress. This is to be deplored as they had named a boulevard after her and she went to see it . . . At first the Empress was inclined to pass the matter over, but her Ministers and everybody round her kept telling her she had been badly treated so that at last she began to believe it herself and the French Court was very sore about the matter.[22]

The French Press railed at the British Queen and her aloofness. Here she was, travelling through France in the Emperor's train and at his expense, and not even bothering to return the Empress's call because she said that she was feeling the heat. It was a strange way to return the compliment of having a boulevard named after her. And it was only natural that the journalists should turn the spotlight on the brawny Scotsman who was the Queen's shadow. It was sad, indeed dangerous, for Napoleon and Eugenie that the relationship between France and Britain should have deteriorated just at this time.

(a) The Queen was travelling incognita as the Countess of Kent.

CHAPTER 20

Suez Interlude

By the end of 1868 things began to go very wrong for Napoleon.

His health was undoubtedly a contributory factor in the decline of his Empire. He was subject to bouts of agony, a combination of rheumatism and the stone in his bladder. Before entering a public gathering he was known to have held his arm to a candle's flame so that he might find relief in the change of pain.[1] Fever had reduced his weight and strength and on occasions he would, without warning, leave important discussions and retire to bed. It was rumoured that he took large quantities of tincture of opium and that he raved as if he was in his last agonies. Somehow he managed to keep the truth from his wife and, though she plagued his doctors, they were bound to silence. A specialist gave his opinion that an immediate operation was necessary, but Napoleon deferred until it was too late. Eugenie only discovered the real truth after he was dead.[2]

The tragedy was deepened by the attacks upon him by the Opposition press. They featured every rumour regarding his illness. The brutality of papers such as 'Rappel', 'Réveil' and 'La Lanterne' was beyond belief. Medical writers were called in to regale their readers with intimate details of how Napoleon would die. Henri Rochefort, editor of 'La Lanterne' boasted in after years: 'That poor man, the Emperor, how I wrung him out like a bundle of linen.'[3]

The more 'freedoms' he handed out – freedom for the Press, freedom to debate – the worse the situation became. A hard winter pushed up the price of bread and there was widespread unemployment. Strikes were frequent and theories of Karl Marx gripped the workers. Once again the strains of the forbidden 'Marseillaise' could be heard in the dark streets and on the 'Day of the Dead' in November memories were revived of those who had died in the *coup d'état*.

When vacancies came in the Legislative Assembly, the Imperial candidates were defeated and the Opposition grew stronger. At the general election in May 1869 the swing was strongly towards the

Republicans, votes for the Government being only four to three, and only one to four in Paris,[4] and in the large cities there were mass gatherings shouting for revolution.

Among the better off, money took preference over patriotism and corruption was rife. Napoleon tried to introduce measures to increase the armed forces. His efforts were not only blocked but met by demands that the amount spent on national defence should on the contrary be cut. Thus France drifted in the direction of war without taking the necessary steps to wage it.

As the danger of war with Germany grew closer there were two people on the international scene whom Bismarck regarded with concern. The first was Lord Clarendon who, to the delight of Napoleon and Eugenie, returned to office as British Foreign Secretary in Mr Gladstone's first administration in December 1868. He was sixty-nine, he was far from well and he commented that he was dragged 'kicking and screaming' back to Whitehall, but in the event he was content to be once again in his old room.[5] Despite his age, he was the man best fitted for the job and the only man whom Bismarck feared. It was a question of whether he had enough years and strength left to prevent mass slaughter in Europe.

The other person whom Bismarck regarded as a danger to his plans was the Empress Eugenie. Yet in France her popularity was on the wane. She was known to be against certain reforms. She was blamed for the Mexican fiasco. She was suspect because of her open support of Austria. She was accused of reckless extravagance. Many disliked her ultramontaine tendencies. In 1869 Persigny,[a] from his retirement, urged the Emperor that she should no longer attend the meetings of the Council. By chance, Eugenie saw the letter and, deeply hurt, agreed that she would attend no more.[6] The time had come for her to absent herself from the scene for a while.

A chance – a glorious chance – to get away from it all came in the summer of 1869. The Khedive of Egypt asked her to open the Suez Canal.

Both Napoleon and Eugenie were enthusiastic '*canalistes*'. His interest was founded on the survey which Napoleon Bonaparte, when in

(a) One of the few remaining of Napoleon's 'old guard'. King Jerome, Mocquard (secretary), Morny and Walewski were all dead.

Egypt in 1768, had ordered to consider the possibility and advantages of piercing the Isthmus of Suez. Then later, while a prisoner in Ham, he had dreamed of joining the waters of the Pacific and the Atlantic and written a paper proposing a Nicaraguan canal. Eugenie's interest was personal. She was the cousin of the man behind the present project, Ferdinand de Lesseps.

In 1854, in Cairo, de Lesseps had obtained a concession to build a canal from Port Said to Suez. The following year he journeyed to London to enlist financial support. There he ran up against Lord Palmerston. The old Prime Minister was in violent opposition to such an idea, considering that the waterway would threaten British communications with India, lay Egypt open to attack by a stronger power and, in any case, was against the laws of nature. It was, he said, 'one of the many bubble schemes that from time to time have been palmed upon gullible capitalists'.[7] De Lesseps looked for help elsewhere. With the influence of Napoleon, the support of Turkey, then overlord of Egypt, was obtained and the *Compagnie Universelle du Canal Maritime de Suez* was formed with French and Egyptian capital. Britain, America and Russia stood aloof.

In 1859 the first spadeful of sand was turned near Port Said. There were endless troubles. Turkey considered that Egypt was becoming too 'independent minded' and raised obstacles. In Britain there was furious outcry about the cruel working conditions of the sweated labour. But with the aid of Napoleon, who was responsible for introducing modern machinery, de Lesseps won through and by the end of the summer of 1869 his dream came true – the waters joined.

Napoleon, too ill to undertake the long journey, was determined that Eugenie should have her hours of starlight, but he had to face a storm of opposition from the Republican press. It was said that a million francs were being frittered away on her expenses and that a woman playing a leading role in such a ceremony would have an undesirable political effect in Mohammedan countries where the feminine status was limited by the harem. Even Mérimée was against her leaving France at this time, but she had set her heart on it and she made her plans.

Eugenie and the distinguished entourage which was to accompany her, attended a series of lectures on Egypt and its monuments.[8] Couturier Worth received one of his largest orders, as many as sixty dresses each for the Empress and her ladies, and he sent his own packers to the Tuileries to lay them correctly in the massive trunks.[9] To avoid criticism, the Emperor settled the bill himself. On the evening of 30th September, at St Cloud, she said goodbye to her husband and her son, and boarded the Imperial train. With her, for company, went her two nieces, the daughters of her sister, Paca.

The trip was vintage Hollywood throughout. On the battlefield of Magenta Eugenie prayed in the moonlight for the souls of the French and Austrian dead. In Venice, coloured lanterns turned the dark waters of the Grand Canal into a pattern of crimson, turquoise and gold, and she was serenaded from the gondolas which escorted her. She heard Mass in San Marco and was received by King Victor Emmanuel.[10] She boarded the Imperial yacht *L'Aigle* and the *bora* was blowing as she sailed down the Adriatic.[11] In Athens a public holiday was proclaimed in her honour and she was taken on a conducted tour of the monuments of Ancient Greece by King George, brother of the Princess of Wales. Then off she set, escorted by French warships, for Constantinople.

Sultan Abdul-Aziz of Turkey was somewhat put out by the Khedive of Egypt's grandiose plans for the opening of the Suez Canal and by the many invitations which he had sent to foreign royalties. He decided that anything the Khedive could do, he could do better. He ordered that the streets of Constantinople should be cleaned and paved. He redecorated the Palace of Begler-beh where the Empress was to stay. He built a State litter for her conveyance on land and a forty-oared *caïque* on the water. This barge had a brow of solid silver and a canopy of scarlet velvet covered the dais on which she was to sit.[12] But the Turks were unaccustomed to receptions such as this and there were incidents.

As *L'Aigle* approached the Bosphorus, a salute was fired by thirty shore batteries. Unfortunately it had not been made clear to the gunners that blank rounds were to be fired with the result that cannon balls rained down around the Imperial yacht.[13] The Sultan came out in the *caïque* to meet his guest and the two sat side by side on the way to the landing stage at Begler-beh. This was an unheard of compliment on the part of the Commander of the Faithful. He even went a step further in his attempt to merge East and West by attempting to kiss Eugenie's hand.[14] But she, partly out of respect for Mussulman custom and partly because she saw the wild look in his eye,[(a)] declined the honour.

That night there was a dinner of eighteen courses at the Sultan's palace. With a tiara of diamonds on her head, a white dress veiled in tulle, and her arms and neck flashing with jewels, she was rowed back through the illuminations to her white palace, and added one more memory to her store of 'unforgettable' experiences.

Yet the ways of the East were new to her and it behoved her to tread with care. She received a visit from the Sultana Valide, who was accompanied by twelve young inmates of the harem. While Eugenie made slow progress in conversation with the Sultana, the attendants, wildly excited at the freedom of an outing, ran shrieking with delight around the palace of Begler-beh, marvelling at the rich, wall-to-wall carpeting and hidden lighting. They discovered Eugenie's French maids and, sheltering behind them, her negro servant, Moussa. Moussa knew well the penalty for laying eyes on harem ladies and thought that his last hour had come. He kept repeating, 'Me no see, me keep eyes shut'.[15]

The Sultana was obviously somewhat suspicious of the West as a result of her visit. Next day Eugenie returned the call. When being shown round the garden by the Sultana's son, she forgot for a moment that she was not at St Cloud and took the boy's arm. Whereat the Sultana gave her a sharp slap '*sur l'estomac*'.[16]

In the retinue of the Empress there were those with time on their hands. One of them was her dentist, Dr Evans, an important member but one whose duties were spasmodic. He decided to try his hand at fishing. He hired a small boat and rowed out on to the Golden Horn. He was ignorant of both channels and local customs.

At the same time the Sultan was accompanying the Empress on a sight-seeing tour in the royal *caïque*. As Evans sat, drowsing in the sunshine, the *caïque* bore down upon him. Now the rule on the water was that the Sultan gave way to nobody. Anyone risking such an encounter was run down, and no notice taken. The Empress saw a small boat ahead. As they neared she recognised the figure of Dr Evans. When she realised that they were on collision course, she could stand the strain no longer, gripped the Sultan's arm and begged him to take avoiding action. He snapped out an order, the small boat was missed by

(a) Abdul-Aziz committed suicide with a pair of scissors in 1876.

feet and Evans woke with a start. He saw the Empress signalling to him. He guessed what had happened and realised that she had saved his life. Within a year he found himself in the strange position where he could repay that debt.[17]

The time came to say goodbye. As a parting gift the Sultan presented his guest with a Turkish carpet. In the centre had been worked a portrait of her husband, human hair being used for the head and the moustache. It was quite frightful and a lady-in-waiting recoiled in horror. Eugenie saw her do so and knew that she must put matters to rights. She enthused about the likeness to the Emperor, she raved about the fineness of the weave, she poured out her eternal gratitude. She was utterly convincing to the Turkish mind and she sailed away towards the Mediterranean assured that her visit had been an overwhelming success.[18]

Next stop, Cairo. She stayed in a palace specially built for her by the Khedive and, after the blaze of the reception was over, she slipped away on the Nile, travelling incognito as the Comtesse de Pierrefonds. It had ever been her dream to do this, to glide in a dahabeeyah to Luxor and Thebes, Edfu and Assouan, and she had been under strain and was in need of rest and relaxation. She was becoming snappy with her entourage, letting slip bitter remarks which she did not really mean, and exercising strict discipline on menus to ensure that her ladies' stomachs did not become upset. No iced drinks and plenty of bananas. She herself ate what she liked without ill effect.

As the days passed the peace of the river soothed her and she became as gay and adventurous as she had been before her marriage. She took her nieces on expeditions to see ruins by moonlight; she explored off the tourists' path. At the Pyramids a fine white donkey awaited her. She set it alight in her Spanish way and raced ahead. The other donkeys played follow-my-leader and a posse of experts on ancient monuments, in attendance upon her, ended on the sand. She wrote to Napoleon:

I write this on my way to Assouan. To say we feel cool would not be absolutely true, but the heat is quite bearable ... Far from men and things one breathes a serenity which is beneficial to body and spirit; and by an effort of the imagination I fancy that all is well with you because I know nothing about what is going on. Amuse yourself. I think distractions are indispensable, for one must build up one's

moral fabric just as one builds up an enfeebled constitution ...
Meanwhile, I enjoy my trip, the sunsets, and this wild yet cultivated
nature on a space fifty yards wide along the banks, behind which is
the desert with its sand hills, and the whole lighted by a burning
sun ...[19]

'*Amuse yourself.*' That was precisely what the Emperor was doing.
As so often happened when Eugenie was away and he was alone with
his son at St Cloud, his health improved. He had more energy for work.
He even looked once again at the ladies. As Queen Sophie of Holland
said, when Eugenie was with him, she was 'like the buzzing bee,
worrying him unceasingly'.[20] He gave small dances for the American
girls who were beginning to invade Paris, culture bound. He flirted
with the Comtesse Louise de Mercy-Argenteau, a social beauty of easy
virtue, bitter tongue and facile pen, a woman whom Eugenie detested.

On 16th November *L'Aigle* was at Port Said and the blessing of the
Canal took place, Allah and the Pope merging noisily but peacefully.
Eugenie was in a pale grey dress touched with lace, a black hat and a
velvet ribbon round her neck. She leaned upon the arm of Emperor
Francis Joseph of Austria.[21] During the next enchanted days he rarely
left her side. This made her particularly happy.[22] Perhaps she would
have been better suited in life as the Empress of Austria.

Next day the journey south began. *L'Aigle* was in the lead, the Empress and de Lesseps on the bridge, and behind, in line astern, sixty-seven
vessels of many nationalities. They came to Ismailia in the evening.
The 18th was the day of greatness – the ceremonial opening. The
display organised by the Khedive stretched the powers of those who
described it – 'Arab horsemen galloped ... burnouses flew ... carbines
cracked ... djerrids whirled ... dervishes howled ... fakirs chanted ...
dromedaries sparkled ...' Over thirty years later the Empress, talking
of her most dazzling memories, recalled:

> The ceremonial opening of the canal was fixed for eight o'clock
> in the morning, in the waters off Ismailia. There was a real Egyptian
> sky, a light of enchantment, a dreamlike resplendence. I was awaited
> by fifty vessels, all beflagged, at the entrance to Lake Timsa. My
> yacht, *L'Aigle*, at once took the head of the procession, and the yachts
> of the Khedive, the Emperor Francis Joseph, the Prince Royal of
> Prussia, Prince Henry of the Netherlands, followed at less than a

cable's length. The spectacle was so supremely magnificent, and proclaimed so proudly the greatness of the French regime, that I could contain myself no longer: I was exultant.[23]

Two days later she was at Suez. The Khedive found her leaning against the rail, staring out across the still Red Sea towards the high mountains. She told him that this view alone made the journey worth while. She ever wanted to see what lay over the hill. She had planned to go on to India, but this had come to the ears of Lord Clarendon and he had quickly put a stop to that. Instead she turned back and headed towards a dreary December in Paris.

In England – represented at the canal celebrations by only a plain 'Mr' from the Foreign Department – there was a mixed sentiment of curiosity and disapproval. Queen Victoria said that she would most certainly not allow any of her sons to be present.[24] Some papers were poking fun at the whole affair, referring to the lovely lady who played the leading part as 'Larmperartreece Eujaynee'. *Punch* was both satiric and prophetic:

> What of this piercing of the sands?
> What of this union of the seas?
> This grasp of unfamiliar hands,
> This blending of strange litanies?
>
> This *pot-pourri* of East and West,
> Pillau and *potage à la bisque*: –
> Circassian belles whom WORTH has drest,
> And Parisiennes *à l'odalisque*!
>
> Riddles that need no Sphinx to put,
> But more than OEDIPUS to read –
> What good or ill from LESSEPS' cut
> Eastward and Westward shall proceed?
>
> Answer in vain the Sphinx invites;
> A darkling veil the future hides:
> We know what seas the work unites,
> Who knows what sovereigns it divides?[25]

When Eugenie reached St Cloud she discovered that Napoleon had been in conversation with Emile Ollivier, the Republican statesman who had led the parliamentary opposition with distinction. Ollivier had joined with Persigny in pressing that the Empress should no longer attend meetings of the Council. Now he had agreed to become her husband's Prime Minister.

Ollivier formed a government and on 2nd January 1870 the Liberal Empire began its short chapter. On the face of it the Emperor's role as active leader was ended and he was restricted to the position of a Constitutional Sovereign. In the event he was still holding the reins. When the British Ambassador, Lord Lyons, criticised Ollivier's appointment, Napoleon replied: 'He has two precious qualities which make me forget his failings. He believes in me and is the eloquent interpreter of my ideas, especially when I let him think they are his own.'[26]

The social reforms introduced by Ollivier's ministers brought with them a mood of relief. Emergency public safety laws were repealed, local government was reorganised, educational grants were increased. In foreign affairs the maintenance of peace was the order of the day – no more adventures like those in Mexico and Italy – international incidents to be settled at once by common sense. The policy suited. The smoke of revolution, noticeable in 1869, blew away.

But Ollivier could not persuade the Legislature to increase France's military strength. On the contrary, a cut of twenty per cent was made in the call up. While Britain imagined that France could muster 600,000 men, the true figure was only half.

In May there was a plebiscite, resulting in 7,257,379 'Ayes' for Napoleon's regime and 1,530,000 'Noes'. The President of the *Corps Législatif* conveyed the result to the Emperor in the Salle des Etats of the Louvre. He announced: 'France says to you, "Sire, the country is with you. Advance confidently in the path of progress ..."'[27] But in analysing the result Napoleon discovered that the army had polled 50,000 votes against him, and that those votes belonged to recruits.

Springtime in Paris ... cavalry trotting on the Champs de Mars, the sun sparkling on the breastplates of the Cuirassiers, picking out the scarlet of the Imperial Guard, the green of the Hussars and the sky-blue of the *Cent Gardes* ... a glittering ball at the Tuileries ... tourists flocking along the Champs Elysées – a false pregnancy for a new life of peace and reform and prosperity.

Beyond the Rhine Bismarck smoked his meerschaum pipe and waited. Every invasion move had been rehearsed a dozen times. 'The stage was set: the pulleys were ready; the back-cloths in position to rise and descend; the men to work them in their places. Only the bell from the auditorium ... *that* had not struck yet. His eye was on the indicator. He watched Napoleon, and he watched Clarendon.'[28]

Lord Clarendon died in harness on 27th June. Eugenie wept and Bismarck smiled.[a] The British Foreign Secretary had done sterling work, in both Paris and Berlin, to keep the peace. His handicaps were ill health and the fact that he was too nice a man to comprehend fully Bismarck's wiles and lack of scruples. He was succeeded by Lord Granville who, on taking office, was informed by his Under-Secretary that there was a great lull in foreign affairs and that there were no important issues to be dealt with.

On 30th June Emile Ollivier declared that 'the peace of Europe never rested on a more secure basis'.[29] To complete the restful scene, Bismarck allowed his generals to go off on leave. On 3rd July the Emperor underwent a medical inspection. He was told that he must take life easily and on no account ride a horse. He made plans for his retirement. He would abdicate when his son became of age in 1874. Thereafter he would spend the summers at Biarritz and the winters at Pau.

Bismarck's moment had come. His excuse was concerned with the candidature of a German, Prince Leopold Hohenzollern, for the throne of Spain, which had been contested by France. To Bismarck's dismay the Prince had now withdrawn his name. But France, in excited mood, foolishly demanded assurances from Germany that his name would not be put forward again. Bismarck edited, and published, a telegram from the King of Prussia in reply, in such a way that the French could only take offence. He later admitted that 'he waved the red flag before the Gallic bull'.[30]

The 'Gallic bull' reacted in the form of crowds milling along the boulevards of Paris, singing the *Marseillaise* and shouting '*A Berlin! A Berlin!*' Politicians made inflammatory speeches. The resolution on war gripped the French people and there was no containing it. Eugenie

---

(a) A year later Bismarck said to Clarendon's daughter, Lady Odo Russell, Ambassadress in Berlin: 'Never in my life, dear lady, was I more glad to hear of anything than I was to hear of your father's death.' When Lady Russell bridled, he explained: 'What I mean is that, if your father had lived, he would have prevented the War.'

was with them, though she told Pauline Metternich: 'May God grant that there be no war. But peace bought at the price of dishonour would be as great a misfortune.'[31]

In the light of what followed, Eugenie may be blamed for her failure to appreciate the seriousness of her husband's illness. Germain Sée, the great surgeon, told her that it was '*abominable* to place a man in such a condition at the head of an Army'. She replied: '*Le vin est tiré, il faut le boire.*'[32] She seemed incapable of understanding that, at an active forty-four, she was married to a spent force.

On the other hand she cannot be blamed for not being aware of France's unpreparedness. She had been assured: 'The army is perfectly supplied in every respect. It will not require the purchase of a single gaiter-button for a year to come – *elle est archiprête.*'[33]

Above all Eugenie knew her Bismarck. She knew that, if he did not come that year, he would most surely come the next . . . or the next . . . Her tragedy was that she no longer had the hand of Lord Clarendon to guide her.

On 19th July 1870 Emperor Napoleon, reluctantly, went to war.

CHAPTER 21

Gotterdammerung

By Heaven's aid, my dear Augusta,
We've gone another awful buster;
Ten thousand Frenchmen gone below,
Praise God from whom all blessings flow.[a]

In the early morning of 28th July 1870 the Imperial train was shunted into the little station by the gates of St Cloud. It was a quaint, thatched building known as 'the Emperor's station', served by a siding off the Sèvres to Montretout line. It had been decided that, in view of Napoleon's health and to avoid disturbances in Paris, he would leave for the front by this quiet route. There was constant movement between the station and the palace as the baggage was loaded. Journalists and artists gathered on the platform. Dr Baron Corvisart arrived with a case of surgical instruments.[2]

Many of the Emperor's family, his Ministers and his friends, had come to the palace to say goodbye and wish him luck. There had been a touching parting with Princess Mathilde. On learning that he was to take command of the army, she had exclaimed: 'But you are in no state to do so   You cannot ride a horse, or even put up with the jolting of a carriage. How will you manage in battle?' Raising his arms in a gesture of fatalism, he answered: 'I am not very handsome or dashing, am I?'[3] His sweetheart of the Strasbourg days was very close to him now. She had acted hostess for him while his wife was away at Suez. She had tried to control her emotions but a few weeks later she was to show her true opinion of Eugenie when she screamed: 'She and she alone has been the cause of all France's misfortunes. This woman has ruined the best and most generous of men . . .'[4]

At half past nine a line of carriages drew up before the palace. Eugenie, now the Regent of France, drove the Emperor in her pony

(a) In Britain sarcastic comment was soon passing on the pious utterances of King William of Prussia. This verse is taken from a skit written in imitation of the King's letters to his wife, Queen Augusta.[1]

198

chaise across the park. In the undress uniform of a General, he sat, slouched and silent, beside her. Behind them came the Prince Imperial, with Princess Clothilde and his Governor.[5] The fourteen-year-old Prince was in a state of high excitement at the thought of accompanying his father to the war. He was in the uniform of a second lieutenant of the Guard. The day before his hair had been cut and his photograph taken. He slapped his sword as he moved about the platform, chatting with everyone.

The order came to join the train. 'Why, it is like a regiment leaving,' commented the Emperor. Eugenie kissed him and he took his seat. She embraced her son and traced the sign of the Cross on his forehead – as she always did when they parted – and said, 'Do your duty, Louis.' He jumped into the carriage after his father. From the window Napoleon spotted a chamberlain whom he had missed. 'Ah, Dumanoir,' he called, 'I have not said goodbye to you.' For many there, those were the last words that they heard the Emperor speak.[6]

The smoke came from the engine, hanging still under a cloudy, sultry sky. As the coaches moved around the bend and out of the park, the white handkerchief of the Prince Imperial fluttered from a window. Eugenie turned and walked erect back to her chaise. It was only as she took the reins and drove away that the tears flooded from her. She wrote to Manuela:

> You are lucky only to have daughters, for at times I feel like a wild animal longing to take my little one far away into the desert and rend anyone who tried to seize him there. Then I reflect and say to myself that I would rather see him dead than dishonoured . . . and leave him in God's hands . . .

The Emperor reached Metz at six o'clock that evening. It did not take the man who had commanded successfully at Magenta and Solferino long to realise that the mobilisation had been a fiasco. The staff officers were bewildered, short of information and could not answer essential questions. There was a pile of unanswered telegrams on his desk.

The truth came out. One third of the regular troops had been on leave when war was declared, and a great many horses had been loaned to farmers. Reservists were crowding the railways all over France, searching for depots which had moved without warning. The newly recruited *Gardes Mobiles* were sullen, completely untrained and considered that their role should be restricted to guarding public buildings in the big cities. There were men without uniforms, horses without harness, guns without ammunition, regiments without tents, cookhouses without utensils or rations. There were stacks of maps of Germany but none of France.[7]

Napoleon had expected to find 385,000 troops mustered along the Rhine; he discovered that the true figure was about 220,000. He sent a message to Eugenie; 'Nothing is ready. We have not troops enough. *Je nous considère d'avance comme perdus*.'[8] As she read it, she felt as if 'her arms and legs had been broken'.

The Emperor realised the absolute importance of sending back to Paris the news of a victory. Not only was this essential for home morale, but only success could bring in Austria and Italy on France's side, remote as that hope was. Accordingly on 2nd August he attacked the small town of Saarbrücken, about two miles across the frontier into Germany. The railway junction gave it the semblance of being an important military objective. The town was garrisoned by one Prussian infantry regiment and three squadrons of cavalry. The invading French force consisted of over 60,000 men. The Prussians put up a lively and determined defence and then retired in good order. The French marched into Saarbrücken and then marched out again. It was to be their sole incursion into enemy territory. The whole operation took some two hours.

The Emperor, the Prince Imperial behind him, rode among the troops. The boy, as any boy of fourteen would have done in such exciting circumstances, picked up a spent round and kept it as a souvenir. For that natural act he was to be lampooned mercilessly in the days ahead. When the Emperor returned to Metz he had to be helped from his horse and he confided in General Lebrun that he was in agony. But he had obtained the cheerful despatch that he so dearly wanted and on the 4th, to the delight of Paris, it appeared in the *Journal Officiel*:

> Today, August 2, at eleven a.m., the French troops had a severe engagement with the Prussians. Our army, assuming the offensive, crossed the frontier and invaded the territory of Prussia. In spite of the strength of the enemy's position . . . our artillery soon drove the enemy from the town. The *élan* of our soldiers was great . . .[9]

Yet on that evening of the 4th, as Paris celebrated, Crown Prince Frederick William, son-in-law of Queen Victoria, commanding III Army on the south of the German line, was writing in his diary: 'A victory over the French under my own eyes God be praised, our very first encounter with the enemy was a success . . .'[10] That was the battle of Wissembourg. The Crown Prince marched on through the harvest fields of France. The villages were deserted – the old, the sick, the children, all had gone, terrified by the rumours that the German soldiers were indulging in cannibalism.[11] On the 6th the diary began: 'I have today completely defeated Marshal MacMahon, putting his troops to utter and disorderly retreat . . .'[12] That was the battle of Worth. From the north news came in of a defeat of the French at Spicheren near Saarbrücken. It was over now.

In those first engagements the French had fought fiercely and bravely and had inflicted heavy losses on the Germans. But they were 'the thin red line' and there was little support. The beaten troops threw away their rifles and badges, or stripped the clothes from dead civilians and took cover in the countryside.

The Crown Prince, who was a brilliant commander but disturbed by the horrors of war, was sick at heart as he rode across the battle-fields. He did his best to help the wounded. He turned sadly away when he came across the dead body of General Douai, French Divisional Commander, his little dog crouched beside him. He interviewed prisoners, who referred to MacMahon as '*un cochon*' and the Emperor as '*une vieille femme*'. He rode through a deserted camp. 'In the French officers' tents were discovered a host of toilet paraphernalia, delicacies of all sorts and copies of plays.' In the baggage of General Ducrot, who had narrowly escaped capture, were found two full sets of ladies' clothes.[13] The German mind could not comprehend that.

On the 6th, as the blood was flowing at Worth, the Empress gave a luncheon for her Ministers at St Cloud. During the meal she suddenly, and most unlike her, began to cry. She later explained that a terrible presentiment of disaster had come over her. Just before midnight, as she was undressing for bed, the duty chamberlain brought her a telegram. It told her of the defeats of the French forces. The message ended: 'Paris must be put into a state of defence immediately.'[14]

She summoned the Ministers to a meeting at the Tuileries in two hours time. She sent a message to the Austrian Ambassador to pick her up as soon as possible. She dressed, all in black, went downstairs and sat by the window, waiting. As soon as she heard the wheels of Prince Metternich's carriage on the gravel, she ran outside and jumped up to the seat beside him. They bowled in the brilliant moonlight through the empty streets. They reached the Tuileries soon after one. Servants, half dressed, were moving about with candles, and the white dust sheets over the furniture peopled the *salons* with ghosts.

From that night onwards it was as if Eugenie was possessed of some strange power. Although she ate little, drinking endless black coffee and taking chloral at nights, her energy was boundless. Her courage amazed those around her. Her blazing temper frightened them. On the 9th she dismissed the Ollivier Government and accepted General de Palikao, a steady and distinguished soldier, as head of a Government of National Defence. To her, honour and the future of France were everything. Death, even that of her husband and her son, took second place.

A suggestion came in from the front that the command should be handed to a professional soldier. To this, Eugenie agreed. Reluctantly, Marshal Bazaine took over, not fully realising that he was being invited to 'carry the can'. Napoleon was now but a hindrance to over-taxed staff officers, his column of baggage wagons an obstacle on the roads, his retinue of liveried servants inciting the wrath of tired and disheartened troops. He realised this, and also how ill he was, and therefore wired for permission to return to Paris. But that Eugenie would not contemplate. A Bonaparte retreating was beyond belief. What would Parisians say, and do, if an ailing Emperor limped back, shed of his glory? So Napoleon decided to join MacMahon at Châlons and there help to re-form the army gathering there.

At Longueville, at dawn on 15th August, the Prince Imperial was awakened by gunfire. His father rushed into the room. 'Quick, Louis,' he shouted, 'the Prussians are here'. The boy looked out of the window. Some officers were breakfasting at a table in the garden. A shell landed among them and their bodies were scattered over the grass.[15] Emperor and Prince mounted and rode for Gravelotte, along roads clogged with refugees and wagons. At Verdun, after nine hours of travel, the station-master produced a shunting engine and a third class carriage to take them on to Châlons.

Châlons, the scene of many brilliant reviews during the Empire, was in chaos. The station was crowded with retreating troops, sleeping, drinking, cursing, fornicating. The pavilion which had been prepared for the Emperor had been looted and his shirts put up for auction. The officers had lost control. On the 17th a Council of War was held. It was attended by the Emperor, Marshal MacMahon, Prince Napoleon, General Trochu and other senior officers. It was resolved that the Emperor should return to Paris and resume control of Government. General Trochu was appointed Governor of Paris and took command of all troops there. MacMahon's army, as soon as it could be re-grouped and organised, should march on the capital and prepare to do battle before it.

General Trochu left at once to take up his duties. But when the decisions taken at Châlons reached Paris, they were brushed aside. The Empress and her Ministers insisted that MacMahon's army must thrust forward to relieve Bazaine. Parisians, they said, would not tolerate a retreat. It was at this news that Napoleon, to all intents and purposes, abdicated. The civilians had chosen to overrule the militarists. He no longer had the strength to resist. He trailed along with Mac-Mahon's forces, his carriages a target for abuse and insult, to Rheims and then towards Sedan. He felt that they were heading towards an abyss. He was right, for MacMahon was moving straight into the trap which had been set by von Moltke.

Napoleon was becoming increasingly worried about the safety of his son and he decided that the boy must stay close to the Belgian frontier so that he might slip across it to safety should the necessity arise. The two said goodbye at Tourterton, midway between Rheims and Sedan. Napoleon was convinced that it was to be their last goodbye. He put the Prince Imperial in the care of three aides, Captains Duperré and Lamey and Comte Clary. They were given an escort of cavalry. Eugenie was not informed of the move, but she soon found out.

Thus began a week of hardship, danger and deep sadness for the fourteen-year-old boy who had already endured four weeks of war. The aides had a most unenviable task. Not only had they to make their own assessment of the safety of towns where they sheltered, but they also had to collect movement orders from the Emperor. Then the Empress joined in, her instructions often in direct contradiction to those of her husband. Mézières was the first halt, and here orders were waiting to move on to Sedan. It was pelting with rain and the Prince caught a feverish cold. Duperré sensed the danger at Sedan and back they trailed to Mézières, threading their way through the refugees and the wounded.

That night, tired out, the boy was wakened and told that they must move again – the Prussians were close. This time he refused point blank, and it was only talk of duty to his father that fetched him from his bed. There followed a seven hour nightmare journey by train to Avesnes. From there they heard the rumble of distant gunfire from Sedan and no order came from the Emperor. The weary, exasperated aides decided that to linger in the battle area was useless and wished to retreat to Amiens.

They appealed to the Empress. She flashed back: 'I do not approve of these wanderings from town to town. You must stand where you are ... You have a care more urgent than security. It is that of honour ... Remember this: I could weep for my son dead or wounded, but a fugitive! I should never forgive you.'[16] News came in of a disaster to MacMahon's army. The aides moved to Maubeuge, nearer the frontier. At last a message came from the Emperor – get the Prince Imperial over the frontier into Belgium.

The Second Empire was ended now and the crowds were rioting in the streets. The Prince Imperial must not be recognised. Louis was dressed in the smock of a peasant lad and smuggled over the frontier. He took a train for Ostend and England.

It was midnight on 30th August when Napoleon reached Sedan. He arrived by train and trudged through the mud to his quarters as, in the darkened hills and woods around, the Prussian pincers closed about the town. Both he and MacMahon had seen the danger and wired to Paris for permission to retreat on Mézières. The blunt answer came back: 'If you leave Bazaine in the lurch, there will be revolution in Paris ...'

Next morning three of MacMahon's Corps reached the environs of Sedan, after a chaotic, punishing night march. The fourth Corps, covering the retreat, came in during the afternoon. There was still a narrow escape route left open for them, between the Belgian frontier and the Meuse, but the men were tired out, and details of the location of the enemy were vague. It was suggested that the Emperor take this chance of escape, but he refused to leave for fear of dispiriting the troops. Instead he sent his last message to the French army: 'Soldiers! prove

Napoleon III and Bismarck at Donchery

Napoleon III leaving Sedan

Above: Le Soleil d'Or – La Rivière de Thibouville
Below: Empress Eugenie and Dr. Evans leaving the Hotel du Casino, Deauville

yourselves worthy of your ancient renown. God will not desert France if each of us only does his duty.'

At first light on 1st September, under cover of a thick mist, the Bavarians attacked. At half past six MacMahon was badly hit and handed over command to General Ducrot.

There then appeared at headquarters the fire-eating General Wimpffen, sent out from Paris to 'inject boldness and decision' into the campaign. He carried the necessary authority to take over from Mac-Mahon in case of accident to the Marshal. Wimpffen was all 'blood and guts' and supremely confident. He reversed existing orders, switching from retreat to attack. Napoleon, angry at not being consulted about the command, remonstrated. He was told: 'Your Majesty may be quite at ease. Within two hours I shall have driven your enemies into the Meuse.'[17]

For five hours Napoleon rode amongst his troops, now dismounting to help with the firing of a gun, now openly courting death by riding along a sky-line. Four of the officers who began the day about him were killed. Hourly the area of battle grew smaller. At last he returned to the town to confer with the wounded MacMahon. He was in obvious agony as he got off his horse. He began to walk, but stumbled and grasped a tree for support. He was half carried into his quarters.

Later he described to his wife the scene which had met his eyes in Sedan: 'I never dreamt of a catastrophe so appalling ... After several hours fighting our troops broke into a rout and tried to re-enter the town. The gates were closed; they clambered over them. The town was then full of a dense crowd, mixed up with vehicles of all descriptions, and on the cluster of human heads the shells rained down ... tearing off the roofs and setting the houses on fire.'[18]

Three Corps Commanders came to him and told him that the position was hopeless and that the fighting must stop. At two o'clock General Lebrun, carrying a white flag, went to headquarters: the flag was torn up. Wimpffen asked the Emperor to join him in an attempt to break out. Napoleon ignored the request and the attack went in without him – a fierce attack, mercilessly repelled.

At three o'clock the Emperor said to Lebrun: 'Why does this useless struggle still go on? An hour and more ago I ordered the white flag to be flown.' Lebrun went in search of Wimpffen, who shouted at him: 'No capitulation! Drop that rag! I mean to fight on.' So Napoleon took matters in his own hands, made his last decision, and ordered the white flag to be hoisted. Wimpffen resigned his command. The Emperor sent for him and thereafter witnessed a scuffle among his Generals. At last Wimpffen was persuaded that it was his duty to arrange terms of surrender.[19]

Under a flag of truce two German staff officers rode up to the gates of Sedan. To their surprise, they were taken to the Emperor – the German commanders did not know that he was in the town. Napoleon told them that General Wimpffen would discuss surrender terms and that shortly he himself would be sending a letter to King William of Prussia. The staff officers returned to their headquarters, shouting, as they galloped up, '*Der Kaiser ist da*'.[20]

It was at a quarter to seven that General Comte Reille rode out into the stubble fields to the spot where the Prussian King stood before a wide semi-circle of armed officers. By him was his son-in-law, Crown Prince Frederick William, who had moved his army north from Worth. Slowly Reille dismounted. There was absolute silence. The cold eyes in the ring of officers bored into him. Disconcerted, he made some adjustment to his breeches. Then, doffing his red cap, he strode up to the King and presented the letter.

No sound but the rasp of the envelope being opened. All eyes still fixed on Reille, bare-headed, miserable. Then the Crown Prince did a nice thing. Reille had been attached to him when he visited Paris with the Crown Princess for the Exhibition in 1867 and they had become friends. Now Frederick William walked up to him, greeted him, commiserated with him at the unpleasantness of his task and asked after his wife and children.[21]

Napoleon's letter read;

> *Monsieur mon frère, n'avant pas pu mourir au milieu de mes troupes, il ne me reste qu'à remettre mon épée entre les mains de Votre Majesté. Je suis, de Votre Majesté, le bon frère Napoleon. Sedan, 1 Sept., 1870.* [a]

The King replied in the same brotherly terms and requested that General Wimpffen should be sent out to discuss terms.[22]

(a) My dear brother, not having been able to die in the midst of my troops, it only remains to me to surrender my sword into Your Majesty's hands. I am, Your Majesty's good brother, Napoleon. Sedan, 1st Sept., 1870.

At around midnight Wimpffen met Bismarck and von Moltke in a house at Donchéry, a little town to the west of Sedan. The Germans wanted complete capitulation – the French could not agree. The only concession gained by Wimpffen was an extension of the truce from four in the morning until nine. They parted without words – '*Ce silence était glacial*,' commented a staff officer. On his return, Wimpffen reported to the Emperor.

A little before six next morning Napoleon drove out of Sedan in an open carriage, accompanied by five aides. He said no goodbyes, for he thought he would be returning. At the town gate Zouaves on duty cried, '*Vive l'Empereur*' – the last time that he was to be thus greeted in France. He was in the undress uniform of a general officer and he was smoking a cigarette. The carriage stopped at the hamlet of Frenois, a mile short of Donchéry, and Reille rode on to inform Bismarck of the presence of the Emperor. Bismarck came at once from his house in the square, in undress uniform and his boots uncleaned. He swung himself on to his big bay horse and followed Reille to Frenois. Thus they met again, the rising star of Germany and the setting sun of France . . . in the early morning, in a lonely village by the frontier . . . remembering the splendour of the military review at Longchamps and the dances at the Tuileries.

Bismarck dismounted, letting his horse go. He walked towards the carriage. Being in uniform, he was about to salute when he saw the Emperor take off his hat. He followed suit. As he did so he saw Napoleon's eyes following the cap downwards to the belt. In the belt, in its holster, was a revolver. When his eyes focussed on the holster, the Emperor shook and went deadly pale.[23] Later Bismarck was to say that he could not account for this, but he did not yet know how ill the other was, and of the sudden spasms which racked him.

Napoleon requested that they should talk in a nearby cottage, thus avoiding a further drive. The cottage belonged to a weaver named Fournaise. His wife agreed that they should talk in a back room, upstairs. To reach it they had to pass through the room where Madame Fournaise had just risen from her bed. There were two hard chairs and a table in the room. The two men talked for a quarter of an hour. Then Bismarck hurried out and, ignoring the warning of the eavesdropping Madame Fournaise, raced down the stairs, mounted his horse and rode off towards Donchéry.[24]

Madame Fournaise entered the room and asked the Emperor if she could do anything for him. Without raising his head from his cupped hands, he asked that the shutters be closed. He sat there for almost an hour. Then he went into the garden, walking up and down on the path between the potatoes, his white gloved hands behind him, smoking cigarette after cigarette. Madame Fournaise noted that his gait was curious. 'He limped slightly on one leg and he waddled in a sideways fashion, the left shoulder forward.'[25]

Bismarck returned, having breakfasted and changed into full dress uniform. He would not go into the cottage again, saying that it was dirty, so the two chairs were placed before the entrance door. The Prussian did most of the talking and asked endless questions. After half an hour he again rode off. At a quarter past nine a troop of Prussian cuirassiers trotted smartly up and surrounded the cottage. They behaved as if the French party did not exist. The officer in charge dismounted two troopers, marched them up behind the Emperor's chair and ordered, 'Draw Swords'. Napoleon swung round in surprise, showing emotion for the first time. The troopers stood like statues.

Half an hour later von Moltke and Bismarck appeared and gave the signal to move. Napoleon called Madame Fournaise and gave her four twenty-franc pieces. As he put them in her hand, he said: 'You have probably given me the last hospitality I shall receive in France.'[(a)] His carriage moved off at walking pace, his 'guard of honour' of cuirassiers about him. They came to the Château de Bellevue, a country house set in the trees to the north of Frenois. He was shown into the drawing-room and there left on his own. The German commanders were determined that he should not meet King William until after the terms were signed.

Meanwhile Wimpffen had been in consultation with his senior officers since first light. All but he were for accepting the surrender terms. For hour after hour the indomitable General procrastinated. At ten o'clock von Moltke sent a message that he had waited long enough and was about to open fire. Reluctantly Wimpffen accompanied the officer who had brought the ultimatum to the Château de Bellevue. There, in the

---

(a) Madame Fournaise kept the coins on proud display for the rest of her life. When she died, thirty-five years later, three of the coins were sold to defray her funeral expenses and the fourth, which bore the head of Napoleon, was buried with her.

dining-room shortly after eleven o'clock, the surrender terms were signed. Bismarck paid tribute to the French commander – 'this brave officer', he called him. Wimpffen was then escorted to the drawing-room. 'The Emperor,' he said, 'with tears in his eyes, approached me, pressed my hand, and embraced me. My sad and painful duty accomplished, I rode back to Sedan, *la mort dans l'âme*.'[26]

King William and the Crown Prince rode down from the hill above Donchéry from where they had been watching events. As they entered the park of Bellevue the Crown Prince stared in amazement. 'All the Imperial baggage wagons and carriages stood drawn up ready for the road; the French household appeared in their well-known rich liveries, and even the postilions were in gala dress and powder as if for a pleasure trip to the Longjumeau racecourse.'[27]

Thus, just before the sun of the Second Empire went down behind the hill, a last bright ray spot-lighted Napoleon. His retinue had entered Sedan on the 31st and camped in the garden behind the Emperor's quarters. In that retinue were men who had been in his service for twenty years and who had been with him at Magenta and Solferino. In that garden, as the battle waged, they had cleaned and polished their equipment and uniforms and groomed their horses. When it was learned that the surrender was signed, they moved out of Sedan, ignoring the abuse hurled at them. Now the column stood, in marching order, on the drive at Bellevue – the massive *fourgons* and the teams of great draught horses, the carriages, the squadron of led horses, the coachmen and the outriders in uniforms of gold and scarlet.

As if he was the host and not the prisoner, the Emperor came down the steps to greet King William. They went inside and talked together for twenty minutes. The Prussian King was kind. When Napoleon said that it had not been his wish to go to war, William said that he knew it, and that it was his advisers who had been at fault. Permission was given to send a cypher telegram to Eugenie.[28]

That afternoon Napoleon spent with his retinue, saying his thanks. In the evening he wrote to Eugenie:

I should have preferred death to the pain of witnessing so disastrous a capitulation. Nevertheless, it was, under the circumstances, the only means of avoiding the slaughter of 80,000 people .... I have just seen the King. He spoke to me with tears in his eyes of the distress I must feel. He has put at my disposal one of his *châteaux* near Cassel. But what does it matter where I go! ... I am in despair. Adieu. I kiss you tenderly.[29]

Before going to bed he went to the bookcase to find something to read. He picked out *The Last of the Barons*, a novel by an old friend of his, Lord Bulwer Lytton .... remember .... it must be all of thirty years ago ... a breakfast at Bulwer's house by the Thames ... Disraeli was there. The book was found open at the page which he had reached as he fell asleep on his last night in France.

In the morning a guard of honour escorted him to the Belgian frontier. He spent two nights in Belgium. Two special trains were provided to carry the Imperial party of over one hundred. At Verviers station he bought a paper. The newsboy was shouting: '*Chute de l'Empire! Fuite de l'Impératrice!*' He reached Wilhemshöhe, three miles north of Cassel, on the evening of the 5th. The *schloss* was not without its Bonaparte connections as it had been the home of his uncle Jerome when King of Westphalia. As he passed along the corridor, picture lined, towards his apartment, Napoleon halted and signalled his aides to leave him. He raised his head. Smiling down at him from a frame was the sweet face of Hortense, his mother.[30]

Part V

FLIGHT

1870

CHAPTER 22

The Lady Vanishes

In the last sad and turbulent days of Paris under the Second Empire there came a violent clash between the Empress Eugenie and General Trochu.

Trochu was a man who liked matters cut and dried. He returned to the capital after the Châlons conference on 19th August with the firm belief that he was to be Governor of Paris and in command of all troops there, that the Emperor would again take up the reins of Government and that MacMahon would withdraw on Paris to re-form his army. Instead, he found that the conference had been overruled and, though his post as Governor had been reluctantly accepted, the Empress had no intention of handing over to her husband. Moreover, MacMahon had been ordered to relieve Bazaine, beleaguered in Metz. He did not like it at all.

Eugenie suspected – and rightly – that the authoritative voice at Châlons had been that of her old enemy, Prince Napoleon, the wily Plon-Plon. Plon-Plon hated to see her wielding the power and, when he heard that she had countermanded the orders, he was furious. He proclaimed that the Empress wanted her husband out of the way, no matter if he were killed. In a rage he left for Italy, on an abortive effort to seek help from his father-in-law, King Victor Emmanuel.

Trochu simply was not her kind of man. He fidgeted in her presence. His large head was bald, his lips were thin and there was a squint in his shifty grey eyes.[1] She disliked men who squinted, as she thought that they brought bad luck. 'An able officer, generally well informed . . .

he was known as a grumbler. When offered a post he would refuse it, but, unable to bear seeing anyone else in it, he would covet it again afterwards. He was one of those uncomfortable people – particularly odious when employed by a government – whose passion is to improve things. "I should like to redress that error," he would often say.'[2] But he had Republican leanings and a following in Paris and his appointment brought a more settled atmosphere, leaving Eugenie to get on with her work.

That work filled most of the hours of every day. She had set up two hospital units in the Tuileries and visited the wounded regularly. 'If they do not want me as Empress, perhaps they will keep me on as a nurse,' she said. She was the power behind the preparations for defence and siege. 'It was the Regent who gave the Ministers the idea of providing the fortifications of Paris with naval guns, of destroying the locks, blowing up bridges and blocking the tunnels.'[3] It was she who arranged for the Crown jewels and the treasures of the museums to be sent to a place of safety. On her own account, she took the precaution of handing her jewels into the care of Pauline Metternich. Her mother's plea that she come to Madrid was firmly rejected. Her courage was beyond belief. 'She is as firm as a rock,' said one of her household. But the strain was telling and on the night that Napoleon trudged through the mud from the railway station to Sedan, she dreamed that she was mad, that all the war news was the result of a disordered brain. When she woke and found that she was not mad, she cried.[4]

Although rumours regarding the surrender at Sedan were circulating in Paris on the evening of 2nd September, it was not until four o'clock on the following afternoon that M. Chevreau, Minister of the Interior, brought to the Tuileries the telegram which Napoleon had been allowed to send from the Château de Bellevue. Many years later the Empress recalled her feelings on that fateful 3rd September:

For three or four days I had received no telegrams, no letters, from the Emperor. And that long and inexplicable silence kept me in a frightful state of anguish. I could not eat, I could not sleep. I was choked with sobs . . . I think I remember that on the previous evening General de Palikao said to me: 'Our communications with Sedan are cut. I am afraid that the army may be surrounded.' Finally, I had just heard that my son, who had been lodged at Mézières, had had to leave abruptly, so concluded that the enemy could not be far from Mézières . . . That was all I knew by the late afternoon of September 3rd, when Chevreau brought me the Emperor's telegram:

> The army has been captured. I have had to surrender my sword. I have just seen King William and am leaving for Wilhelmshöhe.

I summoned my secretaries, Conti and Filon. I summoned them with cries, as one cries for help. I showed them the telegram. And then . . . everything that lay on my heart burst out . . .

When the volcano inside her erupted, she was standing at the head of the narrow, winding staircase which led down from her apartment to that of the Emperor. The two quiet and deferential men looked up at the lovely face which both knew so well. They did not recognise it now. The nerves were working in her cheeks, there were beads of perspiration on her forehead, her eyes were blazing with madness and fury. From her pulpit, she screamed at that cowed audience of two, pointing, accusing, demanding.

'Do you hear what they say – that the Emperor has surrendered. A Napoleon never surrenders! He is dead! Do you hear me? I tell you he is dead. They are trying to hide it from me.' The voice changed note to near a moan. 'Why did he not die? Why is he not buried beneath the walls of Sedan? Could he not see that he was disgracing himself? What a name to leave to his son!'[5]

For weeks past she had been bottling up her emotions, hiding her fears, giving of her strength to others, boosting herself with coffee and chloral. When she broke, it was not only recent trials which flooded from her, but all the disappointments, the insults, the pain which had been her lot since Napoleon left her bed for another's only six months after their marriage.

In her railing, there was not one jot of sympathy for the little man, now white haired, who had been propelled into war against his better judgment, who had endured a month of campaigning when often he was too weak to stand, who, with a stone in his bladder, had sat his horse for near five hours on the field of Sedan and seen his aides killed about him, who every morning and every evening endured the torture of the catheter as the doctor withdrew the urine from his bladder.

She saw only that the legend of the Bonapartes, which the tales of Don Cipriano had planted in her, was smashed, that the enigmatic man on a horse with whom she had fallen in love had not measured up to her standards, and, most important of all, that her son would not become Emperor Napoleon IV.

As suddenly as the fury had possessed her, so it left her. Limp, she sunk to her knees and cried. As Conti and Filon ran up the stairs and put their arms around her, she fainted clean away.[6]

When she had recovered herself, she behaved as if the outburst had never been, washed from her mind and memory as, in reality, it probably was. She called an immediate Ministerial Council. She asked Trochu to call upon her. The answer came back that he had just returned from visiting the defences, was tired and had not yet had his dinner. 'Neither have I had mine,'[7] she snapped, but knew now that she could no longer rely on the Governor of Paris. She was busy until the early hours, opening despatches, receiving callers, burning secret papers. There was a late meeting of the Chamber of Deputies but no one bothered to let her know what had taken place. Then a few hours of uneasy sleep.

Dawn, 4th September 1870 . . . . a mist hung over the Tuileries gardens, heralding a perfect summer's day. The sun rose into a cloudless sky. If rain had been pelting down, France's Second Empire might have lasted a little longer.

The Empress was up at six. Dressed as a Sister of Charity, she visited the wounded in the hospital unit in the palace theatre. She then heard Mass in her private chapel and talked with her chaplain. At half past eight there was a Council of Ministers. General Trochu arrived late, greeting the Empress with the theatrical and meaningless words: '*Madame, voilà l'heure des grands périls! Nous ferons tout ce que nous devons.*'[8] She talked alone with him. When she returned to the Council and was greeted with, '*Eh bien, Madame?*'[9] she did not reply, just raising her eyes and arms in a gesture of despair.

Luncheon was served at half-past eleven. There were twenty-eight at table.[10] The customary etiquette was in no way relaxed, although it was noticeable that some of the servants were carrying revolvers under their jackets. Cries drifted in through an open window and a footman closed it. '*Vive la République! Déchéance! A bas l'Espagnole!*'

During the night the Republican leaders had sent orders to their supporters in the suburbs to rally at the Palais Bourbon when the Chamber met. These strong-arm parties came in from the environs in force, mixing with the Sunday promenaders who were enjoying the sunshine and determined not to miss any excitement that the day might produce.

The Legislative Assembly sat at one o'clock. It was agreed that the Empress Regent should place all her powers in the hands of the Assembly and a deputation hurried to the Tuileries to seek her agreement. She received the party in the Blue drawing-room and immediately realised that she was being asked to abdicate, and that she did not want to do. She was eloquent.

> The times through which I have passed, gentlemen, have been so painful, so horrible, that, believe me, at the present moment the thought of preserving the Crown for the Emperor, or for my son, counts with me for very little. My one care, my one ambition is to fulfil completely the duties which have been imposed on me.

It was only when she was told that her withdrawal might save France from revolution that she agreed, provided that a majority of Ministers wished her to do so. But she had talked too long. By the time the deputation returned to the Palais Bourbon, the Chamber had been occupied by a mob. Two boys were fighting for possession of the presidential chair and another was ringing the presidential bell. Dozens of would-be politicians were pouring out speeches to which no one paid any attention. Women were collecting mementoes. There were shouts of '*Conspuez Bonaparte et sa femme.*' The position was not dangerous, just chaotic. So the Second Empire ended and Jules Favre led the Republicans to the Hôtel de Ville, which, he said, was the right place to declare a Republic.[11] A government of National Defence was set up and Trochu was the President.

Now the cries of the crowds changed – '*Aux Tuileries! Aux Tuileries!*' the tens of thousands chanted. The gilded eagles on the great gates of the gardens were torn away as the Empress's limp flag came down from its high staff for the last time. The gates gave under the pressure and the human tide poured through. It was a motley concourse indeed – revolutionaries, factory workers, men of the National Guard, families out for a Sunday afternoon stroll, foreign visitors. Lord Ronald Gower was among them:

> With the mob I passed across the garden into the palace, through

the principal gateway, the crowd intoning the '*Marseillaise*' as they pushed their way into the home of so many of their former sovereigns . . . Had the Empress been found there and then, her life would have been not worth a moment's purchase. The mob among whom I formed a unit was good tempered, with the good temper of a spoilt child that is allowed to break and destroy what it pleases; for they had it all their own way, and this revolution was indeed what someone called it, *une révolution faite avec de l'eau de rose*; but had anything checked it . . . their good temper would have changed in a moment . . . and the horrors of the massacres of September in 1793 would probably have been repeated . . .[12]

The railings round the private gardens collapsed and the rose beds were trampled flat. Uglier cries could now be heard – '*A bas l'Impératrice! A la guillotine! A la guillotine!*'[13]

Three Ministers hurried to the Empress with the news of the invasion of the Palais Bourbon, and they urged her to flee. Others came with the same advice, Princess Clothilde, Pietri, the Prefect of Police, Prince Richard Metternich and Chevalier Nigra, the Ambassadors of Austria and Italy. She walked to the window and looked out at the wild scenes in the gardens. She asked General Mellinet, in command of the Palace Guard, if he thought that the Tuileries could be defended without bloodshed. 'Madame,' he answered, 'I do not think so.'[14] Still she hesitated. 'I am not afraid to die,' she said. But there was one danger which she did fear – *les tricoteuses*, the viragos who might lift her skirts and defile her.[15]

It was a question of Pietri's which decided her. 'Is it your Majesty's wishes to cause a general massacre of your attendants?' She waited a few seconds before replying: 'Then I will go. I have done my duty.'[16] She gave her hand to her Ministers to be kissed. Her Ladies crowded around her to say goodbye and she told them, 'Go! go! quick'. She walked to the end of the salon and there, turning, she bowed, as only she could bow, as if it was the end of some great state function.[17] She passed through the door into her private apartment, only Metternich, Nigra and Mme Lebreton, her reader, with her.

Prince Metternich now took charge. It was no longer a case of Ambassador and Empress, but of Richard and Eugenie. The two were friends of long standing and they were very fond of one another. He told her to dress at once and Mme Lebreton fetched her a black straw Derby bonnet, a long waterproof cloak and a thick veil. As she put them on, Admiral de la Gravière, of her personal service, M. Conti and Louis Conneau, the doctor's son and the friend of the Prince Imperial, came in to see if they could help. Eugénie looked around her rooms. 'Is it the last time?'[18] she said. She set off down the main staircase towards the door outside which a duty carriage was permanently on duty. Metternich looked through a window, saw the Imperial insignia on the door of the *coupé* and the coachman in livery, and called her back, saying that it was too dangerous and that she would be spotted. She must have his carriage, he said, and he despatched Louis Conneau to fetch it. Louis was soon back with the news that the crowds were forcing their way into the courtyard and that there was no way of getting out. Admiral de la Gravière hurried down the stairs to attempt to keep the intruders back, while Conti led the party to the only escape route left open to them – a door communicating with the Louvre. They hurried behind him, along the wide corridors, through the *Salle des Etats*, and came to the door. It was locked. The crowds were in the Tuileries now and every second their voices grew louder. Metternich banged and shouted, but no one came. It seemed that they were trapped. Then came the sound of running feet and there materialised none other than Charles Thélin, the manservant of Louis Napoleon who had been with him at Strasbourg and Boulogne and who had engineered the escape from Ham. For his services he had been appointed Emperor's Treasurer. He had been looking for the Empress, to try and help her, and he found her in the nick of time. He opened the door with a pass key.

The Louvre was deserted. They hurried through the Great Gallery and the Pavilion of Apollo. The Empress stopped. She said that the party was too big and would attract attention – she would go on alone with the Ambassadors and her lady. She said goodbye to Conti, Thélin and Louis Conneau, bidding the last named to be sure to take off his uniform before venturing out on to the streets. So she passed into the sole care of the representatives of two countries which might well have come to the aid of France but had not done so. The four went down the wide steps into the Egyptian museum and towards a side door opening on to the Place before the Church of St Germain l'Auxerrois. As they approached the door, a gang which had forced its way into the building came shouting along the passage. The four hid in a vestibule. 'Are you frightened?' whispered Nigra to Eugenie. 'You are holding my arm,' she answered. 'Is it shaking?'[19] The shouting died down. 'We must wait a little longer,' said Nigra. 'No,' she cut in. '*Il faut de l'audace.*' And she opened the door and stepped out into the Place.

The revolution had come so quickly that, except where the demonstrators crowded and shouted and forced their way, Paris was as yet undisturbed. Away from the centres of trouble, the streets were deserted. It might have been any Sunday. There was a cab rank on the other side of the Place and Richard Metternich ran over to it, returning with a closed vehicle. As the Empress and Mme Lebreton got into it, a boy on the pavement shouted, '*Voilà l'Impératrice*'. Nigra dived at him, boxed his ears and told him not to talk nonsense. Metternich banged the door, gave an address to the driver, and off went the cab. Neither Ambassador had the chance to say goodbye or wish her luck.

The cab took them to the apartment in the Boulevard Haussmann of M. Besson, a Councillor of State and a trusted friend of Eugenie's. It was on the fourth floor. They pulled the bell but there was no answer. Tired, they sat down on the stairs, hoping that someone would return. After a quarter of an hour Eugenie said, 'I can stand this no longer'. They went down to the street. It was deserted. An open cab came along and they hailed it. They drove, hiding their faces as best they could, to the home, in the Avenue de Wagram, of the Marquis de Piennes, a Chamberlain who had been of the greatest support since the Emperor's departure. Eugenie had no money and her companion only three francs. Having paid off the driver, not daring to argue about the tip, they were without funds. As luck would have it, the Marquis was also out.[20] Now they must walk.

Mme Lebreton suggested that they should seek the safety of the American Embassy. Eugenie decided that a better plan would be to ask the help of her American dentist, Dr Evans, whom she had known for many years and whose life she had saved at Constantinople the previous autumn. They made their way to his house at the corner of Avenue Malakoff, now hiding their faces by looking into shop windows, now sheltering in side streets. They came to the Avenue de l'Impératrice – her graceful street, the name of which was shortly to be changed. Then, at last, and to a relief beyond words, came an answer to their ring. A valet told them that Dr Evans was out but was expected back shortly, and that they might wait in the library. It was five o'clock.

'Le Beau Evans', as the handsome dentist was known in Paris, had spent the day with an American friend, Dr Edward A. Crane, preparing an ambulance unit to receive the wounded due in from Sedan. The two men came in together at six. The valet was waiting. He told of the two ladies waiting in the library. 'One is heavily veiled, sir, but I think I recognise the Empress.'

Evans opened the library door. He saw Eugenie standing erect, her hands on the back of a chair as if for support. She was wearing a black cashmere dress, with white linen collar and cuffs.[21] She said to him: 'Monsieur Evans, I have no friends left but you. I come as a fugitive to beg your help.'[22]

He stared in amazement. He could find no words and it was some seconds before he could mumble that he was completely at Her Majesty's service. She sank, with a sigh, into a deep armchair and the evening light from a window fell on the beautiful face, emphasizing the signs of tiredness, worry and nervous strain. He read the message written there. He told her that she must relax and have something to eat. He asked her only if she had any immediate plans and she answered that she wished to go to England. He left to consider what should be done.

His first reaction was that her presence must be kept secret. Crane and the valet knew but there must be no one else. He talked with them. The immediate difficulty was that he had arranged to give a supper party that evening for twenty, consisting in the main of members of the American Sanitation Committee, of which he was president. His guests were due in half an hour's time and it was too late to cancel. He had no hostess, as his wife was on holiday at the Normandy seaside resort of Deauville. So Crane was given the task of receiving the guests and telling them that their host had been called to an urgent case. The valet was told to light the fire in the library – as Evans had noticed that the Empress was shivering – and also to take up a tray of food. Somehow he had to prepare it without the chef or the footmen seeing him. Both men accomplished their missions, while Evans sat alone in his study, threshing out a plan of action. On his way down to join his guests he looked in at the library. Eugenie, now that she was warm and had eaten, was a different person, smiling and chatting, but Mme

Lebreton was still weepy and fretting. Evans guessed that the Empress did not yet fully appreciate the seriousness of her dilemma.[23]

It seemed to the doctors that the guests would never go. It was half past nine before the dining-room was clear and the servants told that they might go to bed. Then planning began in earnest. The Empress's suggestion was that she should be driven to Poissy, there to catch the night express from St Lazare station to Le Havre. Poissy was fifteen miles away and the train called there at half past one. From Le Havre she would take a steamer to England. But Evans would not accept that. He was sure that the trains would be searched and the ports watched.

Then Eugenie produced a packet from the pocket of her cloak. It contained passports. The one precaution which her staff had taken to cope with a situation such as this was to obtain passes for her to enter certain countries – Britain, Belgium, Austria, Italy. In the wild rush away from the Tuileries, Conti and Metternich had not forgotten this.

Evans thumbed through them. Some bore the signature of Prince Metternich. But the one upon which he seized was the passport for Britain. It was a genuine one, signed by Lord Lyons, the British Ambassador, dated 13th August, but had not been collected. It allowed a British physician, 'Dr C . . .', to take a woman patient, 'Mrs B . . .', and for them to 'pass freely, without let or hindrance'. It was exactly what he wanted. So the plan was finalised. The four of them would drive to Deauville, there to take temporary refuge in the hotel where Mrs Evans was staying, while arrangements were made for a yacht or a hired boat to take the party to England.

Evans ordered his brown landau for five o'clock. Then, leaving the valet on guard, the two doctors went out, Crane to see what was happening around the Hôtel de Ville and the Tuileries, Evans to discover what check was being made at the Porte Maillot, the gate through which they were to pass at dawn. They were back before one. Crane reported that there was little activity but that he had heard that a new Government had been formed. Evans had watched the Porte Maillot from the shadows and it seemed that carriages were passing through with little hindrance.

There was no sleep for any of them. The doctors took over guard from the valet. They were half expecting a sharp ring on the bell, for, if the search for the Empress had begun, the houses of all those who had served her were suspect. They pored over maps, checking distances and estimating times. They thought of every contingency but one – that the lady passengers had not even the essentials for travelling, no spare handkerchiefs, no brush, no soap, no towel.

With no chloral to help her sleep, Eugenie lay back in the deep armchair, watching the firelight's shadows flickering on the ceiling, re-living the agonies and the dangers of the past few days, waiting for the wheels of the brown landau to call her back to reality at five o'clock in the morning.[24]

The Scarlet Pimpernel

First light was streaking the sky as they left the doctor's house in the Avenue Malakoff, trusted coachman Célestin on the box. By the time they reached the Avenue de la Grande Armée, the sun was up. Yawning shopkeepers were taking down their shutters and the street sweepers beginning their work. Milk carts were on their rounds and market wagons were making their way into the city.

Crane was acting the part of the 'Dr C . . .' described on the passport; the Empress was his patient, suffering from 'a severe nervous disorder'; Mme Lebreton was the nurse; and Evans was the patient's brother. Evans held an opened newspaper so that he could shield the 'patient' from enquiring eyes. At the Porte Maillot he leaned out of the carriage window. On learning that he was an American, the guard grunted '*Allez*'. They sat back with sighs of relief – it was clear that the new Government had been too occupied with its formation to put out a net for the Empress.

On along the wide avenue. Here Napoleon I had led his victorious troops and Napoleon III and driven in state with Queen Victoria. Past the bronze statue of the 'Little Corporal' at Courbevoie. Through the village of Rueil and in sight of the church where Empress Josephine and Queen Hortense were buried. By the park of Malmaison, the home of Josephine, re-purchased and restored by Napoleon III. The river to their right and the hills to their left. They came to St Germain-en-Laye and here they expected another check, this time by the *Octroi* to see that no goods subject to toll were smuggled into the town. Evans feared that, if his departure had been noted, the news might have been telegraphed to the guards at St Germain. But their luck held. The *Octroi* obviously considered that a smart landau carrying Americans would hardly likely to be carrying wine or cheese. Célestin was waved on.

Through the shade of the forest now to Poissy, over the Seine and on to the quaint old town of Meulan, whereafter they drove beside the railway which would have taken them to the coast so much more quickly if they had but dared to use it. Over forty kilometres in four hours. The horses had done magnificently, but the time had come for them to rest a while and be watered. Evans ordered Célestin to pull up at a roadside *cabaret*.

As the landau drew up beside the small café, a large black cat came through the window as if jet propelled. Behind it came a broom. For seconds cat and broom kept station in the air. The cat landed first and streaked for the safety of some bushes. Madame appeared and hurled a pithy epithet after it. This was the light relief that the travellers wanted. The two men roared with laughter, the Empress tinkled and even Mme Lebreton, who was taking the adventure very heavily, managed a wan smile.

Madame was round, red of face and cheerful. She produced, for Evans and Crane, an immense roll of bread, cheese, a *saucisson* and *vin du pays*. The men were ravenous and tucked in, but the ladies thought it wise to stay in the carriage. Madame was talkative and Evans had an inkling that she had spotted the Empress[a] but nothing was said and they went on their way, horses refreshed. Evans took with him some bread and sausage wrapped in paper. Eugenie, borrowing his pocket knife, set into the picnic lunch, but Mme Lebreton, shaken by the shock of recent events, would not eat.

At eleven o'clock they were at Limay, a suburb of Mantes la Jolie, and there they halted in the shade. The horses had covered nearly sixty kilometres and could go no further. Leaving Crane in charge, Evans crossed the bridge into Mantes. He bought a newspaper and asked about the hire of a carriage. At the omnibus station he hired, for thirty francs, a landau to take them as far as Pacy-sur-Eure – he had wanted it to take them as far as Evreux but the owner said that this was too far for the horses. Evans had spun his story of a nervous patient, and the two carriages drew up side by side, enabling the ladies to step from one to another without being seen.

As they moved along the riverside road and slowly up the long hill at Rolleboise towards Bonnières, Evans told the Empress of the events which had taken place in Paris. When he informed her that Trochu

(a) The suspicion grew with time and, when France was settled once again, he went back to the *cabaret*. Madame said that she remembered the visit well but would admit nothing about seeing the Empress.

was President of the new Government, she would not believe it until she had read it in the newspaper. 'Traitor!' she spat, recalling his words of loyalty spoken only the day before. It was the betrayal which hurt her, coupled with the memory that it had been Plon-Plon's idea to send Trochu to Paris as Governor.

By two o'clock they had covered the twenty-four kilometres to Pacy. The driver deposited them in the yard of the only establishment which, he said, would hire them a carriage. Then off he set on his return journey and the four felt very lonely and lost. It was at least fortunate that, at this distance from Paris, the Empress's face was less well known.

An elderly woman, hands on her hips, appeared and surveyed them. Yes, she said, if the price was right, she could produce a carriage. But she had only one horse. On being pressed, she said that she might be able to find another, but it was working in the fields, was much smaller than her own and the two had never been in harness together. A small boy was sent off to fetch it. The ladies were shown into the house. The room was dirty and infested with flies. They crawled all over the groceries which were on sale in the shop opening out of it.

The boy brought the horse in from the fields. It was a grey mare and two hands shorter than the big chestnut which stood waiting in the yard. The woman's husband and the the boy went into a shed and dragged forth an amazing contraption which looked as if it had rested there since railways began. In Dr Evans's own words:

> It was a four-wheeled, four-seated, two-horse, closed vehicle, but with large, very large, glass windows at the sides and in front. The leather covering was rusty, and cracked, and creased; and the blue lining on the inside faded, ragged, dirty. It had a green body and yellow wheels. The body was shallow, and the front seat low. The wheels were ramshackle and of questionable solidity. It was once, perhaps, what may have been called a 'calash'; but it had been worn, and torn, and broken, and painted, and patched, and mended, and nailed together, and tied up, until one might have called it anything one liked.

The little grey mare and the big chestnut were attached to it with the aid of rope and string. They set off, Evans on the box with the driver as there was little room for him inside. The rattles and the squeaks made conversation nigh impossible. When they came to hills the two men dismounted to ease the strain on the horses. That long straight road into the west was to remain for ever clear in the memories of those four weary travellers.

At Cambolle, beyond Evreux and one hundred kilometres from Paris, the driver stopped at a café to water his horses. Evans and Crane went inside for a drink. There came to their ears the sound of the *Marseillaise* and cries of '*Vive la République*'. They hurried back to the carriage. The Empress was white as a sheet and Mme Lebreton clearly terrified. Several wagons carrying *Gardes Mobiles* passed by. They had been to a review at Evreux. They were full of wine. They politely raised their hats to the Empress and greeted her with '*Vive la République*'.

On again, in the twilight, to the village of La Commanderie. The driver announced – and it was obvious – that his horses could go no further. He drove into the yard of the old post house where, he said, there lived a farmer who had plenty of fine horses. The farmer appeared and said that he had horses but no carriage. Fortunate indeed was it for the Empress that her dentist was rich. He now suggested to the man from Pacy that he hire the 'calash' and he produced sufficient francs to ensure that his offer was accepted. The farmer produced two horses, attached them as best he could, and off they went at a rattling speed.

Now the power output of the fresh, fine horses was very much in excess of that of their predecessors and the strain proved too much for the vehicle. 'Crack! went a whiffletree,[a] and we were brought suddenly to a standstill, with the traces dangling about the heels of one of the horses.' This was too much for the farmer and he said that he would go no further. Evans and Crane examined the damage as best they could in the darkness and decided that a repair could be made if they had a piece of rope. They looked about and in a box under the front seat they found an old halter. They lashed the whiffletree to the cross-bar and off they went again. It was nearing ten o'clock when they came to La Rivière de Thibouville in the valley of the Risle.

The driver halted before the *auberge* of *Le Soleil d'Or*, with its faded sign of the blazing sun. Evans entered a big room, brightly lit. A fire was burning, women busy about the pots hung above it. Farmers were eating and drinking at a long table. Madame appeared. It would be quite impossible, she said, to hire a carriage in La Rivière at that time of night. And she added, with the relish of her kind, that both of the rooms

(a) The bar to which the traces were fastened.

which she had for letting were occupied and that there was not a bed to be had in the place. Despair came over Evans, as he pictured the possibility of the four of them sitting beside the roadside until the dawn. Whereat Madame relented somewhat and said that she would have beds made up for them in the passage. But Evans considered that *l'Impératrice* and her reader sharing a passage with two American doctors was hardly safe or proper. He then discovered that the two rooms available for letting were occupied by an English coachman and family on the way to pick up his employer at Trouville. Evans spoke to the coachman, stressing the nervous illness of his 'sister' and at the same time dangling the carrot of francs. The coachman agreed that the poor lady should not be inconvenienced, pocketed the money and removed himself and his family into the shelter of the coach.

Evans leading, the Empress following, leaning heavily on the arm of Crane, and Mme Lebreton bringing up the rear, they passed through the parlour and up the rickety staircase to their rooms. Eugenie looked round at the hard beds and the rough wash-stand and collapsed into fits of laughter. '*Oh! Mon Dieu! Mon Dieu, Madame,*' whispered Mme Lebreton. 'How can you laugh in such a situation? There are people next door and they will hear you.' The guillotine was ever before the eyes of the poor woman.

Having arranged for a tray to be sent up to the ladies, the two men ordered dinner in the private dining-room. They ate well and sat up, over brandy and cigars, until one o'clock, reminiscing and planning. No sooner had they got to sleep than all hell was let loose in the court-yard below, horses' hooves clattering, men shouting. Blinded with tiredness, the doctors were convinced that this was the end of the road, that their luck had run out and that a patrol of cavalry had arrived to arrest them. They opened the window and listened. They learned that it was a party of gamekeepers in pursuit of poachers.

Evans was up early, inquiring where he could hire a carriage. Madame told him that the nearest was at Bernay, sixteen kilometres away. But why, she said, go by carriage when the railway station was only a kilometre and a half distant. She was convinced that the party was English and commented – '*Les Anglais sont tellement drôles*'. The doctor learned that La Rivière was on a branch line which connected with the main Paris-Cherbourg line at Serquigny. By taking a train from La Rivière at five minutes past eight, they could connect with the express and be at Lisieux at twenty minutes past nine. The problem now was, how to get to the station. Madame offered her high, two-wheeled gig, but putting Her Imperial Majesty on such lofty and open view was obviously out of the question. As the two were talking, up came a smart carriage, which divulged a smart gentleman in search of breakfast. Evans, by now the experienced 'con man', told his sad story to the smart gentleman and obtained the loan of his carriage for the short trip.

There was no one on La Rivière station but the station-master and the porter collecting tickets. The train came in and the four entered an empty compartment. Then Eugenie made her mistake. Thinking that she was safe from observation, she relaxed and pulled back her veil. But the officious *chef de gare* ran along to check that the carriage door was shut. He stared in amazement and then, as the train moved off, the look of surprise switched to a malicious smile and a leer. A chill ran through the Empress and she shivered. Never throughout the fifty years which lay ahead of her was she to forget that cruel, triumphant leer. She was frightened now, for the first time. Yet she realised that 'sightings' of her must be reaching the police from all over France. Maybe she still had time. There was no wait for the connection at Serquigny and a *pourboire* bought them an empty compartment on the express to Lisieux.

It was raining when they got there and there were only omnibuses in the station yard. Leaving the others to shelter in an archway, Evans went off in search of a carriage. He paid six calls before he was able to hire one at an exorbitant price. He was away for over an hour and the rain pelted down. When he returned, he saw Eugenie standing alone in the doorway, only partly sheltered from the torrent. Her shoes and her skirt were mud stained. The rain dripped off her hat, raced down her veil and spilled on to her cloak. She made a picture of abject misery. There flashed before his eyes a picture of her as he had seen her but a year before. She had been to dinner at the Sultan's palace. It was moonlight and she was gliding across the Golden Horn in the forty-oared *caique* with the silver prow, tiara of diamonds on her head, white dress veiled in tulle, arms and neck flashing with jewels. Now she was a fugitive, wet through, with only two Americans to shield her.

The sun popped in and out of the clouds as they followed the tree-lined road to the coast, through some of the finest farming land in

France. Eugenie's spirits revived, for she drew great strength from the two solid and indefatigable Americans. She brought her two handkerchiefs from her reticule and showed them how clean they were. She had washed them in her hand basin and then pressed and dried them under the mattress. Didn't they think she was clever? At Pont l'Evêque they stopped to water the horses and buy a picnic lunch. At about one o'clock they crossed the bridge linking Trouville with Deauville. Eugenie had never been here before. Deauville owed its existence as a fashionable seaside resort to the efforts and enterprise of the Duc de Morny, her husband's half-brother and adviser. But she and Morny had not seen eye to eye and hence she had avoided the place. She now saw his statue at the end of an avenue.

Evans, on the other hand, was on his own ground, having only parted from his wife at the Hôtel du Casino eight days before. Leaving the others in the carriage, he made his way into the hotel through the side gate and the garden. Fortunately, his wife was in her room. The poor woman had a considerable shock at his news. Soon he was back at the carriage, now carrying an umbrella, as a protection from the rain and to keep off enquiring eyes. They moved off. At the side gate Evans and the Empress got out quickly and hurried across the garden, she hidden by the umbrella. Crane and Mme Lebreton drove on round the block and approached the hotel in the normal way. They booked separate rooms on the first floor. Evans and the Empress slipped up the back stairs and reached the room of Mrs Evans unobserved by the staff. Eugenie greeted the doctor's wife and then collapsed in an armchair:

'Oh, *Mon Dieu, je suis sauvée!*'

CHAPTER 24

Channel Crossing

At two o'clock Evans and Crane crossed to Trouville in the little ferry and began the search for a craft which would take the Empress to England. They had decided that, if necessary, they would hire one for 'a fishing expedition', but they hoped to come across an obliging British yacht owner. They wandered along the Trouville waterfront, crossed the bridge over La Touques and came to the Quai de Marine where the yachts lay. A sailor with *Gazelle* on his cap was leaning against a pile of planks. Tied up nearby was a yacht of that name, and it looked to be suitable. On the Americans showing interest, the sailor told them that the owner was on board and would doubtless show them over.

Sir John Montagu Burgoyne, tenth baronet, was thirty-eight. He was High Sheriff of Bedfordshire and a retired officer of the Grenadier Guards. His seat was Sutton Park, Biggleswade, and his clubs were the Carlton and the Travellers'. He had come over to fetch his wife, who was on holiday in France, but he had been held up for several days by bad weather. He was bored and delighted to be able to talk about his yacht. He took the two doctors on a conducted tour, informing them that the *Gazelle* was forty-two tons, sixty feet long, had a crew of six, and that he was sailing for England at seven o'clock next morning.

Evans saw that the cabin accommodation was sufficient, the boat sound and Sir John obviously an experienced sailor. So, in a somewhat conspiratorial manner, he told his story and asked if the Empress might join as a passenger. As he spoke, he could sense the Englishman freeze. 'I regret, gentlemen,' said Sir John, 'that I am unable to assist you in the matter.'

Evans was astonished and appalled, and spoke his mind. In America, he said, men helped ladies in distress. In this case two Americans had, without notice and regardless of their personal convenience, come to the aid of the Empress, and by so doing had risked arrest and possible

229

imprisonment. He had thought that an Englishman would have done the same. He turned away.

A century ago the gaps between classes, between occupations, between nationalities, were wide and seldom bridged in an intimate way. Evans's immediate reaction against the aristocratic aura of Sir John was as much to be expected as was the Englishman's dislike of being involved in an escapade with a foreign dentist and a member of a sanitary committee. Later Evans was to understand better – that Sir John was worried at the possibility that he might not be able to get out of harbour in the morning and, even if he did, of being landed with a temperamental Empress in a full Channel gale. He also feared that it might be assumed in England that he had been waiting at Deauville for the Empress. 'Larks' of this nature were not appreciated in the circles in which he moved, and most certainly not by Queen Victoria.

As Evans, in a temper, moved away, Crane tried his hand. He was younger, more tactful, and at last Sir John said that he would leave the decision to his wife. The three went below. 'Well, why not?' said Lady Burgoyne. 'Let her come as soon as she likes.' Having arranged to meet Sir John at eleven o'clock in the lumberyard by the quay to settle details, two very relieved Americans returned to the Hôtel du Casino for dinner.

The Empress received the news that she was to embark that night with almost childish delight. She took it for granted that her ordeal was over. She chatted and she laughed. The flight from Paris became a comedy, from which she recalled only the lighter, more human moments . . . the black cat flying through the air . . . slicing the Bologna sausage with a penknife . . . her bedroom at La Rivière. There was fun over dinner. As it was too risky to reveal that there was a stranger in Mrs Evans's room, only a meal for two could be ordered. This was taken from the waiter at the door. Then there was the joking over how to divide the soup and the meat, and who should have the biggest piece of pudding and who would have the next turn with the knife. It was the first sit-down meal for Eugenie since Sunday's lunch at the Tuileries.

As the sun went down into a white-capped sea, she was silent for a few moments. Then she drew a golden locket containing a picture of the Prince Imperial from her pocket. She told them it was the first time that she had looked at it since she had received the Emperor's telegram telling her of the disaster at Sedan and of his surrender. She had thought that she might crack if she did. Now she broke into floods of tears. Mrs Evans led her into the bedroom and in a few minutes the last Empress of the French was fast asleep.

Meanwhile, Sir John Burgoyne, very much on the alert, had visited the Casino, listening to the talk at the tables and the bar. He was considerably perturbed by what he heard. The hunt for the Empress was on in earnest, it was believed that she was in the area and that all Channel ports were being watched. But he had said that he would abide by his wife's decision and there was no withdrawing. At eleven he met Evans among the stacked timber. It was agreed that the Empress should board at midnight. He told the doctor: 'Come to where we are standing now. One of my men will be here with a lantern. I will meet you on the quay by the gang-plank, on which there will be a light.'

At half past eleven two men came on board the *Gazelle*. One of them Sir John knew very slightly, the other he had never seen before. They insisted, despite the lateness of the hour, in seeing over the yacht. By the manner in which they poked and peered about Sir John guessed that they were plain clothes police. When they left, he followed them, using the timber for cover, until he saw them across the bridge into Trouville. Then he hurried back to receive the Empress at the gang-plank.

Evans and the Empress left the Hôtel du Casino via the garden and the side gate, Crane and Mme Lebreton following a few minutes later, using the front door. Mme Lebreton carried a bag in which Mrs Evans had packed essential toilet requisites and some wraps and shawls. It was a blustery night, with heavy clouds racing from the west and their passage across the moon like the switching on and off of a light. There was almost a mile to go and some of the going was rough. There were great puddles on the shore road and this was obviously no time for chivalry. Evans loosed the Empress's arm and they picked their own way, the agile Empress even outpacing her companion. They followed a muddy path across open fields, reached the Rue du Casino, crossed the Place Morny, then, keeping to the middle of the road, on to the docks. Evans picked out the sailor's lantern. They followed him, through the shadows thrown by the baulks of timber, to the *Gazelle*. Blinking, puffing, clothes splashed with sand and mud, water running out of their shoes, they stood in Lady Burgoyne's brightly lit cabin. Little time for ceremonial introduction. Crane and Mme Lebreton arrived – they had fared even worse and had had to wade through water over their ankles. Lady Burgoyne took command. She produced two sets of clothes and took the ladies to their little stateroom to change. She then conjured up a great bowl of hot punch, thus earning the eternal gratitude of the two doctors.

When the ladies had retired to rest, Sir John talked on deck with Evans and Crane. He told them of the news that he had picked up at the Casino, that there was a rumour that Princess Mathilde had been arrested but that as yet there was no news of the fate of the Prince Imperial. He went on to describe the visit of the plain clothes police. On hearing of this, Crane, who was returning to Paris next day to pay some calls and carry out certain business for the Empress, volunteered to stay on board for the night. It was clear that a guard must be kept and, with nine men on board, it should be possible to repulse invaders.

It was a little after seven when the *Gazelle* cleared the harbour and set course for Southampton. 'The weather was thick, a little rain was falling, and the sea rough: but the yacht, with her mainsails set, together with the spinnaker and second jib, and the wind in her favour, began to make good headway.' But at midday a squall blew up, the wind veered into the north-west, and away went the spinnaker boom. All hands were ordered on deck, the jib was run down and the mainsail reefed, everything made fast and a storm-sail set. The yacht was shipping water and Sir John was of the opinion that they should seek shelter in a French harbour. But the Empress would have none of it – she did not wish to share the fate of Marie Antoinette. She was not afraid, she said, and she stood rock steady and she was not sick. Sir John looked at her with unconcealed admiration and said no more about turning back. No one asked the opinion of poor Mme Lebreton who, prostrate on her bunk, was determined that, should she survive this nightmare, she would never again apply for the post of reader to an Empress.

At six the Isle of Wight was sighted in the eye of the wind, and from that moment until midnight all hell was let loose. The gusts became more frequent, the rain fell in torrents, fork lightning split the darkness and thunder cracked overhead. 'As the yacht reeled and staggered in the wild sea that swept over her deck and slapped her sides with tremendous force, it seemed as if she was about to be engulfed, and that the end was near indeed.' Even the Empress later admitted that the noise below was so intense that on several occasions she thought that they were lost. At last the wind swung into the west and the storm abated. With a reef let out in her mainsail, the *Gazelle* scudded towards the Nab Light and at four o'clock anchor was dropped in Ryde Roads. The Empress sent a message of thanks and appreciation to each member of the crew and Evans handed round gold coins as souvenirs of that unforgettable night.[a]

At seven o'clock they left the *Gazelle* and booked rooms, in the name of Thomas, at the York Hotel in George Street. They were wet and travel-worn. By now Evans's role in relation to the Empress was becoming similar to that of John Brown to Queen Victoria. She, who had never undressed herself or bathed without attendance since her marriage, slipped off her dress behind a half opened door, passed it out to the doctor and asked him to cut off the silver 'E' on the belt before taking it down to the kitchen to be dried and ironed.

After breakfast Evans went off to buy a paper. There was much speculative news about French affairs, including a report that the Prince Imperial had landed in England and was on his way to Hastings.

The task of the doctor was, in many ways, more difficult than it had been on the flight from Paris. Then it had been clear cut, the sole object being to get the Empress out of the country unharmed. Now there was a diversity of problems. For example, he had no idea what reception would be the lot of Eugenie in England. Geographically, he was at a disadvantage as he was not as familar with England as he was with France – in fact the Empress, as a result of her visits to Osborne, knew the Isle of Wight better than he did. But what he feared most was a nervous collapse of the woman in his charge. He knew full well the agonies and the trials which she had endured since the news had come through of the first German victories, of how she had sustained herself on chloral and black coffee. He bore in mind how little sleep she had had in the past four days. As a doctor, he considered it advisable that both mother and son should each have a good night's rest before they met. The Prince was also his patient, and he knew that the boy was sentimental and emotional and must have been strained to the limit. Thus it was that Evans only reported that there was a rumour that the Prince Imperial was in England. He added that he considered that it

(a) In the same gale H.M.S. *Captain*, commanded by Captain Hugh Burgoyne, V.C., a close friend of Sir John's, foundered off Cape Finisterre, with the loss of most of her officers and crew, Captain Burgoyne among them.

would be best to go to Brighton where he hoped he would learn something more.

They took the ferry to Southsea, a tram to Portsmouth and caught a train for Brighton. There Evans deposited the ladies in the Queen's Hotel, thinking that it sounded suitable, as indeed it was.

It did not take Evans long to obtain confirmation that the Prince Imperial was at the Marine Hotel,[a] Hastings. He told the Empress over dinner, whereupon she rose from the table and announced that she was going there at once. The fugitive, obedient, uncomplaining, had disappeared and the Empress had returned.

Evans, marvelling at her strength, discovered that there was a train leaving in a few minutes and they climbed into it as it was about to leave. Even now the doctor did not discard his belief that she should rest before the reunion took place and that the boy should be brought to her, not she to the boy. He tried one more ruse – he booked tickets to St Leonards, knowing only that it was the last station before Hastings and that there was a good hotel there.

On alighting, the Empress demanded: 'Is my son here?' When Evans, stammering, explained that he was at the next station, there was an imperial scene. Eugenie demanded that they proceed immediately. Unfortunately for Evans, he did not know that the distance between the towns was so short that he could easily have taken a cab. Instead they waited for the next train and the following twenty-five minutes, in the dark shadows of the platform, were some of the most unfortunate that either he or Mme Lebreton had ever endured.

It was ten o'clock when they reached Hastings. Evans persuaded the two ladies to wait at the Havelock Hotel while he visited the Marine. He found the Prince with his aides in the drawing-room of their private suite. The boy rushed up to him, grasped him and inundated him with questions about the Empress. Evans saw how upset he was and tried to quieten him. He gave away little except to say that his mother was in England. He told the Prince that he hoped to find out more very shortly and told the boy to remain in the drawing-room until he returned. He went back to fetch the Empress.

She did not walk quickly through the streets, she ran. The manager of the Marine thought that, with the cape of her cloak over her head

(a) Soon afterwards demolished to make way for the Hippodrome. At the auction sale of the contents there was brisk bidding for articles connected with the Empress.

and by the intensity of her expression, she was a Sister of Charity, and tried to prevent her going up to the suite. But there was no stopping her and the doctor now and, brushing aside a valet, they went upstairs. Evans had noted, on his previous visit, that the Prince's bedroom could be reached direct from the corridor and also by a communicating door from the drawing-room. He opened the door in the corridor and hurried the Empress in. He then entered the drawing-room. The Prince was waiting there, as he had been instructed to do. Dr Evans simply pointed at the communicating door. The boy ran through it. There came a cry of joy. Then the door closed.

CHAPTER 25

The Last Throw

When the news broke on 9th September that the Empress was at Hastings, every diarist and social gossip in the country took the opportunity to air their views upon her. Generally, the men were kinder and more understanding than the women. Twelve male admirers put houses at her disposal.[1] The Duke of Hamilton made her free of both his Scottish seats and the Duke of Sutherland offered her Trentham.[2] The Prince of Wales invited her to move into Chiswick House, which had been lent to him by the Duke of Devonshire. For this kind thought the Prince received a scolding from the Foreign Secretary, while the Queen dismissed the idea as a 'presumptuous indiscretion.'[3] And the men admired her courage. Mr Gladstone spoke in her defence and Lord Cowley said: 'What she has gone through, poor woman, shows her wonderful pluck. Both before and after leaving Paris, she showed a courage worthy of all admiration.'[4]

The women took little count of the ordeal through which Eugenie had passed, of her month of working a twenty-hour day under great strain at the Tuileries, of her escape and flight or of the nightmare crossing of the Channel. They made a straight comparison between her appearance now and in 1855. They seemed to expect a fashion plate, surrounded by her ladies, as though she had made a leisurely crossing in the Imperial yacht. Princess Mary of Teck found her *sadly changed* since I last saw her – her face worn and wrinkled.'[5] Lady William Russell described her as 'a goose wanting to be *swan* . . .'[6] Queen Victoria confined herself to a series of non-committal, and often

misplaced, adjectives – 'poor, dear, sweet, patient, gentle.' She despatched Lady Ely to Hastings to spy out the land and then wrote to her
eldest daughter, the Crown Princess of Prussia, who was crowing over
the German victories: 'She looks dreadfully ill and altered, coughs
very much and was very poorly dressed in black. . . She is in an uncomfortable, smelling hotel at Hastings, with hot, disagreeable rooms.'[7]

The Empress herself made no complaints either about the heat or
the smells, but she was anxious to leave the Marine for the good reason
that, throughout the daylight hours, a crowd of curious holidaymakers
congregated outside the hotel door in the hope of seeing her emerge.
It was all most restricting. But she decided that, as she was still Regent
of France, she could not compromise herself by accepting the hospitality of a noble lord. With her complete trust in Dr Evans, she asked
him to rent for her a country house within easy reach of London.
Evans, by strange coincidence indeed, selected Camden Place, Chislehurst, where, long ago, Prince Louis Napoleon had courted Emily
Rowles, and, stranger still, which now belonged to an executor of the
late Elizabeth Howard. It was believed by some that the Emperor had
made arrangements against just such an eventuality as the present one
before leaving for the front.

The Empress moved in on 20th September and was there joined by
members of the Imperial staff who had escaped by various means from
Paris. Soon she had quite a Court. The Duc de Bassano arrived with his
worldly possessions in a carpet bag, offered his services and became
head of the Household. Marie de Larminat, a *demoiselle d'honneur*,
joined Mme Lebreton as lady-in-waiting. Faithful Filon took on the
task of tutor to the Prince Imperial. The Comte and Comtesse Clary
made their home in a house in the park. There was no shortage in the
'downstairs' department, refugees from the Tuileries including the
maître d'hôtel, two chefs, a butler and a footman, and, most important
of all to Eugenie, her adored Spanish maid, Pepa. To the joy of the
Prince Imperial, his old nurse, Miss Shaw, drove up in a cab.[8] The
etiquette and way of life of the Tuileries and St Cloud continued as
nearly as possible and somehow the wishes of the Empress were met,
although in the process senior servants gained experience of simple
jobs like laying fires and washing up.

There were many callers, not all welcome in a household restricted
and as yet unorganised. But two were received with delight – the

Duchesse de Mouchy and Princess Pauline Metternich, the latter reporting that the Empress's jewels were safely in a British bank.[9]

Among the unwanted callers was Plon-Plon, who had now set up house in London with his notorious mistress, Cora Pearl.[10] He strutted round the room as if he was Napoleon I, criticising the actions taken during the last days of the Empire and referring to the Palikao Ministry as 'half witted.' 'And where were you on the 4th September?' blazed Eugenie. Flushed with anger, he left the room without answering.[11]

Meanwhile events had been moving so fast in France that the reports reaching the Empress kept her busy far into the night. Despite the Emperor's capitulation the country had kept up the fight and Bismarck moved his forces towards Paris. On the day Eugenie moved into Chislehurst the Crown Prince Frederick William set up his head-quarters at Versailles and the investment of Paris was completed.

That evening the son-in-law of Queen Victoria stood on the terrace of the Palace, watching the sunset. He wrote:

> I could not but recall, as I stood there, the fine, warm Sunday in the year 1867 on which the fountains played here in honour of my father and the Tsar Alexander, and we, in company with a host of princely personages . . . were the guests of Napoleon and Eugenie, who did the honours with an amiable courtesy that charmed us. How swiftly has the star of that Imperial pair faded![12]

Bismarck was also in reminiscent mood. He had installed himself in the magnificent château of Baron Rothschild at Ferrières. The Jewish millionaire had departed in a hurry for Paris, leaving his mansion and priceless cellar in the care of his steward. The game-book was lying on its table. Bismarck opened it, thumbed through the pages and pointed out to his secretary that he had shot there on 3rd November 1856. At dinner the steward refused to produce the required wines. Under a fusillade of Bismarckian fury, he gave in. But this put the Prussian leader in a bad mood and he regaled his staff with stories of the mean-ness of the Rothschilds. 'The Jews,' he said, 'have still no true home, but are a sort of universal Europeans. Their fatherland is Zion.' King William of Prussia was more respectful. The park was well stocked with pheasants and deer, but the King gave strict orders that there was to be no shooting. Bismarck waited until the King was away on a review and then blazed away in the woods. 'They cannot arrest me,' he said, 'for then they would have no one to see after the peace.'[13]

There had already been an attempt to end the war. At the request of the British Ambassador, Lord Lyons, Jules Favre, Minister for Foreign Affairs in the first Republican government, had been received by Bismarck. The Prussian leader had told him:

> We have no concern with the form of your government. If we find that it suits our interest to restore Napoleon, we shall bring him back to Paris . . . You represent nothing but an insignificant minority . . . We have to think of our own future safety, and we shall demand the whole of Alsace, together with a part of Lorraine and the town of Metz.

As Favre picked up his dusty overcoat and crumpled hat, he fired back: 'We will not cede one inch of our territory or one stone of our fortresses!'[14]

Bismarck had, in fact, shifted his ground. A few weeks earlier he had been saying that he was set on the destruction of the Second Empire and the Napoleonic dynasty, and that his real quarrel was not with France. He did not wish to treat with Napoleon, ill, crushed, a prisoner.[15] It was Eugenie with whom Bismarck wished to do business in preference to any Republican government. Not only did he consider that she afforded a better guarantee for the future, but he liked and respected her and he preferred to duel with the strong, even if they were under handicap.

On 5th October Bismarck moved to Versailles. On the 7th one-eyed Gambetta, Minister of the Interior in the new Government, made his sensational escape from encircled Paris in a balloon. From Tours he began organising the defences of France. Thrilled, Eugenie wished to join him there and rally Napoleonic sympathisers in the south. She was politely, but firmly, told that, if she was to embark on such a foolhardy adventure, she would simply be arrested by four *gendarmes*.

Eugenie was in a most difficult position. Politically, she was brave but no tactician. She was short of advisers. Letters from the Emperor took time to arrive and were, of necessity, restrained. She wanted, above all, to save Bazaine's army but she knew that the French people would not accept peace terms which entailed the surrender of territory. Strange emissaries came to Camden Place, with hopeful plans but doubtful authority, and fogged the issue. Her letters to Tsar Alexander and Tsar Francis Joseph brought little result. Then Bismarck sent her his terms. They were:

1. That the army at Metz should declare its continued adhesion to the Empire;
2. That the Empress-Regent should simultaneously invite the French people to pronounce on the form of government they wish to adopt;
3. That the basis of a treaty of peace should be signed by a delegate of the Regency.

On these conditions the Army of Metz might retire 'to some district agreed upon by a military convention'.[16]

When Eugenie read these terms, she cried to General Boyer, who had brought them: 'A blank cheque! Must I give Bismarck a blank cheque? They are asking us to sacrifice our honour.'[17] In her reply she demanded a fortnight's truce, with permission to provision Metz, and declared that she would never agree to a diminution of French territory as a basis for a treaty of peace. On 25th October King William wrote to her saying that the negotiations would be discontinued.[18]

On the 27th the famine-stricken forces in Metz, having eaten their horses, surrendered, and 173,000 Frenchmen followed their comrades of Sedan into captivity. The German army which had contained them was now released and marched west to reinforce the troops besieging Paris. The capital was doomed. Bismarck had tried to deal with the Empress-Regent and he had failed. Now he dismissed her as a power, as a voice of France. And the sad truth was soon to emerge that the terms which she could have obtained were lighter and more favourable than those which the French Government was forced to accept in the new year.

The fall of Metz, the utter disgrace and the tragedy of it, overwhelmed Eugenie. At Camden Place she felt trapped, like a goldfish in a bowl. The rain came down on the typically English park. The house was *triste*, like a large and decaying café, some visitor said. There were the same, few sad faces around her. She was accustomed to space, to changing scenes, to action and movement, and suddenly she could bear her Kentish prison no longer.

After the first two weeks of silence there had been a constant flow of letters between Napoleon and his wife. To him, these letters were of immeasurable relief and comfort, while to her they brought a complete change of heart. Gone were the scorn and contempt which had poured from her in rage when she had castigated him for his surrender at Sedan, as she stood on the winding staircase of the Tuileries. There were many reasons for this. Firstly, his letters showed clearly how much he loved her. 'What have I to cleave to, if not to your affection and that of our son?' 'When I am free, I should like to go to England, and live with you and Louis in a little cottage with bow-windows and a creeper.'[19] Secondly, Napoleon's dignity, reticence, lack of excuses, coupled with tales of his bravery and endurance in battle, had enhanced his international reputation. Thirdly, she had learned the truth about his health. When the Duchesse de Mouchy discovered that she was still in ignorance of his sufferings, she told her the details emerging from the consultation of doctors in July.[20]

Others helped to bridge the rift between husband and wife. Lady Cowley and the Duchess of Hamilton had both talked with the Emperor at Wilhelmshöhe. So had Dr Evans, reporting every detail of the flight. Thus there had grown in Eugenie a new priority – the priority of family life.

On the 29th October she told Pepa to pack a small travelling bag. Taking only Comte Clary and Mme Lebreton with her, she caught the night boat across the English Channel, bound for Wilhelmshöhe.

On the afternoon of Sunday, 30th October, Napoleon was informed that his wife had arrived at Cassel station and was on her way to the castle in a carriage. Although he was taken completely by surprise, he walked down the steps to meet her without a trace of emotion on his face. This was his famous act, the expressionless, unfathomable mask. He did it so well, and his words of greeting were so cold and conventional, that even she wondered if she was welcome. But his retinue made compensation, even kneeling on the gravel to kiss the folds of her black dress. It was only when the door of his study closed, and they were alone, that he clasped her in his arms and the fervour of his embrace brought tears to her eyes.

The German Governor, General von Monts, was intrigued by the visit. He had received a telegram from the King saying the couple were to be allowed to talk undisturbed and that, if the Empress so wished, she could remain at Wilhelmshöhe. But neither Napoleon nor Eugenie were opening themselves to the risk of being accused of living in luxury in a gilded cage while the people of Paris starved. She left, as she had come, without warning, on the evening of 1st November. A hired carriage came to the back of the castle and the three departed as quietly as they had arrived.[21] They wanted no German charity and bought their own tickets at the station. Spies watched her until she crossed the frontier, for the swift visit had aroused the interest of King William of Prussia and his son. What, asked Crown Prince Frederick William, can have induced this woman, who but a few days ago offered to put herself in command of the Metz army and surrender with it, to make this sudden and secret visit to Wilhelmshöhe?[22] It was indeed a delicate position, as his mother-in-law was Queen of England and England had given refuge to the Empress.

Queen Victoria herself fully appreciated the delicacy of the position and in November decided that the time had come for her to pay Eugenie a visit. In the past months she had received a number of rude shocks, outstanding among them being the realisation that not all of Albert's plans and beliefs were as correct and inviolate as she had led herself to believe. In August she had written to Queen Augusta of Prussia – 'How my heart beat when I heard the news of our beloved Fritz's[a] sudden and glorious victories.'[23] Albert's nightmare that the French hordes would cross the Rhine and roll on towards Coburg and Berlin had proved very wrong. It had become obvious that the war was of Germany's making and the result a foregone conclusion. But instead of relations between Britain and Germany becoming closer and more friendly, the reverse had happened. As the Crown Princess made very clear to her mother, Berlin was bitter that Britain had not sided with Germany against the aggressor.[24] On the other hand, the German victories and the setting up of the Third Republic had led to a wide pro-French, anti-German feeling in Britain. At a meeting in Trafalgar Square in September the 'Republic of England' had been proclaimed and at Republican meetings throughout the country the Royal Family was labelled a 'pack of Germans.' There was violent criticism of the goings-on of the Prince of Wales and of the vast income of the Queen. Somewhere the Coburg plan had gone aft agley.

(a) Crown Prince Frederick William.

Thus it was with some misgivings that the Queen travelled to Camden Place on 30th November. She was accompanied only by an equerry, Lady Ely, who had chaperoned Eugenie during a London season twenty years before, and Princess Beatrice. Beatrice was thirteen, a year younger than the Prince Imperial. If little of importance happened that day, at least there was born one of those improbable and immaculate boy-and-girl romances in which Queen Victoria delighted to dabble.

The Queen confined her diary report of the visit to platitudes and sad adjectives. She made one factual statement. It was in a message to the Duc de Bassano, in charge of the Household. The message was that, if she was to come to Camden Place again, the windows must be opened.

Five days later the Empress and her son were invited to Windsor. While Louis explored the castle with the younger members of the Royal Family, the Queen entertained Eugenie by taking her, in the pouring rain, to see the 'dear, reclining statue' of Albert in the Mausoleum.[25]

Christmas in Paris. Nineteen degrees of frost and driving snow. For the majority the festive menu consisted of a rat, a carrot or, at best, a sad lump of horseflesh. On the 27th the German bombardment of the suburbs began. The lovely Palace of St Cloud was wrecked, burned out, its marble reduced to powder. On 5th January the shells began to fall on Paris itself. Six women standing in a food queue were killed.[26] On the 18th, in the stately *Salle des Glaces* of Louis XIV's Palace at Versailles, King William of Prussia was declared Emperor of Germany. On the 20th Jules Favre requested a meeting with Bismarck and at midnight on the 27th the rumble of the cannons ceased. The armistice had come but the people of Paris received the news with anger and almost unbelief. On 1st March the German troops marched into Paris. The streets were empty and the windows draped in black. The time had come for Emperor Napoleon III to join his family in the countryside of Kent.

He left Wilhelmshöhe on 19th March and bid an affectionate farewell to his Governor, General von Monts, at the Belgian frontier. He had been well treated, his health had improved and he had put on weight. The cold, bright weather of the German winter had suited him and he had managed to ride a little and to skate.

On the morning of the 20th the station-master at Chislehurst arrived at Camden Place and informed the Empress that a special train was waiting to take her and the Prince Imperial to Dover. He spoke with a pale and anxious woman, wearing a simple dressing gown and unadorned. He barely recognised the vision whom he received on the platform an hour later. She was radiant, poised, exquisitely dressed and bejewelled.

Dover was a revelation. As the boat came in, the Emperor and his small suite at the rail, the vast crowd cheered. Handkerchiefs were waved and hats went up in the air. Napoleon, looking somewhat bewildered and with tears in his eyes, was welcomed by the former Mayor of Dover who had received him in 1855.[27] As husband and wife embraced, they were pelted with flowers and the police had difficulty in clearing a path for them. It was a wonderful experience for the exiles, but some newspapers, in particular *The Times*, thought that it was somewhat unbecoming.

Queen Victoria noted the popular acclaim and a week later Napoleon was her guest at Windsor:

> At a little before three, went down with our children and Ladies and Gentlemen to receive the Emperor Napoleon. I went to the door with Louise and embraced the Emperor '*comme de rigueur*'. It was a moving moment, when I thought of the last time he came here in '55, in perfect triumph, dearest Albert bringing him from Dover . . . He led me upstairs and we went into the Audience Room. He is grown very stout and grey and his moustaches are no longer curled or waxed as formerly, but otherwise there was the same pleasing, gentle and gracious manner . . . While we were alone he began to allude to the origin of the war, but we were unfortunately interrupted, which was very provoking. At half past three I took him downstairs and he left. The Commune has been elected and is going to sit at Paris![28]

Paris, having survived one ordeal, was quickly faced with another. The extremists, backed by the National Guard, wished France to be divided into a number of self-governing Communes. After scenes of brutality and violence, these extremists occupied the Hôtel de Ville and took control of the city. The Government, in which Thiers had succeeded Trochu, retired to Versailles, gathering round it the remains of the French army. For the next two months the situation was as farcical as it was tragic, as Frenchmen besieged Frenchmen in their own capital and the conquering Germans, encamped on the hills around, kept watch.

Mentally, Napoleon was by no means a spent force. In fact he was probably thinking more clearly than ever before in his life. But he was a man of pattern. After a set-back, he would appear to lose all sense of ambition. He had done this after the Strasbourg adventure, when he had considered becoming an American farmer. He had done the same after his escape from Ham. And now the same thing happened after Sedan. But always, after the shock was over and his health had recovered, the ambition was re-born in him and he began the planning which was the breath of his life. It was difficult, if not impossible, to guess at the workings of his mind.

Having enjoyed a convalescence at Wilhelmshöhe and swallowed the tonic of his ovation at the landing at Dover, he dreamed away the hours at Camden Place by scheming for his return to France. But not yet. When the country was in turmoil, he believed in keeping in the shadows, as he had done when President. He wished to be returned to power by a plebiscite and involvement would prejudice votes. Fortunate indeed was it that he kept his silence, for on 21st May the Government troops from Versailles began to force their way into Paris.

For four terrible days and nights the city was like an abattoir. The followers of the Commune shot scores of hostages, including the Archbishop of Paris. When they saw that they could hold out no longer, they set fire to the principal buildings. The Tuileries and the Hôtel de Ville were destroyed and Notre Dame only saved by a miracle. As they took possession of the blackened ruins, the infuriated 'Versaillist' troops took terrible vengeance, for some days shooting every supporter of the Commune who fell into their hands. Between 20,000 and 30,000 Parisians died and the damage done to Paris by Frenchmen was greater than the whole German army had managed to inflict. But no bloodstain from this degrading tragedy soiled the hands of Emperor Napoleon III.

He seemed well content with his life at Camden Place. He settled down to a routine, reading, writing, playing patience and working at his lathe. He strolled down to the village shop and handed out pennies to the children. He watched the cricket with interest but found it difficult to comprehend that men could expose themselves to such risk without the spur of financial reward. On Sundays parties of Bonapartists would arrive by train and take tea under the cedar tree – if it did not rain, which was seldom. He knew that the Republican government had set spies to list the names of all who came to see him – in fact a duplicate copy of the report was on his breakfast table each morning. The old dog still knew the tricks.

Financially, the exiles were comfortably off but not rich, certainly not rich enough to back an invasion. Napoleon came to England with the equivalent of £13,000 in cash. Eugenie and he between them owned properties in France, Italy, Spain and Switzerland, although there was obvious difficulty in realising the French assets. Eugenie managed to sell, for £60,000, all her jewels except a pearl necklace valued at £12,000.

One day Clary went to Rothschild and told him that he had received a communication from a lady unknown, who said that on a certain day she would come to the Grosvenor Hotel closely veiled, look at the necklace, and if she liked it, would pay the money and carry it off. Clary asked for advice, for as he said, there might be a man lurking behind who would play some trick and be off with the pearls. Rothschild said, 'Well, if it comes to that I can lend you our big porter.' So he did. And the lady came with three veils on, bought the necklace and went away . . .[29]

Eugenie had not the patience of her husband and Camden Place bored her stiff. Each day she looked through her window to see the same number of cows munching the wet English grass. Each day she saw the round and cheerful face of Dr Conneau entering and leaving her husband's room. There were the same few faces at the dining table and the same anecdotes were told over and over again. The same depressing people came down on the train on Sundays. She felt cold and lit fires in August.

In September she broke loose and went to Spain, ostensibly to see her mother, who was losing her sight, and to sell a house. Lord Cowley wrote to the Queen of Holland: 'I hear that the Empress has been enjoying herself in Spain far more than under the circumstances she ought to have done.'[30] Meanwhile the Emperor and his son were on holiday in the West Country. At Torquay they stayed at the Imperial

Hotel. The menu so pleased Napoleon that he sent for the chef to congratulate him. He was confronted by one of his own cooks from the Tuileries.

By the time Eugenie returned home in December, the Prince Imperial had begun a course in physics and mathematics at King's College in the Strand, travelling up daily with M. Filon and Louis Conneau. He understood little of the lectures but at least, as he roamed London's streets, he learned the common touch.

One more glimpse of imperial splendour was to come the way of Napoleon. Before Christmas the Prince of Wales nearly died of typhoid, but made a marvellous recovery, and on 27th February 1872 drove with his mother and family to St Paul's for the Thanksgiving Service. The Queen invited the Emperor and Empress to Buckingham Palace to watch the procession leave. They were received by Princess Beatrice, looking very pretty in a mauve dress trimmed with swansdown,[31] and from a window they watched the glory of their past re-born – the Sovereign's escort, the line of open dress carriages, the postilions, the stands and the decorations, the crowds and the bands. This vast display of loyalty in London's streets marked the end of the Republican movement in Britain. Could the same spirit be stirring in France? By the spring reports showed that, if a plebiscite were to be held, Napoleon would poll between five and six million votes.

The tide in France was turning Napoleon's way. Thiers, who had taken over the political leadership of France, was walking a tightrope and the people of the countryside wished for a return to the comparative stability of the Empire. Napoleon circulated pamphlets in the areas where his support was strongest and made contact with the army. His agents crossed and re-crossed the Channel. He sounded Russia as to his return and received a favourable reply. In deep secret he put out feelers for financial support. He told a visitor to Camden Place: 'I know that I am the only solution. Only it is a pity that I am so ill.'[32]

Eugenie, full of new hope, dreamed of her return. She decided that they would live in the Louvre now that the Tuileries had been destroyed and that the Trianon would take the place of St Cloud.

In the summer Napoleon planned to build up his strength on a holiday at a south German watering place, but he was not well enough to travel. He had to content himself with Bognor and Brighton, while Eugenie took her son on a high-powered tour of Scotland.

The family came together again at a rented villa at Cowes. They sailed with Jennie Jerome[33][(a)] and, to Eugenie's delight, Sir John Burgoyne asked her to try out his new yacht, *Iolanthe*. As *Iolanthe* passed *Gazelle*, the crew cheered so enthusiastically that tears came to her eyes.[34] Then back to Camden Place. In October the Prince Imperial joined the Royal Military Academy at Woolwich.

By November Europe was anticipating a return of the Bonapartes. Although Napoleon's plan was completed, he gave no sign of his intentions and the details remained top secret. The greatest obstacle in his path was his health – he was ill, he said, but the doctors could remedy that. He saw one picture clearly, and that picture was of the Emperor riding into Paris, mounted on a superb horse. He would ride in alone, alone as he had always been.

He said to his wife: 'I cannot walk on foot at the head of the troops. It would have a still worse effect to enter Paris in a carriage. It is necessary that I ride.'[35] So it was that he agreed to the operation which he had long postponed. Once the operation was over, he would convalesce at Cowes. As part of his recuperative programme, he would sail on the yachts of his friends. The spies who watched Camden Place would not suspect an invalid at Cowes. But from one of those yachting trips he would not return.

The date for his disappearance was to be 20th March 1873, four days after the seventeenth birthday of the Prince Imperial. The yacht on which he was to sail was owned by Mr James Ashbury.[36] It was to land him at Ostend. Thereafter he was to travel through Belgium, cross the French frontier and make for Châlons. There between 40,000 and 50,000 troops would be stationed for spring manoeuvres. Information from France indicated that these troops would definitely back the Emperor. The financial side was settled and it was later believed that the source was none other than Bismarck.

In December Sir William Gull, the Queen's physician, made an examination. He called in Sir Henry Thompson, the leading urologist. Sir Henry was appalled at the size of the stone, saying that it would have to be broken down bit by bit and that three operations might be necessary. He began his work on 2nd January and continued it four days later. Napoleon appeared relieved and stronger, but Sir Henry was far from complacent. The final operation was fixed for the morning

(a) Afterwards Lady Randolph Churchill and mother of Sir Winston.

of the 9th. To ensure that the patient slept through the night, Dr Gull prescribed a dose of chloral. Napoleon did not wish to take it. Eugenie insisted.

Knowing that he had slept well, in the morning Eugenie planned to visit her son at Woolwich. As she was about to leave, she was told: '*L'Empereur a une petite crise.*' She took off her hat and moved towards his door. She heard someone shouting urgently for the priest – 'Father Goddard, Father Goddard.'

Napoleon said his last words, to his old friend Dr Conneau who sat by his bed: '*N'est-ce pas, Conneau, que nous n'avons pas été des lâches à Sedan?*'

When he saw Eugenie enter, he sent her the weak message of a kiss. Father Goddard led her away. Five minutes later Napoleon died.[37]

'An enormous name has passed out of the living world into history,' commented *The Times*.

CHAPTER 26

The Gay Adventurer

By the death of Napoleon, Eugenie lost a husband but gained a close and faithful friend – Queen Victoria. 'Dear sisters' they were to be for the next twenty-eight years, ever playing the charade of which should have precedence over the other, as they decided who should go first up the stairs.

'*Après vous, ma chère soeur.*'

'*Mais non, ma chère soeur, après vous.*'[1]

Since the Prince Consort's death, Victoria had been starved of feminine friendship. This was in part owing to her aura of 'oneness' and in part owing to her jealousy of those who had men to share their bed. Now there came into her life a woman linked to her by rank, by widowhood and by memories, and the handicap of Napoleon's schemes was ended.

The Queen, seven years the senior, was definitely the elder sister and the arbiter. Eugenie accepted that, appreciating full well the advantages of the protection of the British Queen. But, as younger sisters are apt to do, she poked some gentle fun at the other behind her back and was not above telling stories about John Brown.[2]

It was on 20th February 1873 that Queen Victoria, with Princess Beatrice, travelled from Windsor to Chislehurst:

> We passed through London, which was wrapped in a thick yellow fog. Drove straight from the station in a closed landau to the small Roman Catholic Chapel of St Mary, a pretty, rural little place, quite a village church. To the right of the altar, or rather below it, behind a railing, in the smallest space possible, rest the earthly remains of the poor Emperor, the coffin covered with a black velvet pall, embroidered with golden bees, and covered with wreaths and flowers of all kinds, many of which are also piled up outside, to which Beatrice and I each added one. The banner of the French 'Ouvriers' was placed near the wreaths. Father Goddard, the priest, a quiet,

youngish man, showed us round and also showed us the plan of the small private chapel, which is to be added on.

From thence drove to Camden House, where at the door, instead of his poor father, who had always received me so kindly, was the Prince Imperial, looking very pale and sad. A few steps further on, in the deepest mourning, looking very ill, very handsome, and the picture of sorrow, was the poor dear Empress, who had insisted on coming down to receive me. Silently we embraced each other and she took my arm in hers, but could not speak for emotion. She led me upstairs to her boudoir, which is very small and full of the souvenirs which she had been able to save . . .

The poor Empress said that . . . Prince Napoleon had behaved very badly, wanting to take the boy, '*tout ce que j'ai*', away from her and not to leave him in England. But she was firm, having been left, by the Emperor's will, her son's guardian. Prince Napoleon wanted her to take him away from Woolwich (which the boy likes very much, and is only half an hour's drive from Chislehurst), saying that Bertie disapproved of his remaining there, which I assured her was precisely the reverse. Prince Napoleon had wanted to take him away, in order to '*faire l'aventure avec lui*', and to ruin him, but the boy was quite determined not to yield to his cousin.[3]

Plon-Plon had not only behaved very badly, he had also been very stupid. After the Emperor's death he had arrived at Camden Place overflowing with authority. He demanded to see the will. It was produced. Made in April 1865, the relevant paragraphs read:

> I leave to the Empress Eugenie all my private property . . . I trust that my memory will be dear to her and that after my death she will forget the griefs I may have caused her. With regard to my son, let him keep as a talisman the seal I used to wear attached to my watch, and which belonged to my mother; let him carefully preserve everything which comes to me from the Emperor my uncle, and let him be convinced that my heart and soul remain with him. I make no mention of my faithful servants – I am convinced that the Empress and my son will never abandon them.[4][a]

(a) The estate totalled some £60,000.

Plon-Plon exploded with anger. He simply could not believe that he had been completely ignored. He insinuated that there had been a later will and that this had been hidden or destroyed. Eugenie took him into her husband's study. There all the drawers had been sealed by secretary Pietri immediately after the death. The Prince tore the seals away and searched through the contents. He insisted that he had seen the Emperor place a highly secret document in a certain drawer, and that now it was not there.[5]

Eugenie, tired out, harrassed by the funeral arrangements, did her best to put matters to rights. She moved towards her husband's cousin, her hands outstretched towards him, and pleaded with him that they should now be friends. He replied that he would consider the suggestion, and left the house. Forty-eight hours later the answer came. It stipulated that, as a condition of friendship, he should be acknowledged as the head of the Bonapartist party and that the Prince Imperial should be given over into his care and taken away from the Military Academy at Woolwich. Eugenie's resultant fury proved both a safety valve for her pent-up emotions and an antidote to her grief.

Plon-Plon was ever convinced that he had a degree of power and influence which surpassed by far the reality. It was this delusion which had led him to irritate Queen Victoria during the State visit to France and now again at the time when she was supporting the Empress in her grief. Unpopular on account of his shabby treatment of his wife, Princess Clothilde, he became a figure of fun when his discarded mistress, Cora Pearl, awarded her lovers with the accolade of allowing them to wear the nightshirt which Plon-Plon had left behind him.[6] Yet Prince Napoleon was by far the cleverest of the Bonapartes apart from the founder of the family. He was a man of most varied abilities. In old age truth came to this fallen Caesar and he said of himself, 'I can succeed in nothing'. When he died in 1891, he was described as 'the most brilliant failure of the nineteenth century'.[7]

Queen Victoria had another part to play at this sad time. To a certain extent she filled the gap left in the life of the Prince Imperial by the death of his father. She was a protecting arm against the schemes of men such as Plon-Plon. She, and she alone, could resurrect for him the way of life to which he had been accustomed since birth. All his memories were of the Tuileries and Compiègne, St Cloud and Biarritz, and these contrasted strangely with the dreary little house in which he lived at Woolwich and with the caricature of a court at Chislehurst. Thus he welcomed visits to Osborne and Windsor. He was not impressed – it was like coming home. As he had always moved among, and chatted with, Kings and Emperors, Prime Ministers and Ambassadors, he was not overcome or shy in the presence of Queen Victoria. And the straightforwardness and confidence of the boy appealed to the Queen. After he had chatted unceasingly to his hostess throughout dinner at Osborne – an occasion which was often gloomy and silent – a member of the Household asked him if he was not frightened of Her Majesty. 'Good gracious, no,' he replied. 'She is my friend.' In fact he took liberties with her which were only equalled by John Brown and the bawdy Lord Fife.

The Queen's faith in him, and her belief that it would be in the best interests of France if, in the foreseeable future, he returned there as Napoleon IV,[8] helped to dilute the bitterness and the pain which the Prince felt at the sustained propaganda poured out by the left wing of the Republican party. It was said that he was degenerate and physically weak and that 'Baby', as they called him, had shown himself to be a coward on the battlefield; that he was a *fruit sec* – a dunce, his examination results at Woolwich being faked by the instructors, and that he was so unpopular that his fellow cadets would not even speak to him. In fact he was well liked at the 'Shop', the best horseman there, and his examination results did not do justice to his progress owing to his lack of knowledge of the English language and his volatile character.

The Prince could not answer back. When he showed signs of exasperation, the example of his father was held up to him, for the Emperor had been of a different temperament, and had been able to ignore criticism and abuse – except for the last charge that he had been a coward at Sedan. The Prince took after his mother, who had blanched with fury when attacks were made upon her before her marriage. But even she, in exile, had learned to ignore the poisoned darts aimed at her. She had to endure a cartoon of herself lying naked on a billiard table. It was entitled '*La Poule*' – 'the tart'.[9]

To reply to such propaganda would only have added to its circulation. The only answer was to ignore the filth. But even then the gibes and the innuendoes ate into the reputation of an absent Prince among the solid country folk who were the main supporters of the Bonapartists.

Yet he was not altogether starved of the sweet sound of cheers, to give him hope and courage. The music came on the two happiest days of his exile in England. The first was his eighteenth birthday, 16th March 1874, when the political situation was still encouraging. There swept over France a wave of emotion, a desire to seek and applaud, the small boy who had been a show-piece of the Second Empire and was now passing into manhood. Paris caught the spirit and *'Partant pour la Syrie'* was played at the theatres. The Republicans ranted in their anger and threatened all manner of punishment for those who travelled to Kent for the celebration. But the Bonapartist supporters ignored the restrictions imposed and packed the Channel steamers and sailed their small boats toward the white cliffs of Dover. Admission to Camden Place was by ticket, issued from Willis's Rooms in London, and the demand far exceeded the supply. The South Eastern Railway saw the opportunity for business and laid on excursion trains from London Bridge and Charing Cross. 'Majority of the Prince Imperial' ran the poster and Londoners flocked to Kent to see how the French behaved *en fête*.[10]

Decorated Chislehurst was chaos that morning of brilliant sunshine. Bells were ringing, bands playing, booth-holders shouting, and the road from the station was solid with carriages and pedestrians. At the gates of Camden Place a force of police was hard pressed sorting out the genuine ticket holders. In the grounds two great marquees had been erected, one, holding three thousand people, in which the Prince was to make his speech, the other for refreshments.

The programme opened with a service at St Mary's, where lay the body of the Emperor. Here only the elite could be accommodated. Father Goddard's impassioned panegyric of the dead man was greeted with loud applause, more suited to a theatre than a quiet country church. Then the congregation moved into the marquee to join the thousands already there.

The flap at the back was raised and the Prince Imperial, his mother on his arm, moved on to the stage. 'The shout that met him was terrifying. It was like a blow, like the buffeting of the sea in fury.'[11] Then dead silence. The Prince rose. He spoke well, with carefully guarded sentences. His reception gave him confidence. His voice gained in strength and emphasis, and filled the marquee. In those few moments he grew up, hypnotised by his new found power.

'If the name of Napoleon should emerge, an eighth time, from the ballot boxes, I am ready to accept the charge imposed on me by the will of the nation . . . Carry my remembrance to the absent – and to France the prayers of one of her children. My courage and life are hers.'

As he bowed and ended, there came a tide of acclamation so strong that it bore the standing audience towards the platform. Stewards, seeing the danger, closed around the Empress and her son and escorted them away. When at last some semblance of order had been restored, the Prince began the ordeal of shaking hands with his army of guests. Slowly they passed, lingering for a word and a touch, and by twilight only half had been received. Those remaining were told that the Prince would be ready for them on the morrow. As the darkness came he stood in a lighted window and the cheering from the undiminished crowd was the sweetest music of all that day. But marvellous as the reception had been, Eugenie was dubious as to the wisdom of it and of the end result. If the celebration had been in France, the flame of enthusiasm might have spread. But it had taken place in a quiet corner of a foreign land. It was only a secondhand version that would reach the French voters. The Republicans had been given clear warning that the embers of Bonapartism could still quickly be fanned into a strong flame. They had been given the chance to take precautions and retaliatory steps. And this, in fact, they did.

The second great day in the life of the Prince in England was the passing-out at the 'Shop'. On 15th February 1875 the Commander-in-Chief, the Duke of Cambridge, wrote in his diary:

Went to Woolwich for the public day of the Royal Academy. Saw the Cadets, who drilled and looked well. The Prince Imperial drilled them remarkably well when called upon. The Empress Eugenie was present throughout the day. She went with me . . . into the Gymnasium, where the Reports were read and the Prizes given. The Prince Imperial took the 7th place in the List, a most excellent position for a Cadet 11 months younger than the greater portion of his class, and who had to study in a foreign language . . . Saw the rides, which were excellent. The Prince Imperial took the first place, also first in fencing.[12]

Although the Prince was seventh overall, he had been first in a preliminary examination, first in the rides and first in fencing. He forgot about the seventh, remembering only those magic placings, FIRST, FIRST, FIRST. If he was to return to France, only the best would do. At a ball that evening he was carried round the floor shoulder-high. That nailed the Republican lie that he was unpopular with his fellows. He spoke at a farewell banquet: 'Never can I forget these years spent at Woolwich, or cease to value the honour of belonging to a corps whose motto is *Ubique quo fas et gloria ducunt.*'

'Everywhere where deeds and glory lead . . .' That now became his motto. Only glory would enable him to ride, alone at the head of a column, along his beloved boulevards of Paris. He began to see his career in the long term, the final target standing far beyond the memorial stone of death. Death was but an awkward happening along the path. France, and all men, must remember him, and think well of him, long after his life was over. He had certainly started well on the path. The Queen wrote to the Duke of Cambridge:

> 'I am truly gratified and pleased at the success of the dear young Prince Imperial . . . The Academy will, I am sure, always feel proud that he distinguished himself in their School, and that he should have acquitted himself so honourably, and, above all, *behaved* so well.'[13]

By 'behaved well', she was recalling the sad affair of her own son, the Prince of Wales. His only military experience had been a summer camp with the Guards at the Curragh in 1861. He had disgraced the Family by spending the last night with an actress, Nellie Clifden, who had been smuggled into his quarters.

When her son came back to Camden Place from Woolwich, the Empress was worried. He had been fully occupied at the 'Shop', but now he would have time on his hands. True, he had received a posting to a battery of the Royal Horse Artillery at Aldershot, but she could not believe that occasional camps and manoeuvres would hold his interest or satisfy his ambitions. Would he now become involved in adventures such as his father had indulged in at a like age? He assured her that he would not, as he dreaded any experience that was 'undignified'. He had no wish to make a small scale, unannounced return to France, be ignominiously arrested, and then banished or imprisoned.

He was prepared to wait for the right moment, which he was convinced would come.

Eugenie took him abroad as much as possible, spending most summers at Arenenberg. She and Napoleon had paid a number of visits to the Swiss château. He had loved it and put everything back in the place where it had been when Queen Hortense was alive.[14] After Sedan he had arranged for the carriage which he had used in the campaign and the Imperial *fourgon* to be sent there.[15] In the days of the Empire Eugenie had considered the house small and unexciting compared with her country homes in France, but now, with its woods and water, it came to take the place of Compiègne.

England, with its insularity, its high opinion of itself, its somewhat patronising approach to exiles, tended to stifle her. In Switzerland she was left alone. The hills were high and the skies clear. Here she and her son were able to meet people, Austrian and Italian, who did not visit Britain. To the ordinary people 'at home', as she now referred to Chislehurst, she was the nice, sad lady at the big house. By the shores of Lake Constance she was still a real Empress, even if she be so in miniature.

One summer the two of them went to Italy and the Prince Imperial was received by the Pope. When he was twenty-two he was despatched on a tour of Scandinavia and proved a great success in royal circles. But, to his deep disappointment, in France the wave of Bonapartist enthusiasm, which had been envisaged in 1874, did not materialise. The unexpected has ever ruled French politics, but few imagined that the image of the Napoleons would fade so quickly from the memories of the mass of voters. The father might have had a chance in 1873, but the unknown son had none five years later. Industrialisation and the railways had played their part. In the elections of October 1877 the Republicans gained a strong majority, 335 to 198. It was clear that only a startling and untoward event could lead to the return of a Napoleon to France.

Being a true son of Napoleon III, it was only natural that the Prince Imperial should seek the amusement and excitements of social life. This was made easy for him as the Prince of Wales absorbed him into the Marlborough House set. The two shared a common liking for pranks and larks. Although 'Bertie' was fifteen years older, as a young man he had been starved of fun by his stern and serious-minded father. He was now making up for lost time. Besides the French Prince, he included among his youthful cronies his youngest brother, Leopold, born in 1853, a haemophiliac but very intelligent and gay, and Prince Louis of Battenberg, born in 1854, a handsome naval officer who was a magnet to the ladies. With these sparks around him, the Heir to the Throne would range around the West End clubs and play havoc at country house weekends. 'Bertie's' current girl friend was Lillie Langtry, up to any mischief. She recalled that, when staying at Mrs Cust's cottage at Cowes, there was an attempt at a séance during which the Prince Imperial poured a sack of flour over 'Bertie's' head. One night the two of them hoisted a donkey up to a first floor window, dressed it up in women's clothes and placed it in the bed of the son of the house.[16]

It was obvious that such goings on must be kept from the Queen. May be she closed her eyes to the activities of the Prince Imperial but she made a clear diagnosis of Prince Louis of Battenberg. Considering his attentions to Princess Beatrice to be somewhat 'fresh', she arranged for him to be sent to distant waters. Her suspicions were proved to be well founded when, on his return, he had a child by Lillie Langtry. Exiled again, this time, fittingly enough, on H.M.S. *Inconstant*, the sailor Prince came back to redeem himself by marrying the Queen's favourite granddaughter, Victoria of Hesse.[17]

From the time that the Prince Imperial left Woolwich, the gossip magazines were busy finding a bride for him. Princess Thyra of Denmark, sister of the Princess of Wales, was one candidate mentioned, but the favourite was Princess Beatrice. The strange point about this was that the Queen did nothing to scotch the rumour, as she had done in the case of Louis of Battenberg. She must have known that the Prince Imperial was often on the milk-train for Chislehurst after cavorting at Marlborough House, and that the type of ladies enter-tained by 'Bertie' would make dead set for him – as, in fact, they did. She knew full well that the Napoleonic strain was not noted for its resistance to temptation. Yet she flashed no warning light.

Beatrice, as a young girl, had been both perky and mischievous. She had cheeked her father and tied her mother to a chair by her apron strings. But when the Prince Consort died, the gloom of the Court swamped the girl. The Queen put out the spark in her. By the time that she reached her 'teens she was so shy that she blushed and stam-mered when spoken to. Never in her life had she been allowed to be alone in a room with a man, not even her brothers.[18] The very mention of engagement to be married was forbidden at the dinner table when she was there. The Queen had determined, in the way of Victorian mammas, 'not to allow her last daughter to go to anyone'.[19] She was to stay at home and play the part of companion and secretary.

Queen Victoria was deep, wily, obstinate and selfish when it came to romance. She had earthy ideas about sex, considering that a young couple had but to be shut in a bedroom for eternal love to sprout. Her main considerations in arranging life unions were self-centered. In the case of the Prince Imperial, a marriage was clearly impossible, as he was a Roman Catholic.

The Prince encouraged the rumours by his approach to Beatrice. He was completely straightforward. He would ride up to her carriage, walk with her in the garden, chatting away in a most natural way, as he did to the Queen, as he did to everybody. If he was attracted to her, who can tell? Probably he was. He was small and swarthy and volatile, she plump, roses and cream, and the opposites call to one another, just as the fair Hesse girls had appealed to the dark Romanoffs, as, later, Beatrice's daughter, Ena, was to attract King Alfonso of Spain. The danger of haemophilia was just ignored.

Perhaps Queen Victoria let the romance trot along in respect for the feelings of the Empress Eugenie, two mammas hatching a little plan. But if the question is asked, was Beatrice in love with the Prince Imperial, the answer must be yes, if love can be attributed to a girl who had never held a man's hand or knew where babies came from. Her subsequent actions showed her feelings. She probably felt the same about Louis of Battenberg – she married his brother.

Yet marriage was not on the cards of the Prince Imperial. At twenty-three he said: 'I have not cared to let my wing be clipped by marriage.'[20] Close as he and his mother were, he followed his father in putting the ideal before any woman. It is difficult to believe that, bred out of such a sire, he was inexperienced in sex. His defamers in the Republican press revealed that he had a 'lower middle-class' mistress whom he had met on the train to Chislehurst. It was said that he had set her up in a flat in south London. If so, it was but an incident.[21]

As he grew to manhood, he began to tire of the social round. He studied political history and wrote pamphlets. He scanned the world for a military adventure which he could join and there win a cloak of military glory. When Austria became involved in trouble in the Balkans, he applied to join the forces of Emperor Francis Joseph, but was quickly rejected. He saw his chance when Britain decided to take punitive action in Zululand.

On 22nd January 1879 the Zulus overran the invading force at Isandhlwana. Eight hundred British troops were killed, more than half of them belonging to the South Wales Borderers. Reinforcements prepared to leave England. Among them was the battery to which the Prince Imperial was attached. The Prince applied to the Duke of Cambridge to be allowed to travel with his unit and his friends. The Empress was with him in the room at Camden Place when the answer came. She was watching his face as he opened the envelope. She saw a look of dismay and unbelief contort his features. He stammered out: 'I have been refused.' Then he burst into tears.

Eugenie had not seen him cry since the day at Biarritz when, as a child, he had been thrown into the sea. She could not bear it, she who had said before Sedan that she would rather see her son dead than dishonoured. Then he had been a boy – now he was a man and an officer.

She hurried to the Horse Guards and interviewed the Commander-in-Chief. Ever as putty in the hands of a pretty woman, the Duke of Cambridge gave ground. The Queen weighed in on the side of the Empress. Disraeli considered the idea to be most 'injudicious' but said that he could do nothing in the face of 'two obstinate old women'. It was agreed that the Prince Imperial should travel out as a civilian and on arrival be attached to the staff of the commanding General in some minor capacity. 'He *must* be very careful not to expose himself unnecessarily, for we know he is very venturesome,' said the Queen.[22]

Observers are not welcomed by commanders in the field. In Africa the Prince Imperial outwitted the officers, already fully occupied, who were detailed to curb him. He courted death as openly as his father had done at Sedan. But while Napoleon had sought death as a relief for his degradation and pain, to his youthful son danger was both an exhilaration and a means to an end.

On 1st June, when the small patrol of which he was a member was surprised by Zulus, he attempted to vault into the saddle of his already moving horse. He had done it many times before – it had been a favourite trick of his father. But this time the strap broke and his right arm was struck by a hoof as he fell. Slowly he rose to his feet and faced the enemy. He moved towards them, revolver in his left hand. He fired three times. Then he ran at them, tripped, and eighteen assegais pierced him as he lay upon the ground.

Next morning his body was recovered and began its journey to the coast. A French journalist who watched the sad procession, wrote: 'I thought how deeply shall they repent, those whose insults drove this unfortunate Prince to prove his manhood even at the cost of his life, when history shall relate how, in this far-off land, the last of the Napoleons brought honour by his very death to the banner of France.'[23]

The news reached England on 19th June and Queen Victoria arranged that it be broken gently to the Empress. Eugenie sat white and motionless for some hours. Soon she wrote:

> I am left alone, the sole remnant of a shipwreck; which proves how vain are the grandeurs of this world ... I cannot even die; and God, in his infinite mercy, will give me a hundred years of life ...[24]

On 11th July the remains of the Prince Imperial reached Chislehurst. One-eyed, mutilated beyond recognition, the sight of him was kept from his mother. It was her old friend and saviour, Dr Evans, who identified a gold filling which he had inserted into a tooth.[25]

The Queen and Princess Beatrice were at Camden Place for the funeral, kneeling before the coffin in the Chapelle Ardente and placing their wreaths upon it. As the procession formed up, they joined the Empress in a shuttered room. It was so dark that they could not see where she sat. A faint voice asked if Beatrice was there. Then she rose like a spectre and kissed the girl.[26]

The Prince of Wales and the Duke of Cambridge were among the pall bearers. The coffin, draped in the flags of France and Britain, was borne on a gun carriage, the Prince's horse behind it. Now St Mary's sheltered the remains of the last Emperor of the French and of his son.

A blankness came over Eugenie and she hid from the eyes of men. All her life was centered around the little church across the common, her only aim to visit the spot where her son had died. Alone with her memories. Ten short years before she had sailed the Mediterranean in the Imperial yacht, been fêted in Turkey, held the eyes of the world as she opened the Suez Canal. Then her husband ruled France and her son was in his schoolroom at St Cloud.

Now – 'I am alone, the sole remnant of a shipwreck ...'

The Gay Adventurer

Queen Victoria did her best to help, fearing that the Empress would suffer a mental or physical collapse under the strain. While she was at Balmoral in the autumn, she invited Eugenie to stay at nearby Abergeldie Castle. The two women walked together by the Dee and picnicked in the shiels, and the holiday did Eugenie good. But it was while she was at Abergeldie that she learned that her mother was dying.

Manuela, eighty-five and almost blind, had not the strength to withstand the shock of her grandson's death and the constant stream of poignant, heart-rending letters which reached her from Camden Place. Eugenie set out for Madrid, having received permission to travel through France. She had almost given up hope that she would hear and see again the clatter on the quay at Calais, the streets of Paris, the countryside over which she had so often gazed as she journeyed to her villa at Biarritz. She arrived in Madrid the day after Manuela died. The Duke of Alba cared for her.

Still her strength held. In March 1880 she set out for the Cape, her party of seven headed by Sir Evelyn and Lady Wood. Eight hundred miles she travelled in a four-horse carriage; fifty nights she slept under canvas. The night of the 1st June, the anniversary of the death of the Prince Imperial, she spent alone by the foot of a stone cross which Queen Victoria had ordered to be erected on the spot where he had fallen. Tapers burned at the foot of the cross. In the utter stillness before the dawn, the flames of the tapers bent and flickered, as if some presence had disturbed their burning. Eugenie thought that her son was by her and she whispered: 'Do you want me to go away, Louis?'

Then she began her long journey back to Kent.

263

CHAPTER 27

The Merry Widow

Eugenie was fifty-four. The forty years left to her were divided into two equal and distinct parts. For the first twenty she was the exiled Empress, the tragic widow who had lost her only son, the protégée of Queen Victoria. For the second twenty, she was *doyenne* among the Sovereigns of Europe.

The mantle of tragedy was placed about her more by custom of the nineteenth century than by truth. In the event, once she had overcome the first, frightful shock of the death of the Prince Imperial and taken steps to ensure that his memory, and that of his father, was suitably enshrined, she led a full and active life. It would not be out of place to describe her as a merry widow, and she was laughing, entertaining and enjoying herself until a few days before her death. She lived to a great age because she did not bottle up, and dwell upon, her grief as Queen Victoria had done. 'Don't dramatise life,' she would say. 'It is quite dramatic enough as it is.'[1] She poured out her emotions – sadness, temper, anger, delight. She filled her life with places and people. Her yacht was a familiar sight in harbours from Scandinavia to Egypt. Her face was to be seen at the windows of the *wagons-lits* of Europe, and she seldom bothered to reserve a seat for rail journeys. She achieved an ambition when exploring Ceylon, a dream born when she was in the Red Sea after the opening of the Suez Canal in 1869. She loved the sun. She surrounded herself with the young, with a preference for the beautiful and the handsome. In the garden of her Riviera villa she built an annex to house the overflow of young bachelors who were her guests.[2] In spirit, if not in action, she followed in the footsteps of Manuela her mother, in the far away gay days at Carabanchel.

She read avidly and built up a splendid library. But, in the main, she lived so long because she did not fret and because she liked fun. She felt that the Empress had died on 4th September 1870 and now that she was a different person, watching the game of life from the side lines. When a visitor called upon her at her hotel in Paris, she took him to the window and, pointing to some steps in the Place de la Concorde, she said: 'That is where King Louis Philippe and Queen Amélie scrambled into a cab and fled.' Then, pointing towards the Louvre, she added: 'And that is where I scrambled into a cab and fled.'³

When she came back from Africa in the summer of 1880, her first task was to build a suitable resting place for her dead. St Mary's Church was too small and she considered purchasing a neighbouring field and enlarging. But the owner, a Protestant, refused to sell.⁴ Eugenie was in no mood to be thwarted and asked Sir Lintorn Simmons, commandant at Woolwich while the Prince Imperial was there, and her lawyers to find her another home. They suggested Farnborough Hill in Hampshire and she agreed their choice. She moved in the following year, anxious now to break the link with Camden Place which held many sad memories.

Farnborough Hill, the property of Mr Longman the publisher, was set in a park of sixty-eight acres. It looked across the valley, where ran the London-Southampton railway, to a pine-clad hill. This land was also purchased by the Empress, giving her 275 acres in all, and here she planned to build a Memorial Church and a mausoleum for her husband and son, and a Priory to house the four monks who would sing masses for their souls.⁽ᵃ⁾ A private bridge spanned the railway line.

Farnborough Hill was pure Victoriana – Norman roof, a touch of the Gothic, bow windows, verandahs. In the grounds were graperies, fernery and orchid-houses. A wooded island graced an artificial lake. A deep shrubbery edged in her privacy. It was all in strong contrast with the homes which she had known in France, but there were hills and many trees, and the rainbow of the rhododendrons and the gold of the gorse, and she came to love her Hampshire home intensely.⁽ᵇ⁾

She engaged a French architect, M. Destailleur. First he made alterations to the house and then began work on the Priory and the Church, which Eugenie decided should be named St Michael's. Soon Farn-

---

(a) The Empress originally intended the red brick house connected with the church for a few secular priests, but she found it impossible to get chantry priests in modern England, so she installed a small community of Premonstratensian canons from Storrington in Sussex . . . In 1895, however, the Premonstratensians withdrew from St Michael's and the Empress requested the Abbot of Solesmes to send a group of monks to take over the care of the Mausoleum. In July 1903 the priory was raised by Pope Leo XIII to the dignity of an abbey. (Dorothy Mostyn – 'Farnborough Hill'.)

(b) See (d) at foot of following page.

borough Hill became a Napoleonic museum. The carriages and the memorabilia of Napoleon I and Queen Hortense came from Arenenberg[a] and, as her private possessions were returned to her by the French authorities, it seemed as if the Second Empire lived again. In the grand gallery hung the seven panels of Gobelins tapestry rescued from her villa at Biarritz. There were the Winterhalters of Paca and the Duchesse de Mouchy and of herself surrounded by her ladies. There were chairs from Compiègne. Cabinets displayed perfect examples of Sèvres china. Side by side stood the little goat-cart in which the Prince Imperial had ridden at St Cloud and the perambulator which had been presented to him by the Prince Consort.[5]

The one sad room in the house was known as 'The Prince's Study'. Here was laid out everything which had belonged to her son, the table on which he had written his will, his smoking-cap, his books and pamphlets, his swords and uniforms and treasured possessions of his Woolwich days. It was as if it was ready for his return. It was as Victoria had done for Albert.

Farnborough became a mecca for visiting royalties. Among them was Princess Marie of Battenberg[b] who wrote:

Windsor, 25th March 1886

Yesterday Liko,[c] Beatrice, and I visited the Empress Eugenie at Farnborough Hill. The Empress is ... particularly attached to Beatrice, because her son, it is said, was deeply in love with her.

We travelled by special train to Frimley, and were driven from there in a green, four-seated open carriage with mourning liveries. The house at Farnborough Hill lies about half an hour's distance from the station, a charming, irregular building[d] ... It is situated on a hill

(a) The Swiss château was handed over to the Canton of Thurgau in 1906.
(b) Princess zu Erbach-Schonberg, aunt of Earl Mountbatten of Burma.
(c) Prince Henry of Battenberg, whom Princess Beatrice had married the previous year.
(d) Dorothy Mostyn writes: 'In some points the architecture of Farnborough Hill is in the early English domestic style. The main block of the building rises from the ground in deep rose brick with stone-mullioned plate-glass windows, as far as the first storey. It then blossoms out into a pattern of teak fleurs-de-lys and arched beams set in pebble-dash, with several beautiful balconies of carved teak supported by stone angels. The square hood moulds around the windows are decorated with delightfully carved corbels representing birds and small animals ... The many gables of the steep-pitched roof ... cluster round a central tower, five storeys high, which dominates the countryside and is a landmark seen from all directions.

in extremely pretty wooded surroundings. The house is prettily furnished, very stately, and quite Imperial. Eugenie received us in the kindest way, but with something of Court formality. She spoke to me in the third person, addressing me as 'Your Highness'. She has white hair prettily done, and is still beautiful, with enchantingly graceful movements and an indescribable charm. She wore black merino with crêpe. After we had sat some time with her in the salon she took us by a wide road through her property to a hill opposite, on which she is having a mausoleum built for her son, which is already almost completed: it is very large, with a cathedral-like cupola, and profuse ornamentation, in white Portland stone. About two o'clock we had luncheon in a wonderful room hung with Gobelin tapestries; we ate off silver with the French arms. On the glasses the famous 'N' in gold was to be seen. The company consisted, beside ourselves, of Madame Lebreton, Monsieur Pietri, and two nieces of the Empress, young Spanish girls with their governess. After luncheon, which was very good, the Empress showed us all her rooms and valuable pictures, and then led us into her son's where everything lies and stands just as he left it when he went to South Africa.

The silver cradle presented to the King of Rome (son of Napoleon I) by the city of Paris is likewise there, and a picture of the place where Prince Louis Napoleon, Eugenie's son, fell. He lies stretched out dead in the sun-dried grass, and on the dim distant horizon the towers of Paris are seen rising like a Fata Morgana.[a] A garland of fresh violets lay in front of the picture. It was all so desperately sad, I could not restrain my tears. We left at four o'clock. I must say it made an extremely strange impression, this echo of French Imperialism on English soil, the refuge of so many and such different exiles.[6]

By the beginning of 1888 St Michael's Church was completed. On 9th January, the fifteenth anniversay of the death of Napoleon III, a battery of the Royal Horse Artillery arrived at St Mary's Church, Chislehurst. The coffins of the Emperor and his son were placed upon gun carriages and began their journey to Farnborough and the crypt of St Michael's. There awaited them two sarcophagi of Aberdeen

(a) A mirage seen in the Straits of Messina.

granite, the gift of Queen Victoria, standing in the transepts to either side of the altar. The task of a wife and a mother was over.

Of all the lost Imperial glories and pleasures, Eugenie missed most her yacht, *L'Aigle*. The sea was her antidote to illness and ennui and she bought *Thistle* from the Duke of Hamilton. As a craft, *Thistle* was not in the 'R.Y.' class, rolling, tossing and pitching in the slightest sea. For this reason offers to sail in her were often, and wisely, declined. But the Empress was proof against seasickness and in storms would climb up to the bridge and enjoy the experience.[7]

Twice yearly invitations arrived from Queen Victoria, in the summer to stay at Osborne Cottage in the Isle of Wight, and in the autumn to Abergeldie Castle on Deeside. Eugenie's love for Scotland all but equalled her passion for the sea, and the stately Castle, with the French influence about it, was the nearest to the standards of Compiègne and St Cloud that she achieved in Britain.

The Queen's progress north was a complicated ritual and intrigued Eugenie. The time-table was printed a month in advance and plans circulated of the carriages and the seats to be occupied by everyone. There was a halt for tea at Leamington in the early hours. Before her first trip on the 'Special' the Empress perused all the instructions and her sense of fun overcame her. She inquired of a lady-in-waiting if one undressed and donned a nightdress. The lady-in-waiting confirmed this procedure. There had been a number of railway accidents about this time and Eugenie remarked that it would surely be rather embarrassing if a naked lady of the royal retinue was to be discovered on the track. During the night journey she bought a newspaper at a station. In it was the story of yet another accident. She cut out the relevant columns and despatched them, by special messenger, to the sleeping lady-in-waiting.[8]

Eugenie's stays on Deeside were made more pleasant owing to her friendship with John Brown. If one wanted to catch a fish or ride a good pony, it was essential to be on amiable terms with the ghillie, and few visitors achieved this. Eugenie understood the strange relationship which existed between the Queen and her Personal Servant, and was duly rewarded. When he died the wreath of the last Empress of the French lay beside that of Queen Victoria on the coffin in old Crathie churchyard.

Culturally, the two women had somewhat different tastes. When

The Emperor, the Empress and the Prince Imperial
at Camden Place, Chiselhurst, Kent

The death of the Prince Imperial

Above: Edward VII and Queen Alexandra at Cowes
Below: Farnborough Abbey from the air

Madame Albani was staying at Mar Lodge, Braemar, the Queen asked the famous singer to perform at Balmoral. To sing with only the two royal ladies as audience was an ordeal, but Madame Albani did her best. While the Queen was obviously delighted, it was plain that the Empress was bored. This riled the opera star and she became determined to make effect. With all the 'stops out', she broke into '*Partant pour la Syrie*', the theme song of the Second Empire which she had sung at the Tuileries in the great days. Eugenie howled.[9]

Despite the close friendship existing between them, Victoria never allowed Eugenie to forget who was dominant. No woman was ever allowed on the same step. One night at Balmoral, when neighbouring nobility were being entertained, the Empress made a slip as to the relationship between families. The Queen snapped at her. Eugenie tried to put matters right, but only made them worse. She then retired to a window seat and refused to discuss any subject but the weather, because, as she said, each time that she opened her mouth she seemed to put her foot in it.[10]

In her own home Eugenie was a very different woman to the one whom Queen Victoria knew – many people noticed the instant deference that came over her when she arrived at Osborne or Balmoral. At Farnborough she was always '*Sa Majesté*'. With her thoughts ever on Fontainebleau and Versailles, Compiègne and the Tuileries, she felt constrained on her Hampshire estate and this was apparent in her moods and temper. On occasion she would bang the dining-table with her fist and make the plates and glasses rattle. When controversial figures such as Garibaldi and Trochu were introduced into the conversation, she would seize a toothpick and flash it about as if it was a stiletto.[11] Some of her staff found that being bottled up with the volcanic exile was too much for their nerves, and returned to France. But the majority of them understood, accepted her as she was and were faithful unto death.

Eugenie became easily bored. Then she would slowly take off the five wedding rings[(a)] which she always wore, and put them back, uttering 'Ah' at intervals as she did so.[12] She found the English gentry heavy on the hand and had her own way of dealing with them. When a dowager called with her daughters, she recounted a distinctly *risqué*

(a) Her own, her husband's, her father's, her mother's, and Paca's.

story about two swans. Mamma gathered her brood about her and bid a hasty retreat.

She was a clever mimic. When really annoyed by someone present, she would discuss his or her faults in the third person, and continue to do so until her victim left the room. It was necessary for her to have an explosive character in her circle of acquaintances, and she found that person in Dame Ethel Smyth.

Composer and Suffragette, rebel and author, Ethel Smyth was dynamic. She was twenty-five when she was introduced to the Empress and they remained friends for life. She would arrive at Farnborough Hill on her new fangled bicycle and wearing trousers. She changed into a tweed skirt in the cover of the shrubbery. Ethel hated regulations. There was a strict rule that no one was allowed to smoke in the presence of the Empress. But if Ethel found herself alone in the house she would plump herself down on a priceless Empire chair, cross her mud stained legs and light up a cigar. This so enraged secretary Pietri that he once chased her out of the house. '*Elle est vraiment trop batailleuse,*' said Eugenie, shaking her head. But this also applied to herself, and after an argument she seized Ethel by the shoulders and marched her out into the passage, telling her to stay there until she had cooled down. They differed in many of their views. When Ethel said that she hated the rich, Eugenie snapped back: 'God, what a fool you are!'[13] But they were good for each other.

Another frequent companion of Eugenie's was Princess Beatrice. Six years after the death of the Prince Imperial, she had married Prince Henry of Battenberg. They met at the Darmstadt wedding of Prince Louis of Battenberg[a] and Princess Victoria of Hesse. Beatrice fell wildly in love, and she showed it, as have all ladies of the British Royal Family when in a like state. Victoria realised this immediately and was furious at the thought of losing the daughter whom she had reserved for herself as companion, secretary and nurse.

For six months she never spoke to her, passing essential information in notes across the breakfast table.[14] Through the efforts of Prince Louis and the Empress, agreement was at last reached and Beatrice and Henry were married in the parish Church of St Mildred's at Whippingham in the Isle of Wight. They had three sons and a daughter. The girl

(a) Prince Henry's brother.

was christened Victoria Eugenie Julia Ena. The Empress was her godmother.

In 1895 came a strange twist of fate. The British decided upon another punitive campaign in Africa, this time in Ashanti. Prince Henry volunteered to take part in it, rather as the Prince Imperial had, although for different reasons. Prince Henry wished to escape the attentions of an amorous lady. The Queen refused permission, but Beatrice insisted that her husband should have the chance of leading an active life. Henry went. He caught fever and died on 20th January 1896.

The Princess was near to collapse. She had loved two men, and both had died on active service in Africa. She had never been parted from her mother for more than a few days but she knew that she must go now. She joined the Empress in the south of France. For five weeks she was lost to the world.

The close bond of Eugenie with both the Queen and Princess Beatrice led to a change of attitude in the Royal Family towards the Catholic Church. Prince Albert had left behind a 'horror of the priestly dominion' and his widow announced that she could not abide 'the bowings, scrapings and confessions'.[15] The death of Napoleon and the Prince Imperial and her feelings for the Empress brought the Queen's vendetta to an end. Under the persuasion of Eugenie, she visited Spain and became the first Protestant woman ever to be received at the Monastry of the Grande Chartreuse near Aix-les-Bains. By 1890 the animosity had completely disappeared and she received a complimentary address from the Archbishop of Chambéry, upon which Dr Davidson, Dean of Windsor, commented:

> I doubt whether any parallel could readily be found in history for an Address couched in these particular terms, emanating from a Roman Catholic dignitary, and addressed to a Protestant Sovereign, to whom he himself owes no direct allegiance. It is no small matter that the excellence and advantage of the principles, not merely of *tolerance*, but of liberality and comprehension, should be thus officially recognised in such a quarter, and it makes one hopeful that some at least of the estrangements and the recriminations which even in modern days have sometimes characterised the mutual relation of Christian Churches may be giving way to a more really 'Christian'

tone and temper. That your Majesty has done something at least to promote such a spirit, both in our own land and elsewhere, must be hereafter recognised as a great fact of English history.[16]

The Empress's relations with the French authorities remained strained – their habit of referring to her as 'the Widow Bonaparte' annoyed her intensely – and it was not until 1883 that she made a short stay in Paris, by so doing winning the admiration of Queen Victoria for her courage.[17]

The reason for her visit was an adventure of Plon-Plon. Infuriated because his son, Victor, had been named in the Prince Imperial's will as the new head of the Bonapartist party, he sought a means to show his power. When Gambetta died, Plon-Plon demanded that there should be a plebiscite in France, and ended in prison for his opportunism. The Bonapartists wished to exclude him from their councils in the future. Eugenie, knowing the dangers of a divided party, went over to Paris to plead his cause. She did not succeed and Plon-Plon went into exile in Italy and Switzerland. But this time he did have the good grace to thank his old adversary, the Empress, for her efforts on his behalf.

It was not until twenty years after her flight from the Tuileries that the Empress was given permission to have a residence in France, and then subject to restrictions. Her household was not to consist of more than eight men, including gardeners and coachman, and she was to be visited each week by a *commissaire*.[18]

Longing for the sun, the site which she chose for a villa was on a tongue of land jutting out into the sea at Cap Martin, between Mentone and Monte Carlo. Here Sarah Bernhardt had camped out in a tent when she wished to escape from the Riviera crowds.[19] Eugenie built in the Italian style, her *loggia* being decorated with Pompeian frescoes. From the window of her sitting-room she could see, on clear mornings, the shadow of Corsica upon the sea. She called her new home Cyrnos, the Greek for Corsica. She edged herself in with pines and banks of multicoloured flowers,[20] and she did not miss a yearly visit to Cap Martin until war came to Europe in 1914.[21]

The local authorities were placed in a somewhat awkward situation by the presence of the 'Widow Bonaparte'. In the 1890s the Riviera was the mecca for holidaying royalty. Queen Victoria was a regular, as were the Prince of Wales, the Duke of Cambridge and the Connaughts. So popular was the Queen that when she arrived at Nice the whole town turned out to greet her and it took four regiments of infantry and a battery of artillery to control the crowd. And each of these visitors called upon the Empress, the indigenous regal product who was not now supposed to exist.

M. Paoli, the famous French detective responsible for the safety of visiting royalty, one day found himself faced with a tricky situation. A guard of honour was provided at the Queen's hotel, ready to present arms to her and distinguished callers. Paoli arrived at the hotel to see the guard being turned out. He enquired who was coming. He was informed that an Empress was on her way. The Empress turned out to be the last of the French. Never was a guard dismissed more quickly, but it was still in view when Eugenie came round the corner. She guessed what had happened.[22]

Empress Elizabeth of Austria was often at Cap Martin, staying at an hotel near Villa Cyrnos. The two women would chatter away for hours, neither listening to what the other said.[23] They bathed together, hiding their jewels behind the same rock.[24] Then Luccheni thrust his dagger into Elizabeth's breast as she boarded a steamer at Geneva, and one more link with the past was severed.

Eugenie was most at peace when at the Villa Cyrnos. There, after dinner, sitting at her favourite spot on the terrace or in the salon, she would entertain her guests with stories of the Empire days. She spoke of the night of the Orsini outrage at the Opéra. In the carriage there was a secret compartment in which two loaded pistols were kept in case of such an emergency. When the first bomb went off, she put her hand into the compartment only to find that the servant responsible had forgotten to put the pistols there. If they had been, she said, she would have shot the assassin who came to the carriage door.[25]

She told of the summer night when she was playing patience with Madame de Pourtalès in the garden at St Cloud. Suddenly a masked and armed man appeared before them and demanded their jewels. They handed them over. At pistol point, he told them to undress. This they began to do. Then Madame de Pourtalès rumbled. 'It's that fool, Poché!' she shouted. Poché was the nickname of Charles de Fitz-James, a young courtier who was for ever playing tricks. The loud recriminations of the two women attracted the attention of the guard, which approached at the double. 'Quick,' said the Empress to Poché and hid him under her crinoline. 'Naughty, wasn't it?' she commented.[26]

At eleven she would rise to retire, replying to the obeisances of her guests with her famous curtsy, leaving behind her the faint smell of violets.

On 1st January 1901 Eugenie received a New Year's card from Osborne bearing a few, scrawled, illegible words in Victoria's hand. Three weeks later the Queen was dead. Eugenie was seventy-five and a great loneliness came over her, as when she had lost Paca, France, her husband and her son.

CHAPTER 28

Sunset

Empress Eugenie was now the senior member of the Sovereign class of Europe. She was four years older than Emperor Francis Joseph of Austria. Her dignity in exile had won her wide respect and she had honoured her husband's wish that silence should be maintained over the causes of the downfall of the Second Empire. She had documentary evidence to refute many of the accusations made, yet she refrained from public argument. As Germany again began the prelude of war, statesmen turned to her to glean from her experience. It was she who had said in 1859, 'If Bismarck barks, then surely he must bite.' Although both as Empress and Regent she had made many mistakes, she had been proved right in her assessment of the German intentions, which led to the war of 1870. Among the statesmen who talked to her was Lord Lansdowne, Foreign Secretary from 1902 to 1906.[1]

With the death of Queen Victoria, Eugenie's influence with the Royal Family increased. King Edward was not only devoted to her, but valued her opinions. And she had friends and admirers in his Household. Sir Arthur Bigge, the Queen's last Private Secretary and thereafter Private Secretary to the Prince of Wales,[a] had been a close friend of the Prince Imperial and he had accompanied her to Africa. She had introduced him to the Queen. Another friend was Frederick Ponsonby,[b] Assistant Private Secretary to the King.

It was only to be expected that, with her Spanish background, the Empress should be consulted on the question of a bride for young King Alfonso XIII of Spain, the boy born a King. His Austrian mother, Queen Maria Christina, acted as Regent until he reached the age of sixteen in 1902. Marriage with the Spanish King was a prize coveted throughout the palaces of Europe. Competition between Mammas with unmarried daughters was intense and further complicated by the then

(a) Afterwards King George V. Sir Arthur was created Lord Stamfordham in 1911. He died in 1931, after fifty-one years in the service of the Royal family.
(b) Afterwards Sir Frederick and Lord Sysonby.

accepted idea that the daughters of an elder sister had preference over those of a younger, to the exclusion of the point of suitability. And Beatrice was a youngest daughter, and not allowed to forget it. Eugenie did nothing about the matter until she received a message from Queen Maria Christina informing her that a British bride would be preferred. Then it was that she sent a photograph of Princess Ena of Battenberg to Madrid.

Eugenie had seen little of her goddaughter in her childhood days. The Battenberg children were part of the royal circus, moving from Osborne to Balmoral and Windsor at order dates. Ena was somewhat of a tomboy and a rebel. The Queen's preference had been for the boys and Ena's life had not been easy. She was once roped to a door as a punishment. When the Empress was a guest for lunch at Osborne, the Queen asked her granddaughter to describe the Epistles. Ena volunteered that they were the wives of the Apostles. The Queen turned to her guest and commented: 'Dear sister, children are insufferable creatures.'

In 1902, when Ena was fifteen, she was invited to stay by herself at Farnborough Hill. There the two came to know, and love, one another. Queen Ena recalled:

> I struck up a strong friendship with my godmother, who took me for long rides in her motor car and told me, in her inimitable accent, marvellous stories about the days of the crinoline. I was also fascinated by Monsieur Pietri, her Corsican secretary. He spat extraordinary jets of saliva, like parabolas, that landed in the chimney. Often they narrowly missed your head, which caused an unpleasant feeling of panic.
>
> The Empress's own private sitting-room was almost entirely decorated with portraits of her son, not as he was alive, young handsome, gay, alert. But as he was dead; the chest bespattered with blood. On retiring and leaving the drawing-room we passed a portrait of the Prince Imperial, set on an easel with a lamp burning in front of it. Before going to bed the Empress would put out the light as if to wish her son Goodnight.[2]

In 1905 King Alfonso visited London, an attempt on his life being made in Paris on the way. He was handsome, smiling and absolutely without fear. He fell head over heels in love with blonde Princess Ena, confiding in her eldest brother that he would remain celibate until he had married her. At the Palace receptions Ena was the target of angry glances from the mothers of unsuccessful candidates.[3]

It was realised that there would be considerable opposition to the niece of the Sovereign marrying a Roman Catholic and the matter had to be handled with care. King Edward sought the advice of the Empress and they met on a number of occasions, under circumstances which would not attract public attention. But those meetings were not without incident.

At Cowes, in August, the King Edward and Queen Alexandra asked Eugenie to tea on the Royal Yacht, *Victoria and Albert*, at five o'clock. Shortly before that time Frederick Ponsonby headed for the shore on the R.Y.'s steam pinnace. From a yacht's deck he saw a parasol being waved. A handkerchief was tied to the end of the parasol. Such signals are unusual at Cowes and he ignored it. Then the thought flashed through his mind that the signal might be meant for him, so he ordered the coxswain to go about and draw alongside the yacht in question. He shouted, but no answer came. He climbed up the ladder and called down the hatchway. Silence. He walked to the stern. There, sitting under her parasol, was the Empress Eugenie. She informed him that the mate of *Thistle* had died and that she had allowed all the members of the crew to attend his funeral, quite forgetting that she was due to take tea with the King and Queen. Would he please take her?

Ponsonby managed to get her down the ladder safely, but there was a bit of a sea running and he could not persuade her to take the sharp step necessary to reach the pinnace. After a time he placed a hand round one of her ankles and provided the necessary impetus. He deposited her upon a seat. She looked up at him and said: 'You pulled my leg.'[4]

Another meeting between King and Empress took place in Paris. Both were travelling incognito, he as the Duke of Lancaster, she as the Comtesse de Pierrefonds. She was staying at the Grand Hotel. The King waited in his car while Ponsonby went to the desk to inquire if the Empress was ready to receive her visitor. The clerk was apparently not impressed by Dukes and Comtesses and in reply to Ponsonby's request that he contact Eugenie, he said '*Bientôt*' and went on sorting the mail. Now King Edward was not a man to be kept waiting, as his Secretary knew only too well. Ponsonby demanded that the clerk hurry up, only to be informed that he must first finish his task of sorting. Whereat Ponsonby shouted that the King of England wished to see Empress Eugenie of the French. This galvanised the clerk into immediate action. At last the King was told that all was in order. Exasperated and annoyed at the delay, he strode quickly into the foyer, convinced, from custom, that everyone would get out of his way. The lift door opened. An American, who had been waiting impatiently for this to happen, strode towards it, travelling at a tangent to the King. He was smoking a fat cigar. King and American collided at the entrance to the lift. The King, having a weight advantage, got the better of the encounter and the cigar went flying. Both men were too winded to do battle on the way to the first floor, but there was a clear break in Anglo-American relations.[5]

When the announcement came of the engagement of Alfonso and Ena, the storm broke. Both the Archbishop of Canterbury and the Bishop of London warned the King of the disapproval of the public. The Church Association and the Protestant Alliance called upon him to refuse his consent. The correspondence columns of the newspapers were crowded with provocative letters. The King showed masterly evasiveness. He said that, as the Princess's father was a German, then she must be German and, as such, the matter had nothing to do with him, thus blandly overlooking the point that Prince Henry had become a naturalised Englishman on his marriage. There then came to him from Princess Beatrice the suggestion that her daughter's preparation for entry into the Roman Catholic Church should take place at the Villa Cyrnos, Cap Martin, under the supervision of the Empress Eugenie. But the King considered that to involve the Empress would only exacerbate matters, and he decreed that the preparation should take place quietly in Paris.[6]

On 31st May 1906 Princess Ena was married at the Church of San Jeronimo in Madrid and became Queen Victoria Eugenia of Spain. On the way back to the Palace the assassin Matteo Morral dropped a flower-wreathed bomb from a balcony upon the wedding procession. There was carnage, over twenty people being killed and a great many injured. Severed heads rolled in the gutters, horses lay legless and the blood of the victims spattered the houses of the Calle Mayor up to the second floor. Yet, as in the case of Napoleon and Eugenie when Orsini made his attempt upon them at the Paris Opera, the King and Queen escaped.

The Empress was eighty and still she circulated Europe and the Mediterranean. In 1906 she climbed Vesuvius.[7] She went on to Venice and then spent three days with Emperor Francis Joseph at Ischl. The Press was convinced, and probably rightly, that she was on an errand for King Edward. Francis Joseph wore only the *légion d'honneur* as decoration when he met her at the station, and his delight at having her as his guest was clear. The shadows lay deep across memory lane as they chatted of a past stretching back to the battle of Solferino and the tragedy of Maximilian and his wife Charlotte, who languished in her château in Belgium. To Francis Joseph, the kindness and companionship which Eugenie had shown to the Empress Elizabeth after the shootings at Mayerling had shattered her, were foremost in his thoughts. He was tired out now, slowing mentally, but his guest was still sprightly, and far his superior in intelligence. Isabel Vesey, Eugenie's young companion, wrote: 'The Empress looked beautiful at dinner last night. Her black silk dress with its long sweeping train, her white hair crowned with a jet diadem, her lovely neck and shoulders . . .'[8]

In the following year Eugenie encountered another Emperor – William of Germany. She was cruising in Norwegian waters and so was the Kaiser, on board his yacht *Hohenzollern* and escorted by men of war. William had made a number of attempts to meet the Empress, but she had taken avoiding action. When *Thistle* steamed into Bergen harbour, German cruisers were thick upon the water. A message arrived from William asking permission to call upon her at eleven o'clock next morning. 'Well,' said Eugenie, to the amusement of her staff, 'we have "slipped" him five times, and, as there is no escape now, I suppose I *must* see him.'[9]

When the Kaiser arrived, in civilian clothes, he was surprised to see the German flag flying. The captain of *Thistle* had borrowed it from *Hohenzollern*.

For two hours Eugenie and William were closeted together – 'interminable hours' they seemed to the Empress's crew and attendants as they struggled to entertain the Kaiser's staff in the pouring rain. There is no record of what passed between the two, except for a complaint by William that his British relations had given him no mementoes of his 'unparalleled grandmama', Queen Victoria, whom he adored. Eugenie rather like William, for he joked with her and did his best to be agreeable. She could handle him, as many women could – it was the men with whom he clashed. The real enmity against England and France lay in his Court and his military staff. As the German ships sailed out past *Thistle*, the Kaiser ordered that the French flag should be flown and that crews should line the deck. Napoleon would have dearly liked to see his wife honoured in this way. Yet she missed the historic moment, as it took place early in the morning and she was sound asleep.[10]

When King Edward died in 1910,[a] the Europe which Eugenie knew came close to its end. Although she was on friendly terms with the new King and Queen, bluff George was an Empire man rather than a European. He knew little of Continental diplomacy and was a stranger to the palaces and hotels in which his father had been a familiar figure, from Vienna to Copenhagen, Hamburg to Biarritz. He was too young to remember the Second Empire.

She was amazingly young for her age, seeming not to appreciate the passing of time as she referred to women in their sixties as 'old'. She absorbed the new, was a friend of Marconi's and arranged for radio to be installed in her yacht. Aviation intrigued her. She had always been thrilled by speed and in 1913 her chauffeur was fined for dangerous driving.[11]

One of the few close friends of the olden days left to her was the Marquis de Alcanizes, the only man with whom she had been truly in love, for whom she had attempted suicide, and to whom she had offered herself before marrying Napoleon. She teased him that, in his eighties, he dyed his beard. It was ridiculous, she said. Then, accusingly: 'He never wanted to marry me!' 'Never, Eugenie,' he replied. 'And I shall not marry you even now.' He was the only person allowed to call her 'Eugenie'.[12]

As the years passed and the impact of the Bonapartes weakened, the Empress drew her Imperial cloak tighter about her. An example was needed to keep the cause alive. When Plon-Plon's son, Prince Victor Napoleon, the head of the House, visited Farnborough, she treated

(a) The Empress placed a card above the holy-water stoup in St Michael's Church, Farnborough: 'Pray for the Repose of the Soul of King Edward VII, the Peacemaker – May 6, 1910.'

him as if he were the Emperor, giving him precedence and curtsying to him.[13] Prince Victor, discreet, intelligent and with a certain audience in France, lacked the dynamism and the ambition of Napoleon III or the confidence of Plon-Plon. She did not anticipate of him the exploits of the earlier Napoleons, but he had been appointed by the Prince Imperial and he had continued the line.

In 1910 he had made a most interesting marriage, his bride being Princess Clementine of Belgium. Her sister, Stephanie, had married Rudolph, Crown Prince of Austria, whose life had ended at Mayerling. Her other sister, Louise, had married Prince Philip of Coburg, whose mother was a daughter of King Louis Philippe. A tangled skein indeed and doubtless one of which Prince Albert would have disapproved. Victor and Clementine had two children, a girl born in 1912 and a boy early in 1914.

Another member of the 'family' who was a frequent visitor to Farnborough was the bastard son of Napoleon III and Contessa Virginie di Castiglione. Virginie was a bad mother. Her other, and legitimate, son, she had dressed as a groom. He lived with the servants and rode behind her carriage. Understandably, he ran away.[14] Napoleon's son was apprenticed to Dr Evans[(a)] and brought up by him, and in time he took over the American dentist's fashionable Paris practice. He was known as Dr Hugenschmidt. Eugenie did not see him until he was a grown man and she was immediately struck by his likeness to the Emperor. The two got on well together, Hugenschmidt advising her on medical matters and even acting as a link between her and politicians in Paris.[15] Strange, after all this time, to meet a walking image of her husband and of her son, who had for so long lain side by side in the crypt of St Michael's.

In July 1914 Eugenie attracted the attention of the Press. After a tour of Italy she stayed in Paris and while there visited her former homes, Fontainebleau, the ruins of St Cloud, Compiègne and Malmaison. It was as if she knew that the lights were going out in Europe and wished to take a farewell look before darkness fell. In the woods at Compiègne she heard a hunting horn and, tensed, she whispered, 'Listen'. At Malmaison she arranged for a memorial to the Prince Imperial.[16] At St Cloud she recognised the chimney piece from her salon lying broken among the briars.[17]

(a) Dr Evans died in 1897.

Of her visit to Fontainebleau, where once she had entertained the King of Prussia and walked with Queen Victoria, the *Daily Telegraph* wrote:

Of what is she thinking, this lone, bereaved, fate-driven figure, as she enters the Château of Fontainebleau, ascends the great horseshoe staircase, and visits room after room consecrated in her mind by wonderful associations? She has a keen and vivid memory, it is clear. She recognises the ivory box which originally belonged to Anne of Austria, and which was presented to her by the Emperor on her marriage. She notices the absence of the 'Diana' of Benvenuto, now removed to the Louvre . . . And looking out on the Carp Pond she can mark with a sigh of regret that her gondola no longer floats on the water. So might the wraith of Marie Antoinette revisit the glimpses of the moon at Trianon and St Cloud . . .[18]

A few days after she returned to England, war was declared. She quickly felt its sting. Prince Victor and Princess Clementine were forced to flee from their home in the Avenue Louise in Brussels, reached Folkestone and, with their children, became the Empress's guests. The yacht *Thistle* was handed over to the Admiralty. Early in November she attended her first Memorial Service for the dead. Prince Maurice of Battenberg, son of Princess Beatrice, had been killed at Ypres. He was the same age as the Prince Imperial when he fell in Zululand. The Empress Eugenie sat with Queen Alexandra in the Chapel Royal, St James's.

A wing of Farnborough Hill became a hospital for wounded officers. It consisted of eight rooms and an operating theatre. The Empress footed the entire cost, releasing some of her capital to do so. She insisted on the best equipment and was to be seen in the corridor trying out a new invalid chair or a pair of crutches.

The wards became her life. She was re-living the days of August 1870 when she had tended the wounded in the hospital units at the Tuileries. And because she had been Empress and Regent then, she was imperious now, brooking no interference with her ideas of administration. She believed that the best treatment for her patients was doses of happiness and laughter, and the antidote to shell-shock was to allow them to flirt. 'It will do them good to fall in love,' she said.[19] Thus young and pretty nurses moved from bed to bed – they were darlings, a patient said. King George and Queen Mary were full of admiration and paid several visits to Farnborough and were among the guests at Eugenie's ninetieth birthday party. The King sent two young men in uniform to see her – David, Prince of Wales and his younger brother, Prince 'Bertie'.[a] They invested the last Empress of the French with the insignia of a Dame Grand Cross of the British Empire.

She thrilled to danger, as she had always done. When, in the night, she heard the deep, menacing drone of Zeppelin engines, she would call to her companion, 'Quick!' and, pulling on a wrap, go out into the garden. When she was warned of the danger of bomb blast, she answered that she was now too old to start learning about how to be afraid.

It was not until September of 1919 that her patients were moved to Aldershot. She told them, before they left, that they must always look upon Farnborough Hill as home. 'Because I have known you in bed, and one cannot be more intimate than that!'[20] And each man, when he had recovered, came back to see her. She was very proud of that.

In December she set out for Paris and Cap Martin. She was nearly blind from cataract and her great age showed in her stooping body, but her mind was bright and clear. She was met at the Gare du Nord by a few devotees, to whom she confided that she was disappointed that she had been unable to travel by air. She returned to a France geographically much the same as it had been in the days of the Empire. A round had been lost, a harder round won. She alone among the leaders had spanned that strange interlude of half a century. Now she warned of the dangers of the peace, seeing, with amazing clarity, the dangers of a third round. In honour and fairness to the two Napoleons, she had one duty to perform, one visit to make – Les Invalides. 'A frail but formidable old woman was seen to stump her way down to the tomb of Napoleon. On reaching it, she took a newspaper from her bag and slowly read out the terms which the Allies had laid down for the German surrender.'[21]

Goodbye, Paris. She stood at the window of her *wagon-lit*, a bunch of hot-house violets in her hands, a quiet smile on her face, seeing, as in a mist, the streets and the churches and the jagged outline of the roofs against the sky.

At the Villa Cyrnos, she was sad. The garden had suffered by her

(a) Afterwards Edward VIII and Duke of Windsor: and George VI.

five years of absence. She missed her old secretary, Pietri, who now lay with his masters in St Michael's. Four years of war, four cold English winters, had taken their toll of her. She feared that she would become totally blind, but no doctor would operate, hesitating to give chloroform to a woman of ninety-three. She spent much of her time in bed, and moods of deep depression swamped her. So few of her contemporaries were left, but she drew comfort from her maid, and friend, Aline Pelletier, who had joined her service as a girl in 1868. Aline knew how matters had been arranged at the Tuileries. But with the spring there came a resurrection. She longed to see Spain again, the gold and blue of the sky, and to escape from the drabness of nonentity which surrounded her in France. Her doctors advised against the trip, but she answered that even she must die some day.

In April 1920 she sailed to Gibraltar, and the Governor called upon her and made much of her. She left 'the Widow Bonaparte' behind and was an Empress once again. The Duke of Alba met her and, with a retinue of relations and old friends, she drove to Jerez and on to Seville. In the Alba palace there, under the palms where she had sat with Paca in the long ago, the smell of minosa, magnolia and honeysuckle brought back the magic of her youth. She gave dinner parties, sat up until the early hours. King Alfonso and Queen Ena called upon her and entertained her as if she were a reigning Sovereign. She was a great star, the outstanding Spanish woman of her century.

At the beginning of May she drove to Madrid – queen of the Palacio de Liria at last. Near eighty years had passed since she had dreamed that Alba would make her mistress there. Callers queued to see her. She joked with the old and the young sat at her feet. A very special visitor was H.E. the French Ambassador. Recognition, and amends at last. Their meeting joined her great memories – driving up the hill to Windsor Castle and Queen Victoria waiting to receive her . . . the cheering of the crowds at the christening of the Prince Imperial at Notre Dame . . . Napoleon riding into Paris at the head of his troops after the victory at Solferino . . . drifting across the torch-lit lake at Annecy, scarlet burnous about her shoulders, and the cry of '*Vive l'Impératrice*' echoing from shore to shore . . . on the bridge of *L'Aigle* as she led the ships of all nations at the opening of the Suez Canal . . .

She was told of a Barcelona doctor who performed the cataract operation without the help of chloroform. Unflinching, she sent for him. He did his work with the aid of suction and a leech.²² When the bandages were taken away a few days later, she found that she could see! She was delirious with excitement. She read a favourite book. She went to a bull fight.

The Duke of Alba was to be married. It was the fulfilment of a long wish of Eugenie and she decided that the wedding should be from Farnborough Hill. She despatched him to England on 9th July and made her travel arrangements to follow three days later. On the 10th she developed a cold and was put to bed. She slipped quietly away. At eight o'clock next morning she died. It was Sunday and the bells were ringing out all over Madrid.

Bibliography

Letters and Diaries

THE LIFE AND LETTERS OF GEORGE WILLIAM FREDERICK, FOURTH EARL OF CLARENDON (2 vols.) By Sir Herbert Maxwell. 1913.

THE WAR DIARY OF EMPEROR FREDERICK III, 1870 – 71. Edited by A. R. Allinson. 1927.

ALICE, GRAND DUCHESS OF HESSE: LETTERS TO H. M. THE QUEEN. 1885.

LETTERS OF QUEEN VICTORIA, 1837 – 1901. 1st Series edited by A. C. Benson and Viscount Esher; 2nd and 3rd Series by G. E. Buckle. 1907 – 32.

FURTHER LETTERS OF QUEEN VICTORIA. Edited by Hector Bolitho. 1938.

LETTERS OF THE PRINCE CONSORT, 1831 – 61. Edited by Dr Jagow. 1938.

LEAVES FROM THE JOURNAL OF OUR LIFE IN THE HIGHLANDS. 1870.

MORE LEAVES FROM THE JOURNAL OF A LIFE IN THE HIGHLANDS. 1885.

DEAREST CHILD. Edited by Roger Fulford. 1964.

DEAREST MAMA. Edited by Roger Fulford. 1968.

YOUR DEAR LETTER. Edited by Roger Fulford. 1971.

LETTERS OF THE EMPRESS FREDERICK. Edited by Sir Frederick Ponsonby. 1928.

GEORGE, DUKE OF CAMBRIDGE. Edited by Edgar Sheppard. 1907.

"MY DEAR DUCHESS" – LETTERS TO THE DUCHESS OF MANCHESTER. Edited by A. L. Kennedy. 1956.

THE EMPRESS FREDERICK WRITES TO SOPHIE. Edited by A. Gould Lee. 1955.

HENRY PONSONBY: HIS LIFE FROM HIS LETTERS. By Arthur Ponsonby. 1942.

GLADSTONE TO HIS WIFE. Edited by A. Tilney Bassett. 1936.

LETTERS OF LADY AUGUSTA STANLEY. Edited by the Dean of Windsor and Hector Bolitho. 1927.

REMINISCENCES OF COURT AND DIPLOMATIC LIFE. (2 vols.). By Lady Bloomfield. 1883.

THE TRAGIC EMPRESS: INTIMATE CONVERSATIONS WITH THE EMPRESS EUGENIE. By Maurice Paléologue. 1928.

JOURNALS AND LETTERS OF REGINALD VISCOUNT ESHER. Edited by M. V. Brett. 1934.

LIFE WITH QUEEN VICTORIA. Edited by Victor Mallet. 1968.

Bibliography

IN MY TOWER. (2 vols.) By Walburga, Lady Paget, 1924.
THE PERSONAL PAPERS OF LORD RENDEL. 1931.
THE GREVILLE MEMOIRS. By Charles Greville. 1888.
QUEEN VICTORIA – LEAVES FROM A JOURNAL, 1855. 1961.

Reminiscences and Memoirs

SOUVENIRS INTIMES DE LA COUR DES TUILERIES. (3 vols.) by Mme Carette. 1891.
MEMOIRS OF THE EMPRESS EUGENIE. By Comte Fleury. 1920.
THE REMINISCENCES OF A SPANISH DIPLOMAT. By Francisco de Reynoso. 1933.
MEMOIRES. By Duc de Persigny. 1896.
THE MEMOIRS OF DR THOMAS W. EVANS (2 vols.) 1894.
REMINISCENCES. By 'J.P.J.' 1929.
REMINISCENCES. By Marie, Princess of Battenberg. 1925.
SUNSHINE AND SHADOWS. By Lady Mary Meynell. 1933.
WHEN MEN HAD TIME TO LOVE. By Agnes de Stoeckl. 1953.
RECOLLECTIONS OF THREE REIGNS. By Sir Frederick Ponsonby. 951.
MY MEMORIES OF SIX REIGNS. By Princess Marie Louise. 1956.
TEN YEARS AT THE COURT OF ST JAMES'. By Baron von Eckardstein. 1921.
MEMOIRS OF PRINCE HOHENLOHE. (2 vols.) 1906.
THE QUEEN THANKS SIR HOWARD. By Mary Howard McClintock. 1946.
COLLECTIONS AND RECOLLECTIONS. By G. W. E. Russell. 1903.
THE PRINCE IMPERIAL. By A. Filon. 1913.
SOUVENIRS SUR L'IMPÉRATRICE EUGENIE. By A. Filon. 1920.
L'INCONNUE – L'IMPÉRATRICE EUGENIE. By Lucien Daudet. 1922.
THE REMINISCENCES OF LADY DOROTHY NEVILL. By Ralph Nevill. 1906.
UNCENSORED RECOLLECTIONS. Anon. 1924.
MEMOIRS OF SARAH BERNHARDT. 1907.
NOT WORTH READING. By Sir George Arthur. 1938.
MEMORIES. By Lord Redesdale. 1915.
MY OWN TIMES. By Lady Dorothy Nevill. 1912.
AS WE WERE. By E. F. Benson. 1932.
A GREAT LADY'S FRIENDSHIPS. Edited by Lady Burghclere. 1933.
LADY DE ROTHSCHILD AND HER DAUGHTERS. By Lucy Cohen. 1935.
THE DAYS BEFORE YESTERDAY. By Lord Frederick Hamilton. 1920.
MY REMINISCENCES. By Lord Ronald Gower. 1895.
MY ROYAL CLIENTS. By Xavier Paoli. Undated.

Bibliography

THE REMINISCENCES OF LADY RANDOLPH CHURCHILL. By Mrs G. Cornwallis-West. 1908.

WHEN I WAS AT COURT. By Lord Ormathwaite. 1937.

MY DAYS OF ADVENTURE. By Ernest Alfred Vizetelly. 1914.

MEMORIES OF FIFTY YEARS. By Lady St Helier. 1909.

THINGS I HAVE SEEN. By Sir Charles Oman. 1933.

THE VANISHED POMPS OF YESTERDAY. Anon. 1919.

STREAKS OF LIFE. By Dame Ethel Smyth. 1920.

SOUVENIRS 1859–1871. By Princess Pauline Metternich. 1922.

REMINISCENCES. By Lady Constance Battersea. 1922.

Biographies and Biographical Studies

DEMOCRATIC DESPOT. By T. A. B. Corley. 1961.

NAPOLEON III IN ENGLAND. By Ivor Guest. 1952.

LIFE OF NAPOLEON III. By Archibald Forbes. 1899.

NAPOLEON THE THIRD. By Walter Geer. 1921.

NAPOLEON III. By W. H. C. Smith. 1972.

NAPOLEON III AND THE WOMEN HE LOVED. By Hector Fleischmann. Undated.

THE RISE OF LOUIS NAPOLEON. By F. A. Simpson. 1925.

THE EMPRESS EUGENIE. By Harold Kurtz. 1964.

THE LIFE OF THE EMPRESS EUGENIE. By Robert Sencourt. 1931.

THE LAST EMPRESS OF THE FRENCH. By Philip W. Sergeant. 1909.

THE LIFE OF THE EMPRESS EUGENIE. By Jane T. Stoddart. 1906.

L'IMPÉRATRICE EUGENIE. By Octave Aubry. 1931.

THE EMPRESS EUGENIE AND HER SON. By Edward Legge. 1916.

THE PRINCE IMPERIAL. By Katherine John. 1939.

THE PRINCE IMPERIAL. By E. E. P. Tisdall. 1959.

THE PRINCESS MATHILDE BONAPARTE. By Philip W. Sergeant. Undated.

IMPERIAL BROTHER: THE LIFE OF THE DUC DE MORNY. By Maristan Chapman. 1931.

PLON-PLON: THE LIFE OF PRINCE NAPOLEON. By Edgar Holt. 1973.

NAPOLEON: BISEXUAL EMPEROR. By Frank Richardson. 1972.

THE AGE OF WORTH. By Edith Saunders. 1954.

QUEEN VICTORIA AND THE BONAPARTES. By Theo Aronson. 1972.

QUEEN VICTORIA. By Sidney Lee. 1902.

QUEEN VICTORIA'S RELATIONS. By Meriel Buchanan. 1954.

QUEEN VICTORIA. By E. F. Benson. 1935.

Bibliography

VICTORIA R. I. By Elizabeth Longford. 1964.

QUEEN VICTORIA (Vol. I). By Cecil Woodham-Smith. 1972.

VICTORIA QUEEN AND RULER. By Emily Crawford. 1903.

CONCERNING QUEEN VICTORIA AND HER SON. By Sir George Arthur, 1943.

THE LIFE OF THE PRINCE CONSORT. By Theodore Martin. 1877.

KING EDWARD THE SEVENTH. By Sir Philip Magnus. 1964.

KING EDWARD VII (2 vols.) By Sir Sidney Lee. 1927.

KING EDWARD VII. By E. F. Benson. 1933.

EDWARDIANS IN LOVE. By Anita Leslie. 1972.

QUEEN ALEXANDRA. By Georgina Battiscombe. 1969.

THE ENGLISH EMPRESS. By E. C. Corti. 1957.

THE EMPRESS FREDERICK. Anon. 1913.

THE PUBLIC AND PRIVATE LIFE OF KAISER WILLIAM II. By Edward Legge. 1915.

THE ROYAL GEORGE. By Giles St Aubyn. 1963.

VICTORIAN GALLERY. By Meriel Buchanan. 1956.

THE LONELY EMPRESS. By Joan Haslip. 1965.

MAXIMILIAN AND CHARLOTTE OF MEXICO. By E. C. Corti. 1928.

THE COBURGS OF BELGIUM. By Theo Aronson. 1969.

KING ALFONSO. By Robert Sencourt. 1942.

DON ALFONSO XIII. By Princess Pilar of Bavaria and D. Chapman-Huston. 1931.

A VANISHED VICTORIAN. By George Villiers. 1938.

DISRAELI. By André Maurois. 1927.

DIZZY. By Hesketh Pearson. 1951.

LORD PALMERSTON. By Jasper Ridley. 1970.

BISMARCK. By Emil Ludwig. 1927.

PRINCE BISMARCK. (2 vols.) By Charles Lowe. 1885.

GARIBALDI. By Jasper Ridley. 1974.

FLORENCE NIGHTINGALE. By Cecil Woodham-Smith. 1950.

CÉSAR RITZ. By Marie Ritz. 1938.

SKITTLES: THE LAST VICTORIAN COURTESAN. By Henry Blyth. 1970.

THE PEARL FROM PLYMOUTH. By W. H. Holden. 1950.

Miscellaneous Works

THE SECOND EMPIRE. By G. P. Gooch. 1960.

THE SECOND EMPIRE. By Philip Guedalla. 1922.

THE ROMANCE OF THE SECOND EMPIRE. By Fitzgerald Molloy. 1904.

Bibliography

THE FALL OF PARIS. By Alistair Horne. 1965.

THE COURT OF THE TUILERIES. 1852 – 1870. By 'Le Petit Homme Rouge'. 1907.

THE GILDED BEAUTIES OF THE SECOND EMPIRE. By Frédéric Loliée. 1919.

A QUEEN AT HOME. By Vera Watson. 1952.

THE ROYAL MARRIAGE MARKET OF EUROPE. By Princess Catherine Radziwill. 1915.

THE DELIGHTFUL PROFESSION. By H. E. Wortham. 1931.

BEHIND THE THRONE. By Paul H. Emden. 1934.

FARNBOROUGH HILL: THE STORY OF A HOUSE. By Dorothy A. Mostyn.

ST MICHAEL'S BENEDICTINE ABBEY: A HISTORY AND A GUIDE. By Dom Placid Higham.

Source References pp. 3 - 59

CHAPTER 2

1 Ludwig: *Napoleon*, p. 6
2 Geer: *Napoleon the Third*, p. 13
3 *The Life of Napoleon Bonaparte*, p. 229.
4 Geer: p. 16
5 Ambès: *Intimate Memoirs*
6 Geer: p. 17
7 *Uncensored Recollections*, p. 15
8 Guedalla: *The Second Empire*, p. 43
9 Ludwig: pp. 345 – 6; Guedalla: p. 50
10 Levett: *Europe since Napoleon*, p. 23
11 Geer: p. 20
12 Guedalla: p. 56
13 Ibid., p. 57
14 *The Life of Napoleon Bonaparte*, p. 390
15 *Life of Napoleon III*
16 Fleischmann: *Napoleon III and the Women He Loved*
17 Geer: p. 33
18 Levett: p. 17
19 *Memoirs of an Ex-Minister*
20 Geer: p. 39
21 Guedalla: p. 64
22 Geer: p. 43

CHAPTER 3

1 Guest: *Napoleon in England*, p. 7 et seq
2 *Victoria in the Highlands*, p. 24
3 Guest: p. 19
4 I.L.N., 23 December 1848
5 Guest: p. 21
6 *Considerations Politiques et Militaires sur la Suisse*
7 Geer: *Napoleon the Third*, p. 58
8 Fleischmann: *Napoleon III and the Women He Loved*
9 Guedalla: *The Second Empire*, p. 84
10 Geer: p. 62

11 Fleischmann: p. 45
12 Guedalla: p. 86
13 Account by Louis Napoleon; Guedalla: pp. 87 – 9
14 Fleischmann: p. 50
15 Guest: p. 25
16 Translation in Geer
17 Guest: p. 29
18 Ibid

CHAPTER 4

1 Geer: *Napoleon the Third*, p. 79
2 Guest: *Napoleon in England*, p. 32
3 Woodham-Smith: *Florence Nightingale*, p. 24
4 Pearson: *Dizzy*, p. 77; Maurois: *Disraeli*, p. 208
5 Geer: p. 85
6 Ibid
7 Russell: *Collections and Recollections*, p. 316
8 Nevill: *Reminiscences*, p. 51
9 Gower: *Bygone Years*, p. 109
10 *The Greville Memoirs*, Vol. IV, p. 173
11 Gower: p. 108
12 Russell: p. 183
13 Guest: p. 50
14 Guedalla: *The Second Empire*, p. 116 et seq
15 Fleischmann: *Napoleon and the Women He Loved*, p. 70
16 Police Report of 19th April 1853
17 Fleischmann: pp. 77 – 85
18 Quoted in Geer

CHAPTER 5

1 Geer: *Napoleon the Third*, p. 115
2 Guest: *Napoleon in England*, pp. 80 – 1

291

3 Blyth: *Skittles, The Last Victorian Courtesan*, p. 115
4 Fleischmann: *Napoleon and the Women He Loved*, p. 103
5 Geer: p. 114
6 Woodham-Smith: *Florence Nightingale*, pp. 63 – 4, 507
7 Bolitho: *The Reign of Queen Victoria*, p. 101
8 Guest: p. 92
9 Guedalla: *The Second Empire*, p. 166
10 Guest: p. 95
11 I.L.N., 16th September 1848
12 Fleischmann: p. 106
13 31st March 1849
14 *Uncensored Recollections*, p. 14
15 Fleischmann: p. 58

CHAPTER 6

1 *Portraits of Eminent Persons*, 1860
2 From a genealogical tree compiled by Mr Campbell Grace, of Dumfries, in 1861
3 Molloy: *The Romance of the Second Empire* p. 294
4 Kirkpatrick: *Kirkpatricks of Closeburn*
5 Maxwell: *The Life and Letters of George William Frederick, Fourth Earl of Clarendon*, Vol. I, p. 48
6 Ibid: Vol. II, p. 180
7 Sencourt: *The Life of the Empress Eugenie*, p. 28
8 Kurtz: p. 12
9 Sergeant: *The Last Empress of the French*, p. 13
10 Maxwell: Vol. I, p. 73
11 Stoddart: *The Life of the Empress Eugenie*, p. 19
12 Sencourt: p. 40
13 Ibid: p. 41
14 Hanotaux: *Lettres de Mérimée - la Comtesse de Montijo*
15 Kurtz: p. 17
16 *Uncensored Recollections*, pp. 15 – 6
17 Maxwell: Vol. I, p. 73
18 *Lettres Familières de l'Impératrice Eugenie*

19 Sencourt: p. 43
20 Belloc, Marie A.: *Eugenie, Empress and Exile*. Lady's Realm, 1897
21 Stoeckl: *When Men had Time to Love*, p. 23
22 Stoddart: p. 30
23 *Memoirs of an Ex-Minister*
24 Sencourt: p. 50
25 Smyth, Ethel: *Streaks of Life*
26 Chapman-Huston: *Don Alfonso XIII*, p. 10
27 Kurtz: p. 32
28 Belloc

CHAPTER 7

1 *Queen Victoria's Letters*, 3rd December 1851
2 I.L.N.
3 Geer: *Napoleon the Third*, p. 135
4 Corley: *Democratic Despot*, p. 104
5 I.L.N.
6 Smith: *Napoleon the Third*, p. 75
7 1st December 1851
8 Geer: p. 141
9 Maxwell: *The Life and Letters of George William Frederick, Fourth Earl of Clarendon*, Vol. I, p. 329

CHAPTER 8

1 Fleischmann: *Napoleon and the Women He Loved*, p. 109
2 Ibid: pp. 111 – 2
3 *The Memoirs of Dr T. W. Evans*, Vol. 1, p. 88
4 Corley: *Democratic Despot*, p. 135
5 Guedalla: *The Second Empire*, p. 229
6 Stoddart: *The Life of the Empress Eugenie*, p. 38
7 Kurtz: *The Empress Eugenie*, p. 37
8 Belloc: *Eugenie, Empress and Exile*
9 Kurtz: p. 39
10 Guedalla: p. 228

CHAPTER 9

1 Aronson: *The Coburgs of Belgium*, p. 32
2 Ibid: p. 33
3 *Life of the Prince Consort*, Vol. II p. 73
4 Sergeant: *The Last Empress of the French*, p. 52
5 Kurtz: *The Empress Eugenie*, p. 45
6 Greville, 12th May 1854
7 Fleischmann: *Napoleon III and the Women He Loved*, p. 122
8 Maurois: *Miss Howard*, p. 77; Corley: *Democratic Despot*, p. 137
9 Stoddart: *The Life of the Empress Eugenie*, p. 41
10 Sencourt: *The Life of the Empress Eugenie*, p. 67
11 Woodham-Smith: *Queen Victoria*, p. 410
12 *Uncensored Recollections*, p. 19
13 Greville, 9th February 1853
14 Kurtz: pp. 48 – 9

CHAPTER 10

1 Gooch: *The Second Empire*, p. 60
2 Sencourt: *The Life of the Empress Eugenie*, p. 71
3 *Morning Post*
4 Stoeckl: *When Men had Time to Love*, p. 26
5 Bolitho: *A Century of British Monarchy*, p. 19
6 Greville, Henry: *Diary*
7 Sencourt: p. 86
8 Stoeckl: p. 33
9 Molloy: *The Romance of the Second Empire*, p. 339
10 *The Memoirs of Dr T. W. Evans*, Vol. I, p. 96
11 Sergeant: *The Last Empress of the French*, p. 81
12 *Queen Victoria's Letters*, 31st January 1853
13 Corley: *Democratic Despot*, p. 141
14 Stoddart: *The Life of the Empress Eugenie*, p. 69
15 Kurtz: *The Empress Eugenie*, p. 67

16 Sencourt: p. 97
17 Gooch: p. 38
18 Kurtz: p. 69
19 Ibid
20 Sencourt: p. 95

CHAPTER 11

1 *Uncensored Recollections:* p. 19
2 Guest: *Napoleon in England*, p. 100
3 *Hessian Tapestry:* p. 65
4 Lee: *Queen Victoria*, p. 238; Greville, 1st February 1854
5 D'Auvergne: *The Coburgs*, p. 220
6 Sheppard: *H.R.H. George, Duke of Cambridge*, Vol. I, p. 118
7 St Aubyn: *The Royal George*, p. 63
8 *Letters of the Prince Consort*, p. 219
9 Queen Victoria: *Leaves from a Journal*, p. 16
10 Martin: *Life of the Prince Consort*, Chapter IV
11 Guest: p. 110
12 Queen Victoria: p. 30
13 Crawford: *Victoria, Queen and Ruler*, p. 294
14 Guest: p. 116
15 Queen Victoria: p. 20
16 Crawford: p. 267
17 Queen Victoria: p. 51
18 Guest: p. 138
19 Ibid: p. 113
20 Watson: *A Queen at Home*, pp. 121 – 2

CHAPTER 12

1 *Letters of the Prince Consort*, p. 232
2 *The Empress Frederick. A Memoir*, p. 20
3 Sencourt: *The Life of the Empress Eugenie*, p. 125
4 Crawford: *Victoria, Queen and Ruler*, pp. 298 – 9
5 Cohen: *Lady Rothschild and Her Daughters*, p. 64
6 Ibid.
7 Queen Victoria: *Leaves from a Journal*, p. 88

8 Ibid., p. 99
9 Villiers: *A Vanished Victorian*, p. 259
10 Ibid.
11 Ibid., pp. 261 – 2
12 Ibid.
13 Queen Victoria, p. 143
14 Ibid., p. 151
15 *Letters of the Prince Consort*, p. 239
16 Taylor: *Fritz of Prussia*, p. 90

CHAPTER 13

1 Kurtz: *The Empress Eugenie*, p. 90
2 Arthur: *Concerning Queen Victoria and Her Son*, p. 82
3 Belloc: *Eugenie, Empress and Exile*
4 Sencourt: *The Life of the Empress Eugenie*, p. 126
5 Knight: *The Prince Imperial*, p. 28
6 Corley: *Democratic Despot*, p. 173
7 Ibid., pp. 178 – 9
8 Ibid., p. 179
9 Carette: *My Mistress the Empress Eugenie*, p. 29
10 Geer: *Napoleon the Third*, p. 178
11 Holden: *The Pearl from Plymouth*, p. 144
12 Arthur: *A Septuagenarian's Scrap Book*, p. 179
13 Sergeant: *The Prince Mathilde Bonaparte*, p. 209
14 Kurtz: p. 102
15 Sencourt: p. 190
16 Kennedy: '*My Dear Duchess*', p. 35
17 *Memoirs of an Ex-Minister*
18 Stoddart: *The Life of the Empress Eugenie*, p. 135
19 Aronson: *Queen Victoria and the Bonapartes*, p. 77
20 Ibid: p. 81
21 Martin: *Life of the Prince Consort*, Ch. LXXIX
22 Geer: p. 180
23 *Le Moniteur*
24 Stoddart: p. 111
25 Sencourt: p. 136
26 Corley: p. 198

CHAPTER 14

1 Kennedy: '*My Dear Duchess*', p. 22
2 Martin: *Life of the Prince Consort* Ch. LXXXVI
3 Stoddart: *The Life of the Empress Eugenie*, p. 124
4 Corley: *The Democratic Despot*, p. 215
5 Ibid: pp. 216 – 7
6 Ridley: *Garibaldi*, p. 413
7 Richardson: *Napoleon, Bisexual Emperor*, p. 33
8 Ibid: p. 19
9 *Memoirs*, p. 133
10 Pearson: *Dizzy*, p. 157
11 Ibid: *The Court of the Tuileries*, p. 308
12 Geer: *Napoleon the Third*, p. 207
13 Evans; Geer; John: *The Prince Imperial*, p. 49
14 Lee: *Queen Victoria*, p. 301

CHAPTER 15

1 Sergeant: *The Last Empress of the French*, p. 258
2 Kurtz: *The Empress Eugenie*, p. 151
3 Stoddart: *The Life of the Empress Eugenie*, p. 141
4 Gooch: *The Second Empire*, p. 56
5 Sencourt: *The Life of the Empress Eugenie*, p. 149
6 Corley: *Democratic Despot*, p. 232
7 Sergeant: p. 258
8 Sencourt: p. 152
9 Kurtz: p. 155
10 Stoeckl: *When Men had Time to Love*, p. 84
11 Sencourt: p. 154
12 *Letters of the Prince Consort*, p. 353
13 Stoddart: p. 149
14 Fulford: '*Dearest Child*', p. 284
15 *Letters of Lady Augusta Stanley*, p. 15
16 Sergeant, p. 263
17 '*Dearest Child*', p. 284
18 Kennedy: '*My Dear Duchess*', p. 121
19 '*Dearest Child*', p. 291

CHAPTER 16

1 *Queen Victoria's Letters*, 24th December 1861
2 Corti: *The English Empress*, p. 59
3 Corley: *Democratic Despot*, p. 223
4 *The Empress Eugenie*, p. 192
5 *Early Years of the Prince Consort*, p. 244
6 Kennedy: '*My Dearest Duchess*', p. 127
7 Kronberg Archives
8 Corley: p. 224
9 Ibid: p. 243
10 Sencourt: *Life of the Empress Eugenie*, p. 159
11 Gooch: *The Second Empire*, p. 41
12 Sencourt: p. 157
13 *The Court of the Tuileries*, p. 256
14 Molloy: *The Romance of the Second Empire*, p. 454
15 Gooch: p. 2
16 Stoddart: *The Life of the Empress Eugenie*, p. 54
17 Ibid., p. 148
18 *Victoria Travels*, p. 280
19 Ludwig: *Bismarck*, p. 208
20 Ibid., p. 209
21 Loliée: p. 14
22 Loliée: *The Gilded Beauties of the Second Empire*, p. 282
23 *The Court of the Tuileries*, p. 202
24 Fleischman: *Napoleon III and the Women he Loved*, Ch. IV
25 Sencourt: p. 181
26 Loliée: p. 286
27 Sencourt: p. 181
28 Fleury: *Memoirs of the Empress Eugenie*, pp. 275 – 280
29 Ibid.
30 Sencourt: p. 181
31 Kurtz: *The Empress Eugenie*, p. 186
32 Ibid.
33 Holden: *The Pearl from Plymouth*, p. 144
34 *The Personal Papers of Lord Rendel*, pp. 132 – 3
35 Lee: *Queen Victoria*, p. 367
36 Battenberg: *Reminiscences*, p. 69
37 Paleologue: *Entretiens*

38 Sencourt: p. 194
39 Kurtz: p. 205

CHAPTER 17

1 Legge: *The Last Empress of the French*, p. 270
2 *The Court of the Tuileries*, p. 283
3 John: *The Prince Imperial*, p. 99
4 Sencourt: *The Life of Princess Eugenie*, p. 161
5 Kurtz: *The Empress Eugenie*, p. 189
6 Burghclere: *A Great Lady's Friendships*, p. 107
7 *Uncensored Recollections*, pp. 77 – 9
8 Buchanan: *Victorian Gallery*, p. 9
9 Stoeckl: *When Men had Time to Love*, p. 67
10 John, p. 106
11 Ibid., p. 96
12 Buchanan, p. 25
13 Metternich: *My Years in Paris*
14 Molloy: *The Romance of the Second Empire*, p. 501
15 *The Court of the Tuileries*, p. 380
16 Molloy: p. 502
17 John: *The Prince Imperial*, p. 55
18 Ibid., p. 53
19 Molloy: p. 502
20 *The Court of the Tuileries*, p. 377
21 Molloy: p. 511
22 Ibid., p. 503
23 Ibid. p. 506
24 John: p. 112
25 Kurtz: *The Empress Eugenie*, p. 208
26 Kenyon: *I, Eugenie*, p. 214

CHAPTER 18

1 *Queen Victoria's Letters*, 16th June 1857
2 Paléologue: *The Tragic Empress*, p. 119
3 Messervy: *The Quick Step of an Emperor*, p. 233
4 Burghclere: *A Great Lady's Friendships*, p. 49

5 John: *The Prince Imperial*, p. 114
6 Burghclere, p. 49
7 Carette: *My Mistress the Empress Eugenie*, pp. 281 – 2
8 Burghclere, p. 49
9 Gooch: *The Second Empire*, p. 82
10 Corti: *Maximilian and Charlotte in Mexico*, Vol. II, p. 686
11 Sencourt: *The Life of the Empress Eugenie*, pp. 199 - 200
12 Fulford: *Your Dear Letter*, p. 102

CHAPTER 19

1 I.L.N.
2 Fulford: *Your Dear Letter*, p. 145
3 *Queen Victoria's Letters*, 24th July 1867
4 *The Court of the Tuileries*, p. 273
5 John: *The Prince Imperial*, p. 116
6 *The Court of the Tuileries*, p. 272
7 Guedalla: *The Second Empire*, p. 377
8 Legge: *The Last Empress of the French*, p. 316
9 Kurtz: *The Empress Eugenie*, p. 220
10 Geer: *Napoleon the Third*, p. 220
11 John, p. 120
12 I.L.N.
13 Ibid.
14 Legge, p. 166
15 John, p. 117
16 Kurtz: p. 220
17 *The Court of the Tuileries*, p. 315
18 Corti: *Maximilian and Charlotte in Mexico*, Vol. II, p. 829
19 I.L.N.
20 Sencourt: *Life of the Empress Eugenie*, p. 209
21 I.L.N.
22 Arthur: *Concerning Queen Victoria and Her Son*, p. 144

CHAPTER 20

1 Molloy: *The Romance of the Second Empire*, p. 518
2 Kurtz: *The Empress Eugenie*, p. 233

3 Corley: *Democratic Despot*, p. 301
4 Gooch: *The Second Empire*, p. 180
5 Villiers: *A Vanished Victorian*, pp. 345 – 7
6 Gooch, p. 48
7 Dangerfield: *Victoria's Heir*, p. 202
8 Sencourt: *The Life of the Empress Eugenie*, p. 226
9 Saunders: *The Age of Worth*, p. 169
10 Molloy, p. 521
11 Guedalla: *The Second Empire*, p. 397
12. Legge: *The Last Empress of the French*, p. 329: Molloy, p. 521
13 Reynoso: *Reminiscences of a Spanish Diplomat*, p. 181
14 Fleury: *Memoirs of the Empress Eugenie*, p. 291
15 Sencourt, p. 229
16 Longford: *Victoria R.I.*, p. 408
17 Meynell: *Sunshine and Shadows*, p. 125
18 Sencourt, p. 230
19 Fleury, p. 299
20 Burghclere: *A Great Lady's Friendships*, p. 226
21 Legge, p. 330
22 Kurtz, p. 226
23 Paléologue: *The Tragic Empress*, p. 32
24 Fulford: *Your Dear Letter*, p. 246
25 29th November 1869
26 Corley, p. 314
27 Forbes: *Life of Napoleon III*, p. 262
28 Villiers, p. 350
29 Forbes, p. 264
30 Kurtz, p. 234
31 Ibid., p. 235
32 Burghclere, p. 248
33 Forbes, p. 277

CHAPTER 21

1 *Leaves from the Note-Books of Lady Dorothy Nevill*, p. 307
2 Visetelly: *My Days of Adventure*, p.45; Fleury: *Memoirs of the Empress Eugenie*, p. 122 – 4
3 Paléologue: *Entretiens*, p. 157
4 Gooch: *The Second Empire*, p. 51
5 John: *The Prince Imperial*, p. 180

6 Molloy: *The Romance of the Second Empire*, p. 543
7 Gooch, p. 52
8 John, p. 185
9 Forbes: *Life of Napoleon III*, p. 282
10 *War Diary of Emperor Frederick III*, p. 22
11 Ibid., p. 29
12 Ibid., p. 31
13 Ibid., p. 49
14 Sencourt: *Life of the Empress Eugenie*, p. 251
15 Forbes, p. 289
16 John, p. 227
17 Forbes, p. 308
18 *Memoirs of Dr T. W. Evans*, Vol. I, p. 278
19 Forbes, pp. 310 – 3
20 Ibid., p. 316
21 *War Diary of the Emperor Frederick*, p. 93
22 *Oeuvres Posthumes de Napoleon III*, p. 325
23 Corley: *Democratic Despot*, p. 341
24 Forbes, p. 321
25 Ibid., p. 322
26 Ibid., p. 324
27 *War Diary of the Emperor Frederick*, p. 97
28 Ibid., p. 98
29 *Memoirs of Dr T. W. Evans*, Vol. I, p. 277
30 Molloy, p. 561

CHAPTER 22

1 Turnbull: *Eugenie of the French*, p. 265
2 Sencourt: *Life of the Empress Eugenie*, p. 256
3 Kurtz: *The Empress Eugenie*, p. 246
4 Sencourt, p. 261
5 Paléologue: *The Tragic Empress*, p. 194
6 Ibid.
7 *Memoirs of Dr T. W. Evans*, Vol. I, p. 292
8 *L'Empire et la Défence de Paris*, p. 428

9 *Enquete Parlementaire*, Vol. I, p. 267
10 *The Court of the Tuileries*, p. 404
11 John: *The Prince Imperial*, p. 238
12 Gower: *My Reminiscences*, pp. 247 – 8
13 Molloy: *The Romance of the Second Empire*, p. 570
14 Sencourt, p. 272
15 John, p. 239
16 Molloy, p. 567
17 *Court of the Tuileries*, p. 407
18 Evans, Vol. II, p. 330
19 Sencourt, p. 275
20 Molloy, p. 572
21 Stoddart: *The Life of the Empress Eugenie*, p. 213
22 Stoeckl: *When Men had Time to Love*, p. 107
23 Evans, Vol. II, Chap. X
24 Ibid.

CHAPTER 23

The Memoirs of Dr T. W. Evans, Vol. II, Chaps. XI – XIII

CHAPTER 24

The Memoirs of Dr T. W. Evans, Vol. II, Chaps. XIII & XIV
Queen Victoria's Letters, 15th September 1870 (Report by Sir John M. Burgoyne to Colonel Ponsonby).

CHAPTER 25

1 Burghclere: *A Great Lady's Friendships*, p. 280
2 Bassett: *Gladstone to His Wife*, p. 177
3 Lee: *King Edward VII*, Vol. I, p. 309
4 Burghclere, p. 284
5 Kinloch Cooke: *H.R.H. Princess Mary Adelaide*, Vol. II, p. 37
6 Burghclere, p. 279
7 Fulford: *Your Dear Letter*, p. 301
8 Guest: *Napoleon III in England*, p. 167
9 Buchanan: *Victorian Gallery*, pp. 15 – 6

10 Holden: *The Pearl from Plymouth*, p. 108
11 John: *The Prince Imperial*, p. 251
12 *War Diary of the Emperor Frederick*, p. 128
13 Lowe: *Prince Bismarck*, Vol. I, pp. 570 – 2
14 Ludwig: *Bismarck*, p. 364
15 Corley: *Democratic Despot*, p. 345
16 Lowe, p. 593
17 Sencourt: *The Life of the Empress Eugenie*, p. 297
18 Lowe, p. 594
19 Corley, pp. 345 – 6
20 Legge: *The Last Empress of the French*, p. 389
21 Legge: *The Empress Eugenie and Her Son*, pp. 178 – 81
22 *War Diary of the Emperor Frederick*, pp. 170 & 176
23 Bolitho: *Further Letters of Queen Victoria*, p. 172
24 *Queen Victoria's Letters*, 7th November 1870
25 Ibid., 30th November and 5th December 1870
26 Horne: *The Fall of Paris*, p. 213
27 Guest, p. 174
28 *Queen Victoria's Letters*, 27th March 1871
29 *Journals and Letters of Reginald Viscount Esher*, Vol. I, p. 29
30 Burghclere, p. 320
31 *Queen Victoria's Letters*, 27th February 1872
32 Knight: *The Prince Imperial*, p. 280
33 *Reminiscences of Lady Randolph Churchill*, p. 30
34 Guest, p. 190
35 Forbes: *Life of Napoleon III*, p. 341
36 Ibid., p. 342
37 Guest, p. 195; *Queen Victoria's Letters*, 20th February 1873

CHAPTER 26

1 Princess Marie Louise: *My Memories of Six Reigns*, p. 117

2 Longford: *Victoria R.I.*, p. 344
3 *Queen Victoria's Letters*, 20th February 1873
4 Forbes: *Life of Napoleon III*, p. 343
5 Turnbull: *Eugenie of the French*, p. 323
6 Blyth: *Skittles*, p. 202
7 *Annual Register*, March 1891
8 Kurtz: *The Empress Eugenie*, p. 289
9 Holt: *Plon-Plon*, pp. 256 – 7
10 John: *The Prince Imperial*, p. 324
11 Ibid., p. 325
12 Sheppard: *H.R.H. George Duke of Cambridge*, Vol. II, p. 53
13 Ibid., p. 325
14 *Princess Alice*, p. 182
15 Geer: *Napoleon the Third*, p. 30
16 Wortham: *The Delightful Profession*, p. 173
17 Hough: *Louis and Victoria*, p. 97
18 Marquess of Carisbrooke
19 Hough, p. 74
20 Turnbull, p. 348
21 Ibid., pp. 344 – 5
22 Kurtz, p. 297
23 *Figaro*
24 *The Shy Princess*, p. 89
25 Legge: *The Empress Eugenie and Her Son*, Ch. XXII
26 *Queen Victoria's Letters*, 12th July 1879

CHAPTER 27

1 Turnbull: *Eugenie of the French*, p. 386
2 Chapman-Huston: *Daisy Princess of Pless*, p. 189
3 Stoeckl: *When Men Had Time to Love*, p. 231
4 Legge: *Empress Eugenie and Her Son*, p. 138
5 Stoddart: *The Life of the Empress Eugenie*, pp. 284 – 90; Fleury: *Memoirs of the Empress Eugenie*, pp. 466 – 8
6 *Reminiscences*, p. 232
7 Kurtz: *The Empress Eugenie*, p. 332
8 Sencourt: *The Life of the Empress Eugenie*, p. 344
9 Meynell: *Sunshine and Shadows*, p. 67
10 Ponsonby: *Henry Ponsonby*, p. 382

11 Sencourt, p. 347
12 Legge, p. 119
13 Smyth: *Streaks of Life*
14 Marquess of Carisbrooke
15 *Victoria Travels*, p. 264
16 *Queen Victoria's Letters*, 9th April 1890
17 *Queen Victoria's Letters*, 29th January 1883
18 Ormathwaite: *When I was at Court*, p. 83
19 *Memoirs of Sarah Bernhardt*, p. 289
20 Belloc: *Eugenie, Empress and Exile*
21 Legge, p. 21
22 Paoli: *My Royal Clients*, p. 335
23 Haslip: *The Lonely Empress*, p. 431
24 Brown: *Royal Riviera*
25 Stoeckl, p. 226
26 Ibid., p. 177

CHAPTER 28

1 Sencourt: *The Life of Empress Eugenie*, p. 353
2 *Reminiscences*

3 Marquess of Carisbrooke
4 Ponsonby: *Recollections of Three Reigns*, p. 217
5 Ibid., p. 218
6 Lee: *King Edward VII*, Vol. II, p. 513
7 Sergeant: *The Last Empress of the French*, p. 404
8 Kurtz: *The Empress Eugenie*, p. 353
9 Legge: *Public and Private Life of Kaiser William II*, p. 174
10 Vesey MS: Kurtz, p. 350
11 Legge: *The Empress Eugenie and Her Son*, p. 317
12 Sencourt, p. 350
13 Kurtz, p. 354
14 Fleischmann: *Napoleon III and the Women He Loved*, p. 186
15 Kurtz, p. 355
16 *Evening Standard*, 30th July 1914
17 *The Times*, 14th July 1914
18 14th July 1914
19 Sencourt, p. 357
20 Ibid., p. 358
21 Blyth: *Skittles*, p. 244
22 Sencourt, p. 368

TRANSLATION OF NAPOLEON'S LETTER QUOTED ON pp.6–7

You are governing this nation too monkishly. A king's benevolence should have an air of majesty, not monkishness . . .

Your quarrels with the ex Queen are reaching the public ear. In your private life show the mild and paternal qualities that you display in government, and in government the same rigorousness that you show at home. You are treating a young woman as if you were commanding a regiment . . .

You have the best and most virtuous of wives and you are making her unhappy. Let her dance as much as she wants to; it's her age. My own wife is forty, yet I write from the battlefield urging her to attend a ball; and you expect a girl of twenty, who sees her life slipping away and has all her illusions still intact, to live in a cloister, and be like a nursemaid for ever bathing the baby . . . It is a pity you have a virtuous wife; if you had a flirtatious one she would twist you round her little finger.

Index

Index

Index

Index

Index

by King Louis Philippe 18, In London
19–21, Suspicions about his activities 21–2,
Returns to Arenenberg 22, Death of
Napoleon II 22–3, Summoned to family
conference in London 23, Joins Swiss army
23–4, Meets Persigny 24–5, The Strasbourg
attempt 25–8, Arrested 28, Shipped to
America 29–30, In New York 30–1, Fêted
there 30–1, Hears of illness of mother 31,
Hurries to London 31, Attempts to detain
him there 32, Escapes and reaches
Switzerland 32, Death of Queen Hortense
32–3, France demands his expulsion from
Switzerland 33–4, Leaves voluntarily 34,
His London establishment 34, His friends
34, Takes part in the Eglinton Tournament
35, Count D'Orsay and Lady Blessington
36–8, His attachment to Emily Rowles 38,
Watched by French authorities 38–9, His
invasion plans 39, Charters the *Edinburgh
Castle* 39, The landing at Wimereux 40,
Routed at Boulogne 41, Trial in Paris 42,
Imprisoned at Ham 42–4, His life in prison
43–4, Affair with Eleanora Vergeot 45, His
escape 45–6, Reaches London 47, Regains
his health 48–9, Meets Elizabeth Howard
50–2, Visits Paris after 1848 revolution 53,
Special constable during Chartist rising 53,
Elected by four French departments 54,
Returns to Paris 56, Elected President of
the Republic 56–7, Cares for relatives and
friends 57, Sets up Miss Howard 57, Early
steps as President 73–4, the *Coup d'Etat*
74–80, Plebiscite confirms his ten-year
period as President 81, Discards Elizabeth
Howard 83, Candidates to be his bride 83–4,
Falls in love with Eugenie de Montijo
85–6, Becomes Emperor 87, Attempts to
marry Queen Victoria's niece 90–4, Stages
hunting party for Eugenie at Compiègne
91–3, Proposes marriage 95, The anger of
Elizabeth Howard 97, Defends his choice of
Eugenie 98, The wedding 99–102, The
honeymoon 102–3, Grief when Eugenie
loses child 104, Plans State Visit to England
107–10, The Crimean War 108–9, Meets
Prince Albert at Boulogne 110–11, Receives
invitation to England 111, The journey 112,
At Windsor 112, Receives Order of the
Garter 112–13, At Buckingham Palace 113,
His friendly relations with the Queen
113–15, The return visit to Paris 117–23,
At Les Invalides 123, Birth of son 126–7,
The christening 128, Medical check-up
128–30, His affair with the Contessa di
Castiglione 131–2, And Marianne Walewska
133, Visits Osborne 134–5, The Orsini
bomb attempt 135–6, Invites Queen
Victoria and Prince Albert to meet him at
Cherbourg 137, Strained relations 138,
Decides to free Italy from Austrian yoke 138,
Battles of Magenta and Solferino
139–41, Peace of Villafranca 141–2,
Triumphant return to Paris 142–3, Gains
Nice and Savoy 143, Visits Savoy, Corsica
and Algeria 144–6, Withholds news of
Paca's death from Eugenie 146, Her anger
and visit to Britain 146–50, His illness
154–5, Meets Marguerite Bellanger 158,
His last affair 158–61, Relations with
Bismarck 161–2, Entertains him at Biarritz
162–3, The Schleswig-Holstein and Seven
Weeks' Wars 162–3, Ill, he refuses to take
aggressive steps against Prussia 163–4,
Spoils his son 169–71, The Mexican tragedy
174–5, Refuses Empress Charlotte's plea for
help 176, Stages Paris Exhibition of 1867
179–80, With Russian Tsar during
assassination attempt 181–2, Receives news
of the execution of Emperor Maximilian
182, Visits Emperor Francis Joseph 183–4,
Deteriorating relations with Britain 186,
Swing towards Republicanism in France
187–8, His worsening health 187, Press
attacks upon him 187, Agrees that Eugenie
should open the Suez Canal 189, Letters
from her from Egypt 192–3, Appoints
Ollivier Prime Minister 194–5, The Liberal
Empire 195–6, Plans retirement 196, The
Spanish Succession 196, Declaration of war
against Prussia 197, Leaves for front 198–9,
Disillusionment on reaching Metz 199–200,
Minor victory at Saarbrücken 200, Retreats
to Châlons 202, Request to return to Paris
refused 202–3, Decides that son must leave
front line 203, Reaches Sedan 204, The
battle 204–6, He urges surrender 205,
Disagreement with General Wimpffen
205–6, His letter of surrender to the King
of Prussia 206, Drives out to meet
Bismarck 207, At the weaver's cottage
207–8, Taken to Château de Bellevue 208,
His imperial retinue 209, His meeting with
King William 209, Last night in France
210, The journey to Wilhelmshöhe 210,
Worried by lack of news of Empress
240–2, Her surprise visit to Wilhelmshöhe
242–3, Leaves Germany 244, His reception
at Dover 245, Guest of Queen Victoria at
Windsor 245, His life at Chislehurst 246–7,
At Torquay 247, At Buckingham Palace
248, Plans for return to France 248–9,
Undergoes operation 249, Death of 250,
His will 252, Memorial service at
Chislehurst on occasion of eighteenth
birthday of the Prince Imperial 255,
Remains transferred to Farnborough
267–8
Napoleon, Charles, 5
Napoleon, Prince (Plon-Plon), 93, 99, 122,
127, 154, 171, 203, 211, 239, 252–3, 272

Index

Index